Standards-Based Learning
in Action

Moving From Theory to Practice

Tom Schimmer

Garnet Hillman

Mandy Stalets

Solution Tree | Press

a division of
Solution Tree

the **Solution Tree**
Assessment Center

555 North Morton Street
Bloomington, IN 47404
800.733.6786 (toll free) / 812.336.7700
FAX: 812.336.7790

email: info@SolutionTree.com
SolutionTree.com

Visit **go.SolutionTree.com/assessment** to download the free reproducibles in this book.

Printed in the United States of America

Library of Congress Cataloging-in-Publication Data

Names: Schimmer, Tom, author. | Hillman, Garnet, author. | Stalets, Mandy, author.
Title: Standards-based learning in action : moving from theory to practice /
    Tom Schimmer, Garnet Hillman, and Mandy Stalets.
Description: Bloomington, IN : Solution Tree Press, [2018] | Includes
    bibliographical references and index.
Identifiers: LCCN 2017037236 | ISBN 9781945349010 (perfect bound)
Subjects: LCSH: Education--Standards.
Classification: LCC LB3060.82 .S734 2018 | DDC 379.1/58--dc23 LC record available
at https://lccn.loc.gov/2017037236

Solution Tree
Jeffrey C. Jones, CEO
Edmund M. Ackerman, President

Solution Tree Press
President and Publisher: Douglas M. Rife
Editorial Director: Sarah Payne-Mills
Art Director: Rian Anderson
Managing Production Editor: Caroline Cascio
Senior Production Editor: Tonya Maddox Cupp
Senior Editor: Amy Rubenstein
Copy Editor: Miranda Addonizio
Proofreader: Jessi Finn
Cover Designer: Rian Anderson
Editorial Assistants: Jessi Finn and Kendra Slayton

Acknowledgments

First and foremost, we would like to thank our greatest supports—our families.

Tom would like to thank his wife, Monica, as well as his two children, Samantha and Adrian, for their continued love and support! The sacrifices you all continue to make so I can pursue and fulfill my professional passion are inspiring. My professional journey would be meaningless without you!

Garnet would like to thank her husband, Shawn, and sons, Julian and Jackson, for their incredible love and support throughout the process of writing this book. You inspire my work and are a constant reminder of its importance. Thanks for your willingness to sacrifice family time and your continual reminders that being an author was not only possible but also an endeavor worth pursuing.

Mandy would like to thank her husband, Luke, and daughters, Eva and Alex, for the endless support they have shown through the writing of this book. Your ongoing love, encouragement, and flexibility made this dream a possibility! You are my biggest cheerleaders and I couldn't have done this without you!

Beyond family, we are all thankful for the inspirational educators we have had the privilege to work with, past and present. The work you do every day is so meaningful. Thank you for pushing us, educating us, and helping us do what we love.

We would also like to thank thought leaders in the field of assessment, especially the associates of the Solution Tree Assessment Center. Your commitment, dedication, and contributions to the field are inspiring, and our work would not be possible without you.

Finally, we would like to thank the wonderful people at Solution Tree who helped make this book a reality.

Solution Tree Press would like to thank the following reviewers:

Aaron Blackwelder
English Teacher
Woodland High School
Woodland, Washington

Sarah Bosch
6–12 Director of Curriculum and Instruction
Elkhorn Area School District
Elkhorn, Wisconsin

Lori Colasuonno
English Teacher
Charles J. Colgan Senior High School
Manassas, Virginia

Steve Mefford
Facilitator of Curriculum and Professional Learning
Urbandale Community School District
Urbandale, Iowa

Visit **go.SolutionTree.com/assessment** to download the free reproducibles in this book.

Table of Contents

9 Proficiency Scales and Rubrics in Action . . 165

10 Standards-Based Reporting in Action 187

Epilogue 211

References and Resources 213

Index 223

About the Authors

Tom Schimmer is an author and a speaker with expertise in assessment, grading, leadership, and behavioral support. Tom is a former district-level leader, school administrator, and teacher. As a district-level leader, he was a member of the senior management team responsible for overseeing the efforts to support and build the instructional and assessment capacities of teachers and administrators.

Tom is a sought-after speaker who presents internationally for schools and districts. He has worked extensively throughout North America, as well as in Vietnam, Myanmar, China, Thailand, Japan, India, Qatar, Bahrain, Spain, the United Kingdom, and the United Arab Emirates. He earned a teaching degree from Boise State University and a master's degree in curriculum and instruction from the University of British Columbia.

To learn more about Tom's work, visit All Things Assessment (http://allthings assessment.info) or follow @TomSchimmer on Twitter.

Garnet Hillman is an educator, writer, presenter, and learner. She was a Spanish teacher at Lockport Township High School and served as an instructional coach at Caruso Middle School, both in Illinois. She consults around the United States on the topics of assessment, grading, and student motivation. A passionate educator, Garnet values student learning above all else.

Garnet has published writing within *Assessment 3.0* by Mark Barnes and *What Connected Educators Do Differently* by Todd Whitaker, Jeffrey Zoul, and Jimmy Casas. She is a member of the Association for Middle Level Education as well as the American Council on the Teaching of Foreign Languages.

Through her consulting work, Garnet emphasizes healthy grading and sound assessment practices. She has worked with a variety of school districts that desire to improve instruction, provide relevant and respectful assessment, cultivate grading practices that support learning, and increase student motivation. She provides rationale for a paradigm shift in grading methods and a step-by-step process to implement it.

Garnet holds a master's degree in educational leadership from Aurora University as well as a bachelor's degree in Spanish from Ohio University. She has also completed graduate coursework in instructional technology.

To learn more about Garnet's work, follow @garnet_hillman on Twitter.

 **Mandy Stalets** is a teacher and learner who focuses on sound grading practices and standards-based learning. She is currently a high school mathematics teacher at Illinois State University's laboratory schools and was previously a middle school mathematics teacher.

In 2010, Mandy implemented standards-based learning and grading in her own classroom and has been successfully using that system in her middle and high school mathematics classroom ever since. Mandy works with a wide variety of teachers, undergraduate students, and school districts to improve assessment and grading practices to maximize communication and student success. She provides rationale for the need for change in our current grading practices, as well as practical steps to implement it.

Mandy received her undergraduate degree in secondary mathematics education and graduate degree in teaching and learning from Illinois State University.

To learn more about Mandy's work, follow @MandyStalets on Twitter.

To book Tom Schimmer, Garnet Hillman, or Mandy Stalets for professional development, contact pd@SolutionTree.com.

Introduction

It's easier to act your way into a new way of thinking, than to think your way into a new way of acting.

—Richard Pascale, Jerry Sternin, and Monique Sternin

The National Commission on Excellence in Education's (1983) report *A Nation at Risk* submits that the United States "lost sight of the basic purposes of schooling, and of the high expectations and disciplined effort needed to attain them" (pp. 5–6). Following its release, educators began exploring what establishing higher standards for the public education system would mean (Brown, 2009; Hamilton, 2003; Holme, Richards, Jimerson, & Cohen, 2010). Since the mid-1990s, we have measured the success of our education systems against the achievement of curricular standards. That era's standards movement changed the instructional paradigm from one that compares students to each other to one that compares students' work to identified performance standards. Research on standards-based learning also addresses models for English learners and special education educators (Echevarria, Short, & Powers, 2010; Jung & Guskey, 2012; Leko, Brownell, Sindelar, & Kiely, 2015).

Yet teachers persistently hesitate to commit to standards-based teaching and learning. Since the early 1990s, almost every jurisdiction has mandated curricular standards, but still there are classrooms in which the primary experience hinges on doing activities, accumulating points, and complying behaviorally. As you will read several times throughout the book, the existence of standards is simply not enough to transform classrooms. Accurate and holistic standards-based reporting requires acknowledging (either formally or informally) each of its three sides—(1) growth, (2) achievement, and (3) student attributes.

The Knowing-Doing Gap: How Smart Companies Turn Knowledge Into Action, by Jeffrey Pfeffer and Robert I. Sutton (1999), outlines the causes of this somewhat predictable gap between what organizations *know* and what they *do*. Although the authors primarily focus on the business world, educators worldwide experience the same knowing-doing gap when it comes to implementing promising practices within their specific contexts.

Educators may know that standards-based learning helps increase achievement and engagement, but be unable to make the transition. Point accumulation and behavioral compliance tied together with academic grading don't—at least in their traditional iteration—square with standards-based learning; chapters 1 and 2 (pages 9 and 31, respectively) highlight the ways curricular standards and desirable student behaviors can be articulated and (separately) assessed. While activities still exist and behavioral compliance remains important in standards-based classrooms, the emphasis on reaching academic proficiency turns activities into a *means to an end* and removes behavioral compliance from having any role in determining a student's proficiency grade. This book's tools and starting points can help you begin to bridge the knowing-doing gap. In the following sections, we explain what that looks like, as well as more about this book's approach and what is within each chapter.

The Knowing-Doing Gap

We have adapted Pfeffer and Sutton's (1999) guidelines for bridging the knowing-doing gap to transform classrooms into standards-based learning environments. Those guidelines include putting *why* before *how*, avoiding smart talk, learning by doing, embracing mistakes, acting fearlessly, eliminating competition, measuring what matters, and letting leaders set the pace of change.

Put *Why* Before *How*

Putting the *why* before the *how* may be the simplest guideline to both understand and execute. Because teachers expect students to reach proficiency within each subject's standards, it only makes sense that they use those standards to teach, assess, organize evidence, and report. The challenge, of course, is that teachers most often find that a state or national organization imposes these standards on them. Although some may still resist the idea of teaching to standards, the majority of teachers recognize that standards in some iteration are an ingrained part of the education system. Change, especially mandated change, is not always easy to execute, but once teachers move past resistance or hesitation, we believe they will see that the *why* of developing a standards-based learning environment is obvious; if students are expected to reach proficiency, then it seems logical that teachers would create learning experiences anchored on those very same curricular standards.

Avoid Smart Talk

The ubiquity of smart talk is a critical reason for this book. Smart *talk* about assessment is ubiquitous; smart *action* is less so. Smart talk without smart action leaves teachers in a never-ending cycle of preparing to prepare. There are several possibilities that explain why some teachers have not implemented the practice.

- **They may feel that experimenting with unfamiliar practices in the classroom is risky:** Teachers, for all the right reasons, are planners who want to get things right. Although trying things on a whim is not the best approach, the desire for perfection can leave teachers in a perpetual state of *analysis paralysis*—preparing to prepare. Many of our colleagues have suffered through this state over the years.

- **Initiative burnout occurs:** Teachers with lots of experience have seen several initiatives come and go over the course of their careers. After a while, investing in something new feels futile because each seems doomed to a short life. Sometimes that mindset is more cynical than is professionally healthy, but sometimes it is simply the residual effect of a career's worth of experience.

- **Old habits die hard:** Most teachers develop meaningful relationships, maximize student success, and even provide a kind of mentorship that has a lifelong impact. When results are good it can be difficult to envision something better. The tools in this book are a path to better results.

There is no shortage of research, professional literature, and real-life examples of how teachers have already transformed their classrooms. However, most of the professional literature is heavy on research and light on examples; we aim to flip the script on this by leaning heavily toward the implementation side of standards-based learning.

Learn by Doing

Metacognition—the thinking about one's own thinking—is another way to bridge the knowing-doing gap. Teachers, to transform their classrooms through purposeful efforts, must employ it. Educational researcher and former dean of the Ontario Institute for Studies in Education Michael Fullan (2011) asserts that effective change leaders "walk into the future through examining their own and others' best practices, looking for insights they had hitherto not noticed" (p. 11). Research shows that students, through formative assessment, can develop the metacognitive awareness needed to plan, monitor, and assess their learning (Andrade, 2013; Clark, 2012; Jones, 2007). We submit the same holds true for teachers. Teachers who contemplate their own assessment thinking can plan, monitor, and assess as they walk into their standards-based learning future.

Embrace Mistakes

Moving forward means being aware that not everything will necessarily play out according to plan. Success in a standards-based learning environment occurs when teachers develop a habit of reflecting and refining to best suit the needs of the learners they serve. Sometimes their mistakes may stem from implementation error; sometimes they simply mismatch past practice and current learners. In either case, teachers who accept mistakes as part of their professional growth will bridge the gap between what they know and what they do. Teachers don't expect students to become proficient without practicing, making mistakes, and reflecting on and refining their work; teachers shouldn't expect that of themselves, either.

Act Fearlessly

Fearing mistakes is an easily understood response to any potential change. Parents, colleagues, stakeholders, and even students can push back against any changes that might seem new or out of the ordinary. Obviously, teachers need to be thoughtful about any potential changes they might make to their practice, but fear of getting it wrong can prevent teachers from ultimately getting it right. Being fearless is not being careless. By embracing their own expertise and experience, teachers can thoughtfully act on their knowledge to create a more standards-focused learning environment.

Eliminate Competition

Many of our traditional assessment and grading practices fuel competition by inadvertently or intentionally creating learning environments where success is contingent upon factors either tangential or unrelated to learning. In cultures of competition, students will be reluctant to help one another since their standing is determined through a comparison to other students. Why would a student contribute to another student's learning if there is a built-in competition between students? Some competition in life is unavoidable, and it can even be productive in the right places, but the classroom is not one of those places. The competition is students versus standards, not students versus each other.

Measure Only What Matters

Establishing clear and consistent performance criteria is essential in a standards-based classroom. We reiterate this throughout the book. These criteria are how teachers will know whether their newly implemented practices are producing the desired results. In this book, we define *proficiency scales* as the levels with holistic descriptors teachers use to communicate proficiency across grade levels and content areas. *Rubrics* expand on these descriptors, making them more specific to a subject, class, standard, skill, or standards-based assessment.

We know success breeds success, so maintaining a laser-like focus on desirable outcomes is non-negotiable. Doing so allows teachers the opportunity to measure their own success and know which, if any, adjustments they must make going forward.

Let Leaders Set the Pace

Leaders, whether in that position through title or influence, must navigate the transformation pace with some finesse. They can help keep teachers from taking on too much too soon by avoiding changing everything at once. Although there is an urgency to move to standards-based learning, good leaders pair that urgency with patience. Urgency comes with the expectation of change; patience comes through the collective determination of how long change could or should take. You must consider institutional history, long-standing practices, and current policies as both teachers and administrators determine a reasonable timeline for how standards-based learning will unfold. Leaders should avoid exerting a disproportionate amount of pressure (related to the agreed-upon timeline) for change to occur. Teachers need to become familiar with how standards-based and traditional learning differ so they can determine which of their practices can remain and what changes they must consider and implement. Early adopters—leaders through influence—can do the same for themselves by reminding one another that long-term plans manifest through short-term victories. The team approach is quite useful in this regard. How ready any school, team, or teacher is determines how fast the pace should be and, so long as stagnation doesn't set in, schools will find the sweet spot between urgency and patience.

About This Book

This book leans heavily on the practical side of implementing the practices and processes that align with standards-based learning. Throughout, we intentionally emphasize how to put theory into practice. We know that the professional literature is filled with books that meticulously make the case for sound assessment practices through a thorough examination of the research, followed by a few supplemental examples of what it might look like. Our goal is just the opposite. We aim to provide readers with abundant strategies for putting standards-based learning into action; we supplement and synthesize these strategies with research.

As bottom up as possible, as top down as necessary—that's another approach we take. This book's primary audience is K–12 classroom teachers because the move to solidify a standards-based learning environment is the cumulative effect of what classroom teachers do. The bottom-up focus ensures that teachers exert maximum influence over what they do with their students each day. The most critical element of standards-based learning is simply a decision to begin the process of aligning teaching, assessment, and reporting to standards.

Because some aspects of standards-based learning require administrative support or initiative, some aspects must be top down. As the secondary audience of this book, school and district administrators play an integral role in the long-term success of establishing a standards-based learning environment. This is not to say that leaders can afford to be authoritarian or exclusive during decision making; they can't. However, they can link individual change efforts to create schoolwide alignment in practice. Consider that administrators have access to every classroom, department, or grade-level team. This affords them the opportunity to take what individual teachers are doing and begin to facilitate across the school some alignment and consistency with practices and processes. District leaders have access to multiple schools and can facilitate the same kind of alignment at a district level, should that be desirable and plausible. By developing their fluency and capacity with standards-based learning, coupled with their experience in leadership, administrators create a best-case scenario for schools as they align consistent practices with what research indicates are the more favorable courses of action.

Within Each Chapter

Each chapter addresses a topic specifically in light of standards-based learning implementation. Chapter 1 lays down the foundation by explaining how to put standards planning, communicating, and sequencing into action. This chapter also stresses the importance of separating behaviors from academics to implement standards-based learning with fidelity. Establishing student accountability, measuring growth, and changing the language of grading while communicating with parents also appear in this chapter. We cover achieving standards alignment in chapter 2. Chapter 3 and chapter 4 break down formative assessment and feedback, respectively, to ensure clear communication with students. Chapter 5 guides teachers toward meaningful homework and chapter 6 helps them teach students how to self-assess. We focus on summative assessment in chapter 7. Chapter 8 explains the differences among retakes, reassessments, and redos; chapter 9 explains how to put proficiency scales and rubrics into action in standards-based learning. Finally, chapter 10 details standards-based reporting.

Each chapter continues by encapsulating the most salient research. Wherever possible, we've sought to include the most up-to-date research while also honoring the long-standing research that has stood the test of time. In either case, the research is included to lay the foundation for the strategies we subsequently explore throughout the bulk of the chapter. This initial section is not intended to be a literature review; the research foundation is there to support the positions, advice, and practices that teachers can use to establish a standards-based learning environment. We have intentionally clustered the research references in this one section to allow readers to consume the practical strategies and tools more seamlessly. We dedicate most of each chapter to the particular aspect or strategy in action, thoroughly examining the practical implementation processes and strategies. This section is full of tools and strategies that teachers can adopt and adapt to create the most optimal standards-based learning experience for their students. We also include personal narratives from the field gathered during our work with educators from 2015 to 2016.

A short section follows that we devote to talking to learners. Too often we target change *to* students, rather than work *with* them to change; we seek to shift that mindset by providing readers with some guidance on how to engage learners in a conversation about what's changing, why it's changing, and how they can meaningfully participate in the change from the outset.

Each chapter continues with a short section on talking to parents. As with students, it is important to keep parents informed ahead of changes. We advise teachers to craft messages about standards-based learning ahead of time, rather than face a rash of individual emails, texts, and phone calls from parents. The quick bullet points in the Getting Started section are for teachers who need some guidance on what to do first. Finally, each chapter closes with reflective questions that ask readers to consider what aspects of their current practices this book reaffirms, which aspects it challenges, and what their subsequent actions could or should be.

The time for action is now. Teachers will not be able to implement the subsequent practices and processes we put forth in this book all at once. Getting to a standards-focused learning environment is a transition, and it requires a thoughtful examination of current practices and a purposeful effort toward aligning instruction, assessment, and grades. Be reflective, be progressive, be collaborative, and be transparent. The result will be a more learning-focused classroom, and the side effect will be a more authentic, meaningful relationship with your students.

1

Standards-Based Learning in Action

The past 20 years have seen an accelerating growth in studies of formative assessment. However, this has not been matched by a corresponding development in summative assessment. The net effect has been that the changes have not improved the state of discord between these two functions.

—Paul Black

A move to standards-based learning requires some fundamental and significant shifts in how teachers organize, execute, and assess their students. After they have identified the standards, it becomes clearer to teachers what they should teach and assess—and what they should not. Most teachers would have to go out of their way to avoid *covering* the mandated standards by topic; however, the existence of standards doesn't always equate to *teaching* to standards. Standards-based learning is anchored on a teacher's commitment to designing instructional experiences and assessment that make proficiency against standards (not the accumulation of points) the priority outcome.

Moving From Rationale to Action

The latest research provides the rationale for standards-based learning and helps create the tools teachers need to put these ideas into action.

The Research

The research we explore in the following sections focuses on clearer, more purposeful instruction toward curricular standards, as well as the behavioral attributes and characteristics that are transferable to any context. Separating academic achievement from behavioral attributes brings profile and attention to the characteristics that can otherwise be buried or marginalized in a system where all reporting is reduced to a singular symbol. Separation raises the level of attention toward those characteristics, making them an obvious parallel residual effect of the school experience.

Clearer, More Purposeful Instruction

The potential advantage to establishing curricular standards is the clarity and consistency that teachers can bring to classrooms across multiple contexts. This level of specificity provides teachers the opportunity to plan with the end in mind because, in advance of instruction, they can develop specific performance criteria for each standard. In some cases, teachers may even involve students in co-constructing performance criteria. Standards lead to more precise and efficient instructional choices.

Standards also help create consistency from year to year; student demonstrations of learning are expected to align with standards and the corresponding criteria. The scoring and grading scales remain constant (meaning they are criterion-referenced assessments) instead of varying, as when teachers compare students to one another, which is a norm-referenced approach (Brookhart, 2013b). Writing the best essay in the class is no longer equivalent to the highest performance level if the essay itself does not meet the established criteria. Table 1.1 contrasts the key differences between norm referencing and criterion referencing.

Conceptually, the shift to criterion-referenced assessments is simple and straightforward; however, there are still some habits that are hard to break. This means many teachers still, in practicality, sit somewhere in between. Although most teachers *know* assessments today should be based on a certain level of achievement against specific criteria, student-to-student comparisons are still an alluring element of past practices. Teachers need to continue to work with one another to ensure that students are judged solely on their individual ability to meet the specific established criteria.

Characteristics and Attributes

Proficiency grades might get students into college, but 21st century characteristics and skills allow them to graduate from college and maintain careers (American Institute of Certified Public Accountants, 2011; Williams, 2015). Those crucial 21st century requirements include critical thinking, communication, collaboration, and creativity, also known as the *four Cs* (Partnership for 21st Century Learning, n.d.).

Table 1.1: Criterion- Versus Norm-Referenced Assessment

Dimension	Criterion-Referenced Assessment	Norm-Referenced Assessment
Purpose	• Determines whether each student has achieved specific skills or concepts • Determines how much students know before and following instruction	• Ranks each student with respect to others' achievement in broad areas of knowledge • Discriminates between high and low achievers
Content	• Measures teacher- and curriculum expert–identified skills that make up a designated curriculum • Presents each skill as an instructional objective	• Measures broad skill areas sampled from a variety of textbooks, syllabi, and the judgments of curriculum experts
Item characteristics	• Assesses each skill with at least four items to ensure an adequate sample and minimize the effect of guessing • Assesses any given skill at parallel difficulty	• Tests each skill with fewer than four items • Tests with items of varying difficulty levels • Tests with items that discriminate between high and low achievers
Score interpretation	• Compares individuals with a preset standard for acceptable achievement • Reports achievement on quality or consistency of skill level • Reports achievement on individual skills	• Compares individuals with other examinees and assigns a score—usually expressed as a percentile, a grade-equivalent score, or a stanine • Reports achievement for broad skill areas (although some tests do report student achievement for individual skills)

Source: Adapted from Huitt, 1996.

Standards-based learning separates behavior from standards proficiency. A common misconception is that separating them means these behaviors and skills are irrelevant. That is not the case; they remain relevant regardless of the split. If separating academic performance and behavioral characteristics results in a diminished focus on the importance of behavior, it is an error in execution (Durlak, Weissberg, Dymnicki, Taylor, & Schellinger, 2011). The right way is for teachers to help students learn to act accordingly by teaching and assessing behavioral attributes similarly to how they handle academics. Like academic standards, students need clear, specific criteria and intentional assessment to learn behavioral attributes.

In Action

Many schools try to make the shift to standards-based grading without first changing their educators' mindsets about classroom culture, learning, and grading. In a traditional system, the focus in the classroom is often on the grade; students complete assignments for points, teachers judge assessments by how many questions are incorrect, and extra credit bumps up grades even if a student's demonstration of a skill has not improved.

In this traditional system, experience has trained students to play the game of school. Schools dangle the carrot (the academic grade) in front of their faces and encourage students to chase it. With these practices, schools have created a culture of compliance. Becoming standards based is about changing to a culture of learning. "Complete this assignment to get these points" changes to "Complete this assignment to improve your learning." To change the culture, it is not necessary to start with changing grading practices. In fact, that should be one of the *last* things to change to avoid shocking learners and parents. (They, too, require mindset shifts.) When changing to a standards-based learning classroom, teachers must do the heavy lifting where it matters—in classroom instruction, instructional alignment to the standards, and assessment practices. Educators have trained learners to focus on the academic grade; they can coach them out of this assumption.

Although most educators can agree, at least in principle, that standards proficiency, positive behavior, and academic growth are three distinct areas of success, challenges often arise in execution; what do these look like in the classroom? This chapter focuses on how to "begin with the end in mind" by examining the potential results of separating academics and behavioral competence (Covey, 2004, p. 95). Here, teachers discover how to plan around the standards, communicate the learning, and then sequence assessments intentionally. Following that, they may need help pinpointing the most prudent behaviors and teaching them, holding students accountable, communicating growth (versus grades), and generally adopting a language of learning.

Planning the Destination Before the Journey

Implementing standards-based learning in the classroom is a lot like planning a vacation; decide on the destination (proficiency with the standards) and then plan the path to arrive there (the instruction). With that clarity, teachers can mindfully plan the means to support learners in meeting their goals. As they plan, teachers should ask themselves the following questions; subsequent chapters help answer them.

- **"What are the standards?"** Teachers must have a deep understanding of the standards to effectively communicate them to students and parents. Rather than saying, "The next unit covers poetry," clearly state the unit's standards. For example, "Determine a theme of a story, drama, or poem from details in the text" (RL.4.2 National Governors Association Center for Best Practices [NGA] & Council of Chief State School Officers [CCSSO], 2010a). Have a target for student learning and provide learners with a goal. Chapter 2 (page 31) explains how to deeply understand the standards.

- **"How do I unpack standards for students? How clear are they?"** The language in academic standards can often overwhelm teachers, learners, and families. Breaking down standards into manageable learning targets provides a road map for learning. Students must master these smaller pieces in order to achieve the larger goal—proficiency with the standard. Chapter 2 explains how to unpack and communicate standards.

- **"How will I summatively assess standards?"** Keeping in mind the standards for summative assessment, determine the best way to assess student proficiency. By planning the summative assessment first, teachers clarify what evidence they want students to produce. Some may say this is teaching to the test; it's not. This is teaching to the *standards*. We cover summative assessment in chapter 7 (page 125).

- **"What are the formative checks? Do they address all standards?"** Teachers should next plan how they will measure progress toward the end goal. Intentionally sequencing formative checkpoints throughout the unit of study allows educators to stop, re-evaluate, and plan next steps for instruction. Chapter 3 (page 51) details formative assessment.

- **"Are there opportunities for practice in my instructional plan? Have I established success criteria?"** Daily instruction comes last as teachers plan standards-based units; formative assessment drives instruction. After collecting rich formative data, teachers better understand student needs. From there, they create instruction that is more focused and meaningful.

After intentionally planning the way they will approach learning in their classrooms, teachers can be more mindful about how they will communicate the targets.

Communicating the Journey

Communicating the learning targets is multifaceted. A key piece of the communication is the way teachers talk to learners about the learning targets and standards.

Providing students with the standards and learning targets in advance of instruction (and revisiting those often) allows them to see the course ahead. Often, as seen in the following example, these learning targets are presented in the form *I can* to incorporate student-friendly language. This allows learners to understand what success looks like so they can more accurately gauge where they are in relation to the assessed standard. Figure 1.1 is an example of a standard from the Common Core State Standards (CCSS; NGA & CCSSO, 2010b) and its learning targets that students in a seventh-grade mathematics class might receive.

Standard: CCSS.Math-Content.7.G.B.4	
Know the formulas for the area and circumference of a circle and use them to solve problems; give an informal derivation of the relationship between the circumference and area of a circle.	
Knowledge targets (What I need to know)	• I can explain what the radius and diameter of a circle are. • I can explain what the circumference and area of a circle are. • I can explain how to use exponents. • I know the formulas for circumference and area.
Reasoning targets (What I can do with what I know)	• I can summarize when and how I would need to find the circumference and area of a circle in real-life situations. • I can identify radius and diameter of a circle. • I can find the radius of a circle given the diameter. • I can find the diameter of a circle given the radius.
Skill targets (What I can demonstrate)	• I can calculate the circumference of a circle when given the radius or diameter. • I can calculate the area of a circle when given the radius of the diameter. • I can provide an informal derivation of the relationship between circumference and area of a circle.

Product targets
 	
(What I can make to show my learning)
	• I can solve real-life problems involving circumference and area of a circle.
	  • I can calculate the amount of fencing needed to enclose a circular garden.
	  • I can calculate the amount of paint needed to paint a circular area of a playground.

Source for standard: NGA & CCSSO, 2010b.

Figure 1.1: Mathematics standard with learning targets.

Visit go.SolutionTree.com/assessment for a free reproducible version of this figure.

Having this reference point not only provides teachers with instructional clarity, but offers students a checklist of what they need to know, understand, and do.

The classroom culture changes as learners do the following.

- Target their questions.
- Understand and communicate their learning.
- Understand and communicate their needs.
- Identify deficit skills to focus their learning.
- Understand next steps in learning.

PERSONAL NARRATIVE

Brittney Minton

Fourth-Grade Teacher, Thomas Metcalf School, Normal, Illinois

After lunch and recess, students slam their locker doors after putting their coats away, grab a drink, and hustle back into our fourth-grade classroom to work on mathematics. I ask them to grab their whiteboards from their desks so that we can do some quick formative checking before heading out into small-group time after the minilesson. A few students check in to remind me that they have already mastered this skill. They are at a 4 (on our school's four-point proficiency scale) and will be in the back room working on a practice sheet that involves solving word problems with two-by-two-digit multiplication.

"Perfect," I tell them, and then reassure them I will check in after I introduce this skill to the rest of the class. At the beginning of each unit, I offer students a variety of practice sheets all labeled with the specific standard each focuses on within the unit so that students always know what resources will help them with the skill they need to be working on.

We are currently immersed in a multiplication unit which has three standards; learners are working at a variety of places on different skills and standards within the unit. Ten years ago this would have made me nervous, asking, "Not everyone has to work on the same thing at the same time? Students know themselves better than me? Students decide what skill they need to work on within the mathematics workshop? They aren't in the same group throughout the entire unit? They know what standards we will cover in the next unit and the rest of the year?"

continued →

The rest of the class comes back to the front, and I announce that I am getting ready to explicitly teach and model the second core standard of our unit, which is a numbers and base ten standard that says that we can multiply two-digit numbers by two-digit numbers using what we know about operations and place value. I have already presented the standard to students in visual form, first on their preassessment before starting the unit, on their practice sheets, on the classroom website that offers reinforcement lessons, and on the top of the chart that serves as a visual anchor for the lesson. I will display and refer to it throughout the unit. I remind students of what the standard says we should be able to do and break it down so that they tell me what the purpose of the lesson is. This is how we start each minilesson. It establishes a purpose for their learning and encourages them to work toward this goal throughout the block. Before starting any lesson in our standards-based classroom, I ensure that students understand what the standard says and what it means they can do.

I ask them to hold their hands and fingers in front of their chests to show me where they feel they are in accordance with that standard on our four-point proficiency scale. I see mostly 3s, meaning they feel they are proficient with the skill and ready for the new lesson. There are, of course, a few students holding up a 2. Some still need to work on proficiency for solving two-by-one-digit problems. The beautiful thing is, they know that. Why? Because of the standards-based learning environment they're a part of each day.

I model how to solve a two-by-two-digit multiplication problem. Then, I allow students the chance to solve one on their whiteboards. Again, I check and ask them to self-assess. During this part of the lesson, many decide to go out into small groups and practice this skill. I have a handful of students stay with me at the front for another model and chance to practice. At the end of this, a few more students leave, telling me what they're going to work on when they head into the next part of the workshop. The few students I have left ask to work on two-by-one-digit multiplication problems. I ask them what they need me to do. Some say they just need time to practice. One or two ask if I can model another one-by-two. I do. Then, they say they are going to work on one independently and check back in with me or a trusted peer from the back room who has already mastered the skill.

I check in with students in the back room who consider themselves proficient with the skills in this lesson. Some are excited to show me how they have mastered two-by-twos. A couple are working on multistep word problems that include the multiplication skills. One is working on some basic algebra that she has been wanting to learn. Two are working on long division because they know that will be the focus of the next unit. One even wants to show me how he can solve a long-division problem. I compliment him, then ask what he plans on working on next. "Well, I thought about working on long division with a two-digit divisor, but is that a fourth-grade standard? If not, I think I will start exploring fractions."

Being in a university lab school, we have many visitors and observers each day. They often ask me how I balance my mathematics block with students working on a variety of skills. "Easy," I say. The students know what they are learning. They know end goals. They know what the grade-level standards ask of them. Because of this, they have control of their learning. And I wouldn't have it any other way. Such a beautiful thing.

Sequencing Assessments Intentionally

Intentionally sequencing assessments in advance of instruction provides checkpoints, wherein teachers can pause, re-evaluate, differentiate, and communicate. Teacher teams intentionally design these checkpoints to collect real-time data as an opportunity to check progress, redirect learners toward the target, and collaborate with team members to plan future instruction. Figure 1.2 provides a sample assessment plan that a teacher might design before a unit begins.

Key
P = Practice
F = Formative assessment
S = Summative assessment
X = Assessment data are collected

	P1	P2	F1	P3	F2	P4	P5	F3	S
Standard 1	X	X	X					X	X
Standard 2		X		X	X	X		X	X
Standard 3						X	X	X	X

Source: Adapted from Vagle, 2013.

Figure 1.2: Intentionally sequencing assessments.

*Visit **go.SolutionTree.com/assessment** for a free reproducible version of this figure.*

Designing an assessment plan in this way allows educators to ensure that learners have practiced and received feedback on each standard several times. While there is no magic number as to how often data must be collected to determine proficiency, planning assessment in advance of instruction provides clarity within the process.

Moving Beyond Academics

A standards-based learning classroom involves so much more than clearly defined academic learning standards. Educators want students to be reflective, hardworking, timely, responsible, respectful—and more. In a traditional classroom, a single grade has become a potpourri of academic and nonacademic factors. Academic achievement, classroom behaviors, and growth are all important—just different. Thus, teachers must address academics and behaviors in both instruction and reporting.

Many schools claim to teach desired classroom behaviors and life skills. However, that is not often the case. For example, it is common to reduce an academic score for turning in an assignment late. When teachers do this, two things happen.

1. **They compromise the validity of academic reporting:** Does this student know less because he or she handed an assignment in late? What part of the standard was the student missing because he or she missed the deadline? Having an academic penalty for a behavioral misstep doesn't make sense, yet it has become common practice in the classroom.

2. **They penalize students instead of teaching them the desired skill:** Has this student learned executive-functioning skills? Does he or she know how to manage time and understand the importance of deadlines? When students struggle with academic content, schools lend instructional support. When students struggle with how to manage their time outside the classroom, schools often penalize them.

Standards-based learning cultures instead discern between academics and behaviors, explain what behaviors they want to see in students, and then teach them how to practice these behaviors. They also determine what the response will look like when there is a deficit and provide support when learners don't meet expectations.

To be clear, consequences and instruction are not mutually exclusive; an undesirable behavior could result in both consequences and instruction. For example, a student who consistently misses deadlines could face the immediate *consequence* of having to complete the missing assignments during free time (such as during lunch or after school) and join a targeted *instructional* grouping that focuses on developing the skill of staying on task and organized in advance of a deadline. Consequences disjointed from the behavior are unreasonable and unfair; how much students know and when they hand in their assignments are two separate constructs. The consequence for not doing the work should be doing the work; the consequence for not meeting a deadline should be learning how to meet a deadline.

Determining Behavioral Characteristics

Determining behaviors for the classroom or school often proves more challenging than determining academic standards because they aren't clearly outlined for teachers and the classes they teach. As the teacher or team of teachers determine the desired behaviors and share those with students and parents, they see not only the academic standards, but also the classroom behaviors that need improvement. Despite the reality that many schools lack a separate place on the report card to share each element, teachers must not distort the grade by including behaviors on the academic side. Articulating and teaching these behaviors and skills, in addition to separately reporting their growth—before a standards-based report card is in place—also provides a clearer picture of the whole child.

Determining which behaviors to report can be a challenge. A school's standards-based learning committee might sit down and determine what qualities it wants students to possess by the end of the year or the time they graduate from the school. The committee could then communicate with the rest of the staff for changes and approval. It is important that teachers in the school have a voice in this process because they will be responsible for teaching these skills.

The following are examples of possible behavioral characteristics for reporting.

- Work completion
- Participation
- Timeliness
- Attitude
- Initiative
- Problem solving
- Determination and perseverance
- Punctuality
- Ability to work with peers or a group
- Self-awareness and reflection
- Work habits
- Critical thinking

Whether a school calls them *behaviors, work habits,* or *process standards,* students must know what teachers expect of them in class. Schools must determine which behaviors to use for reporting, how to assess them, and what the response will look like when there is a deficit. For example, when looking at *timeliness,* an educator might provide support in the following ways.

- Requiring signatures in the assignment notebook

- Scheduling periodic check-ins with long-term assignments

- Requiring after-school sessions to complete work

- Meeting with parents about time management at home

The assessment of the important behavioral characteristics matters; the subsequent actions and support to ensure growth matter more.

Reporting on these behaviors, even if not on a report card, requires rubrics or descriptors that show student progression as well as assessment procedures that allow teachers to document student growth. For example, a teacher may measure behavior on a frequency scale—like that which indicates *consistently, often, sometimes,* and *rarely.* Without a scale or shared understanding of the descriptors, reporting of those behaviors can become inaccurate and inconsistent between classrooms. Figure 1.3 provides an example of the behavior *work completion* with performance criteria.

Behavioral: Work completion			
Rarely	**Sometimes**	**Often**	**Consistently**
Rarely hands in or completes practice assignments	Sometimes hands in or completes practice assignments	Often hands in or completes practice assignments	Consistently hands in or completes practice assignments

Figure 1.3: Scale for work completion behavior with performance criteria.

When creating a team or schoolwide frequency scale, it is important to stay away from descriptors such as *one to two assignments missing* because of the variation between different classrooms and teachers. Some teachers might only report three assignments throughout the period, while others might assign twenty. This variation makes that criterion unfair and impossible to score accurately. Descriptors such as *consistently, frequently, usually, often, sometimes, seldom,* and *rarely* offer a chance for more clear and consistent communication with the student about the expected behavior. Figure 1.4 assesses on a continuum of a student possessing the skill of self-awareness.

Behavioral: Self-awareness		
Beginning	**Developing**	**Distinguished**
The student is self-aware in some aspects of his or her learning, such as where and with whom he or she works best, but often needs help making decisions regarding learning.	With support, the student is able to make decisions about learning and what is best for him or her and is able to communicate those needs.	The student is very aware of him- or herself as a learner. The student can identify strengths and next steps, and often take steps to improve as a learner and reflect on those decisions.

Figure 1.4: Scale for self-awareness behavior with performance criteria.

When schools or teams clearly establish and communicate behavioral characteristics, teachers, students, and parents have a better picture of classroom expectations and how they can measure their success against those behaviors.

Figure 1.5 provides an example for teachers who are exploring implementing standards-based learning with separate behavioral standards prior to schoolwide implementation.

Learner Characteristics			
Student: _____ Grade: _____			
Class: _____ Quarter: _____			
Teacher: _____			
Respects others' rights, feelings, and property	Rarely	Sometimes	Consistently
Follows directions	Rarely	Sometimes	Consistently
Completes assignments with attention to quality and timeliness	Rarely	Sometimes	Consistently
Exhibits effort, commitment, and perseverance	Rarely	Sometimes	Consistently
Comments:			

Source: Adapted from Deerfield Public Schools District 109, 2016.

Figure 1.5: Sample behavioral characteristics.

*Visit **go.SolutionTree.com/assessment** for a free reproducible version of this figure.*

When teaching in a system that still requires traditional letter grades and report cards, teachers can send home forms like the one in figure 1.5 with the report card (if administration gives permission) or separately with students or through email. This communicates the importance of learner qualities in the classroom and gives parents insight into how to help their children succeed.

Holding Students Accountable

One of the big concerns when making the transition to a standards-based learning classroom is student accountability. Teachers have a resounding fear that if they don't grade it, students won't do it. Additionally, they worry that if they do not set deadlines, students will flood them with late papers and last-minute revision attempts at the end of the reporting period. When educators implement standards-based learning practices correctly, these worries could not be further from the truth.

If students do not place importance on completing their practice, they often don't care about their academic grades either. Hurting their academic grade for incomplete work compromises grade accuracy and allows students the choice to not do the work. After all, the best consequence for the absence of an assignment is requiring that assignment's completion. Figure 1.6 illustrates an example of how team members could assist one another with the common concern of work completion and accountability.

A teacher team shares this chart, which teachers can easily use in elementary, middle, or high school settings. Teachers add to the document when a student has missing work so that any other educator can access it to help support these students and remind them of their expectations in the classroom. Having established policies (such as a student who appears on the list three times being required to receive additional support after school) helps communicate to students that missing work is not an option. Teachers can visit this document daily, at weekly team meetings, or as often as they see fit.

Communicating Growth

The final piece in a standards-based learning classroom involves honoring students' academic growth. Not only do teachers, students, and parents care how students are doing at the time they get a report, but they also care how they got there. Teachers can mindfully note student growth throughout marking periods and report that to students and parents. This growth mindfulness could include goal setting with students, tracking formative progress with standards, and celebrating that progress with students.

Missing Work
English
Mathematics
Science
Social Studies
Music
Foreign Language

Source: Adapted from Hill & Nave, 2012.

Figure 1.6: Missing work accountability chart.

Although chapter 10 (page 187) focuses on standards-based reporting, it is import-ant to think about what reporting growth could look like early on in planning. By knowing how they will report academic growth, teachers can be mindful about how they collect and record data. Looking at and reporting growth often provides more insight into student learning than any other form of reporting because of its ability to address each student's characteristics.

Student growth is hard to quantify, so teachers often communicate it through nar-rative comments. Whether a teacher has 25 or 125 students, this can be daunting and time consuming. Figure 1.7 provides a template to guide teachers in collecting these data throughout the marking period that they can share with students and parents.

Student:			
Quarter 1	**Quarter 2**	**Quarter 3**	**Quarter 4**
Strength:	Strength:	Strength:	Strength:
Growth:	Growth:	Growth:	Growth:
Goal:	Goal:	Goal:	Goal:

Figure 1.7: Sample growth document.

Visit go.SolutionTree.com/assessment for a free reproducible version of this figure.

Taking brief notes in a single document throughout units or after summative assessment and organizing data before a parent-teacher conference or at the end of the reporting period becomes more manageable with a tool like the sample growth document in figure 1.7. Keeping multiple marking periods in one document means teachers can reference earlier goals and more easily report growth and progress.

Creating a Standards-Based Learning Classroom

Once the culture shifts, teachers view grades as communication, nothing more or less. Teachers with a standards-based mindset understand that an academic grade should represent the achievement of the academic standards (Schimmer, 2016). They also acknowledge that when they include nonacademic factors in grades, they compromise their accuracy. This mindset must extend to both students and parents.

Adopting a language of learning is a critical step in this process. This common language brings students and parents into the picture and allows them to become partners in the journey. By making this communication change, the classroom transforms from a culture of compliance to a culture of learning. Remember to communicate early and often with parents about such a change. Explain why it's occurring and how it will benefit both students and parents. Explain what will change for students and what will remain the same.

The following ideas can help teachers start shifting language with students and parents.

- **Communicate the standards, their learning targets, and what success looks like:** Learning should not be a guessing game. Be open. Let students know exactly what you expect of them and how they will know when they are successful.

- **Explain why the assigned work is important:** Be mindful about what you assign and how it will benefit student learning. When students view the work as critical to their learning, their buy-in is a natural outcome. Chapter 5 (page 89) talks more about homework.

- **Involve students in the learning process and allow some choice:** When students believe they have mastered a standard, allow them an opportunity to show it. If they have shown proficiency, provide ways to delve more deeply and keep moving forward. Speak with learners early and often about this approach. Teach students to own their learning.

- **Use effective, individualized feedback:** Each student is different and each should receive his or her own feedback. Because standards have provided the map, use feedback to keep students on track and push them along. Keep the language focused on the learning instead of the points. Chapter 4 (page 69) discusses effective feedback in depth.

Teachers must use the language of learning so students will follow suit.

The remainder of this book focuses on changing classroom practices. These include a balanced assessment system, effective feedback, and a consistent focus on standards, evidence, and proficiency.

PERSONAL NARRATIVE

Mandy Stalets

Author and High School Mathematics Teacher,
Illinois State University, Normal, Illinois

When I first made the change to standards-based learning, I made the mistake of grading assessments I categorized as formative and even weighted them in the gradebook at 10 percent. I made this choice because I truly believed that if I didn't grade it, they wouldn't do it. Fast-forward to year two. On the first day of school, I designed an activity in which students had to create their dream classroom. They were to come up with ten *wants* and then prioritize them.

Teaching middle school, I assumed that their number one might be that they were allowed to choose their seats or listen to music during work time. Those items were definitely on their list, but I was shocked to see their number one was "formative assessment weighted at 0 percent." When I asked students why this was so important to them, they began to tell me how I shouldn't punish them for early mistakes, how they value the feedback more than the grade, and how it often crushes their confidence to see early scores since they were just beginning to learn the standards. This was the moment when I realized things were going well. My students' focus was where it belonged—on their learning. They understood that growth and reflection were part of the learning process.

Talking to Learners

It is important that learners understand that standards-based learning is all about recognizing (and eventually reporting on) their whole selves. Outlining expectations, both behavioral and academic, provides learners with clear knowledge of what teachers expect of them in the classroom.

Just as you might post rules on the classroom walls and articulate them to students, make it a point to do the same with academic standards. Start a unit by sharing the standards and their learning targets. Put these standards on the class website and in parent newsletters or other communications. Let learners know exactly where they are headed early in learning, instead of making it a guessing game. Outline to learners what the standards are by starting lessons with statements such as, "Today, we will start learning to recognize and draw shapes having specified attributes, such as a given number of angles or a given number of equal faces. We will also identify triangles, quadrilaterals, pentagons, hexagons, and cubes" (2.MD.G.A.1; NGA & CCSSO, 2010b). Break apart that standard for learners. Define words. Involve students in the deconstruction by asking them what learning targets they see in the standard. Preassess on the spot by asking what part of the standard they are familiar with and what they still need to learn. This allows learners to begin with the end in mind.

It is also crucial that learners understand that their teachers recognize the effort, care, attention, focus, and perseverance they put in throughout units of study, the behaviors they display in class and with their work, and the growth they undergo throughout their learning journey. Figure 1.8 highlights some questions students might ask when it comes to standards-based learning and possible teacher responses.

Student Question	Teacher Response
Why do we have standards?	Standards are there to keep us on track and have a goal to work toward. Standards tell me what to teach and tell you what you are going to learn.
How do I know what will be on the test?	I teach to and assess the standards. Look at the standard and learning targets and let that be your guide.
Why do we assess so often?	I am constantly assessing and adjusting my instruction to better meet your needs. I want to constantly give you feedback to narrow the target for you.

Figure 1.8: Student questions and teacher responses about standards-based learning.

Communicate to learners that as teachers look at growth, they want to honor the natural learning process. Learners are unique and learn at a variety of paces; teachers want to respect that. The effort that a student puts forth during a unit might not match up with the ending proficiency level; teachers should also respect that and report all aspects of student learning. Through this, students learn that the journey is just as important as the destination. In fact, teachers know and understand that some learners who work the hardest might not have the highest grades, yet they don't want to overlook one of the most important parts—*how far the learner has come*!

Talking to Parents

When approaching this topic with parents, start by explaining that the purpose of grading is to communicate proficiency with the academic standards. This can be a challenge for parents because most grew up with the traditional 101-level grading system. Open their eyes to see that traditional grades have lost meaning because nonacademic factors can falsely inflate or deflate them. Talk with them about the desire to provide accurate information on how they can help their child be successful.

Starting with standards-based learning—teaching to the standards and changing the way we communicate—should be an exciting change for all involved. We want parents to be involved and active with their child's education and we would like to give them as much information as possible. Although traditional letter grades provide comfort and are the current status quo, they do not give a clear picture of the whole child, do not communicate what he or she learned, and do not provide parents with information about next steps and how they can support him or her at home.

Ask parents to answer the following questions based on their children's most recent letter grade.

- What are your child's strengths?
- What are academic areas he or she needs to work on?
- What are next steps?
- How is your child performing in the classroom?

Parents should answer the same questions *after* you provide (via a digital gradebook or separate communication) the academic standards their children are learning and their most recent achievement on each of those standards. We need to train parents to think about learning and grades differently. Standards-based reporting communicates more meaningful information as parents get a true glimpse of their child's strengths and areas for growth.

Getting Started With Standards-Based Learning

Making the shift to a standards-based learning classroom does not start with grading. Changing classroom practices happens first. Some ideas for getting started with standards-based learning follow.

- Get to know your standards. Deconstruct them, outline learning targets, and communicate those learning targets to parents and students.

- Rethink the way you plan units. Start with the end in mind (the standards). Use the learning targets to plan your journey.

- Change your language in the classroom. Make your focus the standards and student learning.

- Separate behaviors from academic grades.

- When reporting, make sure that you are communicating academic achievement, behavioral attributes, and growth. Deliberately plan how you will communicate these.

Questions for Learning Teams

Pose these questions during teacher team meetings, planning meetings, or book study.

- What quote or passage encapsulates your biggest takeaway from this chapter? What immediate action (large or small) will you take? Explain both to your team.

- How can we guarantee that we honor academic achievement, behaviors, and growth and communicate each one?

- How can we communicate standards and learning targets to students and families in a meaningful way?

- How can we plan units to make them standards based?

- How can we teach accountability without using grades?

- What types of learner behaviors are essential for students (during school and as they become adults)? How can we communicate and teach them?

- How can our classroom language focus more on learning and standards?

Standards Alignment in Action

These educational objectives become the criteria by which materials are selected, content is outlined, instructional procedures are developed and tests and examinations are prepared.

—Ralph Tyler

Standards represent the outcome that educators intend for the instructional process, and they are often *subject neutral* in that many have latitudinal applicability across multiple subjects; this allows educators who teach different subjects to establish alignment with instructional processes. For example, formulating an argument and supporting it with relevant details in a cohesive manner is applicable in English language arts, social studies, science, mathematics, and other subjects. The *curriculum*, or topic, is the means through which teachers bring standards to life within specific subject areas, while *instruction* is the process through which teachers fuse the curriculum and standards to create a vibrant learning experience.

Alignment between standards and instruction is the process of analyzing and unpacking standards to create meaningful learning progressions that allow students to move from the simplest to the most sophisticated demonstrations of learning. Strong alignment makes the instructional sequencing and progression transparent, so students understand how individual skill development (for example) contributes to higher-level thinking. Weak alignment does just the opposite, where each instructional experience is viewed as an isolated, unrelated occurrence. The alignment among standards, curriculum, and instruction is not automatic; teachers must purposefully work to create the necessary alignment.

Moving From Rationale to Action

The biggest idea is that the existence of standards doesn't guarantee that teachers are actually teaching to those standards, nor does it guarantee that the existing standards are aligned to what happens day to day in the classrooms. While the curriculum is often non-negotiable and is often discipline specific, the alignment between standards and instruction is a universal process of analyzing and unpacking standards to create meaningful learning progressions that allow students to move from the simplest to the most sophisticated demonstrations of learning.

The Research

The research we explore in the following sections focuses on aligning standards and instruction; analyzing and unpacking standards; and creating purposeful learning progressions.

Aligning Standards and Instruction

Standards are the *what* of learning, and instruction is the *how*. The alignment between the two maximizes both effectiveness and efficiency for learners and teachers. Practically speaking, instructional time at the macro level (term, semester, or school year) is fixed, which usually results in teachers running out of time before they run out of topics. Therefore, the intentional alignment between the *means* (instruction) and the *ends* (standards proficiency) is irrefutably necessary to maximize outcomes for learners.

In a standards-based instructional paradigm, meeting *standards* is the goal, so it is essential that proficiency against standards be the priority of the instructional process (Guskey, Swan, & Jung, 2010; McMunn, Schenck, & McColskey, 2003). Analyzing standards and developing clear learning progressions help teachers more effectively and efficiently *use* standards in a relevant and meaningful way.

Analyzing and Unpacking Standards

Analyzing and unpacking standards are the first steps to creating the necessary instructional alignment. Through analysis, teachers identify the level of cognitive complexity of the standards and do so again for each learning target; this allows teachers to match the assessment method to the specific complexity of the standard or target (Chappuis, Stiggins, Chappuis, & Arter, 2012). Once the teacher analyzes a standard, he or she can then *unpack* it, which means identifying the learning targets and underpinnings that make up the standard.

Educators identify cognitive complexity in different ways, including Bloom's (1956) taxonomy, Webb's (1997) Depth of Knowledge (DOK), or Fink's (2003) taxonomy. We use DOK in this book because it has served as a reference point for the development of several curricular standards, but teachers are free to use whichever model they prefer. The key is to use a model that assists with pinpointing the cognitive complexity, which, in turn, allows for the identification of specific learning progressions. If, for example, a teacher recognizes that a standard is set at a Level 3 on Webb's DOK, then he or she knows that the result of the instructional process should be the demonstration of strategic thinking (Webb, 1997). That level necessitates multiple steps, sources, or answers.

It is not uncommon to inadvertently mismatch the expected level of complexity and the required demonstrations. Knowing a standard is at DOK Level 3 but only requiring students to demonstrate their learning at a Level 2 is misleading to both teachers and students. It is one thing to *recall* (DOK 1) the meaning of poetic devices (such as personification or metaphor), but another to *use context clues* (DOK 2) to locate those within the context of a poem; it is yet another thing to be able to *critique* (DOK 3) the effectiveness with which a poet used those devices. It creates a false perception of proficiency because most Level 2 demonstrations would not fully encapsulate a Level 3 standard and might lead the teacher to (wrongly) conclude that no further instruction is necessary, when, in fact, the student hasn't demonstrated the expected depth and breadth of the standard. Students, too, misunderstand their own proficiency and may conclude that they have mastered a standard when they haven't. Plus, given the fact that most national or state standardized assessments align to the appropriate DOK, the requirements of those assessments could blindside students; they will not have demonstrated their proficiency at that level before.

Once teachers have analyzed a standard, they need to unpack it into their enabling targets and underpinnings. (Later in this chapter [page 37], we outline several processes that teachers can use to analyze and unpack standards.) To be sure, many of the underpinnings will overlap several standards so teachers aren't starting from scratch, but, for example, if students were to use dramatic irony within their writing, they would need to know the definition of *dramatic irony* and, quite likely, be able to aptly identify the use of dramatic irony within the context of several pieces of literature before being able to effectively use dramatic irony within their original compositions. The *knowing* and *identifying* of dramatic irony are the underpinnings and targets that lead to proficiency.

As stand-alones, these targets and underpinnings don't fully encapsulate the standard, but when teachers intentionally organize them into a cohesive pathway, they lead students to demonstrate their proficiency at the appropriate level of complexity against the standards; this intentional pathway is called a *learning progression*. Teachers must put learning targets back together as a cohesive standard for summative assessment. It is the process of unpacking standards—that is to say, building and using formative assessment with the identified targets within a learning progression to advance proficiency—that ultimately leads to the repacking of the standard. The repacking of a standard simply means students are demonstrating their learning at the full depth and breadth (the full complexity) of the standard, hopefully at a level of mastery. This is what forms the optimum learning experience for students.

Creating Purposeful Learning Progressions

Learning progressions provide teachers with a blueprint for instruction and assessment; their value for classroom assessment is that they identify both what to assess and when to assess it (Andrade, 2013). Learning progressions do essentially two things: (1) lay out, in successive steps, more sophisticated understandings and (2) describe the typical development of a student's understanding over an extended period of time (Heritage, 2013; Smith, Wiser, Anderson, & Krajcik, 2006).

The development of learning progressions is about intentionally sequencing instruction from the simplest (targets) to the most sophisticated (standards) demonstrations of learning. Some schools and districts develop *macro* progressions that examine how standards grow in sophistication longitudinally through successive grade levels; that's not the focus of this chapter. Instead, we discuss *micro* progressions within standards whereby teachers organize the underpinnings or targets into a specific instructional order.

After developing learning progressions, teachers can use effective assessment strategies to identify where instruction should begin; this is where they can gain instructional efficiency. Students rarely start from scratch, so effective preassessment can determine their individual and collective levels of readiness for new learning, and because standards often overlap and spiral through and between grade levels, teachers need not always begin from the beginning. Teachers need to personalize learning somewhat from year to year in that the scope and sequence from last year may not be applicable this year. Pacing plans and sound instructional practices do provide a solid predictor of where most students will be following instruction, but flexibility is necessary.

In Action

Standards are at the heart of all learning experiences for students. They anchor units of study, which means it is essential for teachers to examine how to make them meaningful and infuse them into their daily practice. Doing this takes an immense amount of work and includes, before anything else, knowing and aligning academic standards. This chapter explains how to accomplish those imperatives. Additionally, it helps teachers create learning progressions and addresses how to unpack standards. Finally, this chapter explains how to best communicate to students about standards, learning targets, and behavioral expectations.

Knowing the Standards First

To begin, teachers must know what the standards mean, and although this may seem simple on the surface, it can present challenges. Standards are broad statements that are often written using complex language. Delving deeply to strengthen understanding of the standards is an ongoing task for all teachers. Before students can clearly know what their teachers expect of them, and before teachers can use the standards to guide students, teachers have to model the process. For example, teachers can select a standard and show students how to break it down into learning targets. Through this process, teachers and students enhance their understanding as they grow and progress together.

When teachers don't fully comprehend standards, they run the risk of students not understanding them either. When the learning destination is, at best, opaque, teachers seriously compromise students' ability to efficiently and effectively meet the standards. Teachers must spend the necessary time to explore their standards deeply, have collaborative conversations to further clarify their understanding of the standards, and commit to use this understanding to guide their decisions throughout a unit of study. As their knowledge of the standards increases, teachers are better equipped to break them down in new ways that benefit both them and their learners.

Aligning Academic Standards

Every standard contains at least one verb that reveals the complexity of evidence and depth of knowledge required to show proficiency. Standards are typically skill based or content based (often tied to a specific skill). For those that are solely skill based, the content can vary depending on the curriculum. Content-specific standards demand that students demonstrate the skill within the context of the content. It is important that teachers are clear on the specifics of the standards at hand.

Two examples of skill-based standards follow. The grades 9 and 10 English language arts standard from the NGA and CCSSO (2010a) asks that students "cite strong and thorough textual evidence to support analysis of what the text says explicitly as well as inferences drawn from the text" (RL.9–10.1). The College, Career, and Civic Life (C3) Framework for Social Studies' standard for grades 3 through 5 asks that students "describe ways in which people benefit from and are challenged by working together, including through government, workplaces, voluntary organizations, and families" (National Council for the Social Studies, 2013, p. 32).

Both of these examples are purely skill based: *cite* evidence, *support* analysis, and *describe* benefits. A variety of content, texts, and themes could frame units of study while fulfilling these skill requirements; this gives schools and teachers the autonomy to use the best fit for their students, building, or district.

We do not find skill-based standards only in English language arts and social studies, of course. The mathematical practices from the Common Core State Standards provide standards that span not only the varied content areas in mathematics, but also grades K–12. The science and engineering practices from the Next Generation Science Standards (NGSS; NGSS Lead States, 2013) also cross multiple content areas and grade levels.

Again, it is possible to achieve alignment with these standards in various ways. Teachers can have candid conversations about what the standards mean and how they can consistently apply them regardless of whether they are utilizing the same content or concepts. For example, students could be reading different novels in a ninth-grade language arts class while using the same standards for reading literature. That said, it may be advantageous for teachers in the same school or district to select the same content to achieve the standards. Teachers should clearly communicate to both students and parents the manner in which students will access, practice, and demonstrate the standards. However, if different schools or districts choose different content, it is certainly feasible to achieve the same standards. Common standards, rather than common content, drive alignment.

The following two excerpts highlight content-based standards that are tied to skills: (1) "Know the formulas for the area and circumference of a circle and use them to solve problems; give an informal derivation of the relationship between the circumference and area of a circle" (7.G.B.4; NGA & CCSSO, 2010b) and (2) "Make observations to determine the effect of sunlight on Earth's surface" (K-PS3-1; NGSS, 2013).

These standards require a skill (*know* formulas, *give* a derivation, *make* observations, and *determine* the effect) as well as specific content knowledge (area and circumference of circles, sunlight and the Earth's surface) when showing proficiency. Teachers must be mindful that some standards, including these examples, can include multiple skills, each of which they must account for.

Determining Depth of Knowledge

Another consideration when aligning standards is to take into account the Depth of Knowledge level that each requires (Webb, 1997). A standard that asks students to *know formulas* is very different from one that demands application or analysis. When examining verbs within standards, teachers should dedicate some thought to the task's complexity. The verbs alone don't completely reveal each standard's cognitive complexity, but they can offer clues. If the complexity is high, more support along the way may be necessary compared to less demanding standards.

Teachers can use a chart like that in figure 2.1 to identify the DOK level.

Standard	Type	Verbs	Content, If Applicable	DOK Level
23.A.1a—Identify basic parts of body systems and their functions.	Skill and content	Identify	Body systems and functions	1 (Recall)
23.A.3a—Explain how body systems interact with each other.	Skill and content	Explain	Body systems and functions	2 (Skill or concept)

Source for standard: Illinois State Board of Education, 2010.

Figure 2.1: Standard type and depth of knowledge example.

Visit go.SolutionTree.com/assessment for a free reproducible version of this figure.

Once teachers are clear on the cognitive complexity of a standard, it is essential that they take into account all the facets of a standard by *unpacking* it into more specific learning targets. These targets guide the formative process, including instruction, practice, and assessment. When the DOK is clear, creating learning progressions that lead to the desired level of proficiency becomes straightforward.

Unpacking Standards

Standards, when teachers present them in sum, can overwhelm students. Breaking them down into digestible pieces clears a path forward for the journey students take to proficiency. Again, the deconstructed elements are commonly called *learning targets*. No matter the terminology, the important point is that the teacher breaks down the standards so students can access and make sense of what they should know and be able to do. With proper execution, the learning process with attainable yet challenging targets builds student confidence.

There are a variety of ways to deconstruct standards into manageable and meaningful pieces for students. The following are four possible methods for unpacking standards.

1. *I can* statements

2. Know, understand, and do (KUD) statements

3. Benchmarks from the academic state or provincial or national standards

4. Learning goals ladders (Vagle, 2014)

I Can *Statements*

I can statements are user friendly. They are a positive way to communicate what learners will practice along the way as well as what they will put together in the end to show proficiency. Although we discuss this further in chapter 7 (page 125), teachers must deconstruct standards into learning targets to drive instruction and practice. Then, in turn, they should put these practiced skills back together for summative assessment.

Teachers can integrate *I can* statements with one of the other systems for deconstructing standards (in the preceding section) or have them serve as stand-alone learning targets. We put them in their own section to highlight their potential use as a stand-alone. Whether part of another system, or on their own, *I can* statements communicate powerfully to students that these are attainable goals that will lead them to proficiency with the standards in sum. Figure 2.2 is an example of a standard deconstructed with *I can* statements from an eighth-grade science class.

Providing students a chance to focus on what they can do instead of worrying about what they cannot yet do is a positive side effect of this exercise, which works nicely at the introduction of every new standard.

KUD Statements

Based on the work of Carol Ann Tomlinson and Cindy Strickland (2005), creating KUD statements can break down broad standards into categories of knowledge, overarching understandings, and skills that, when blended, create an environment where students can showcase mastery.

The concepts and vocabulary that learners need from the Know section are used with the skills in the Do section, and then the Understand section frames them. Simply demonstrating the Know portion is a lower Depth of Knowledge level than what the standards demand; however, it is a starting place as students build their learning. The *do* statements are, in essence, *I can* statements and show learners the

---

Standard: Analyze factors that affect weather and climate and create models that account for regional differences.

I Can Statements

- I can describe the importance and function of Earth's atmospheric layers and the major gases found in the atmosphere.

- I can describe and use the various weather instruments that measure current weather conditions and describe how to use them to predict future weather.

- I can describe the three forms of heat transfer and their effect on regional and global weather and climate.

- I can explain how air masses flow from regions of high pressure to low pressure, causing weather to change over time.

- I can explain how the unequal heating of the Earth causes patterns of atmospheric and oceanic circulation that vary by latitude, altitude, and geographic land distribution.

- I can develop a model to show how sudden changes in weather can result when different air masses collide.

- I can describe how the Coriolis effect produces atmospheric winds and ocean circulation, resulting in the transfer of heat by the global ocean and air convection cycle.

Source: © 2017 by L. Odden. Source for standard: Adapted from the NGSS MS-ESS2-6.

Figure 2.2: *I can* statements.

---

skills they will use to demonstrate proficiency with the standards. The Understand section guides learners to put the learning targets back together to show their learning via the standards.

At the end of the unit, students must put the KUD statements together to demonstrate proficiency with the standards. Figure 2.3 (page 40) encompasses multiple standards in the unit breakdown of a Spanish II language course. In this model, once learners and teachers develop confidence with the deconstructed pieces of the standards, it is time to put them together to produce the final product to confirm proficiency—summative assessment. The content must be used with the skills to show their understanding.

Thematic Unit: The City

Standards:

- Narrate in the past using locations, people, and activities pertaining to the city in written form.
- Describe locations, people, and activities pertaining to the city in spoken form.
- Read and respond appropriately concerning the city.
- Listen and respond appropriately concerning the city.

By the end of the thematic unit you should know, understand, and be able to do the following.

Know	Understand	Do
• Vocabulary pertaining to occupations, stores, purchases, locations in the city, directions, and prepositions of location • Indirect object pronouns • Conjugations of *dar*, *decir*, *saber*, *conocer*, *ser*, and *estar* in the present tense • Conjugations of regular verbs, *-car*, *-gar*, and *-zar* verbs, *conocer*, *andar*, *venir*, *tener*, *dar*, *ver*, *hacer*, and *ir* in the preterite tense	• Verbs must be conjugated to show who is doing the activity and when the activity takes place. • There are two past tenses in Spanish that have different uses. • There are several ways to talk about the verb *to know* in Spanish. • There are several ways to express commands in Spanish, including the imperative tense. • There are recognizable language patterns in Spanish.	• Conjugate a variety of verbs in the present tense. • Conjugate a variety of verbs in the preterite tense. • Describe occupations. • Talk about knowing people, places, facts, and information. • State where someone went and what he or she did. • Ask for clarification. • State business hours, names of stores, and items purchased. • Use impersonal and passive *se* to talk about what is done, what is allowed, or what is prohibited. • Use the preterite tense to talk about completed past actions. • Infer meaning from text and audio sources.

Figure 2.3: KUD statements.

Benchmarks From the Academic State or Provincial or National Standards

The state, provincial, or federal government may benchmark some standards for teachers. These benchmarks can be learning targets, but it is important that teachers review them to ensure understanding of the language, purpose, and focus before using them with students. Teachers must prepare themselves to show students the connections between the learning targets and the standards, so a careful review of these targets is critical.

Figure 2.4 displays a third-grade mathematics standard and the Minnesota Department of Education's (2007) benchmarks.

Standard: 3.1.1—Compare and represent whole numbers up to 100,000 with an emphasis on place value and equality.
Benchmarks
3.1.1.1—Read, write and represent whole numbers up to 100,000.
3.1.1.2—Use place value to describe whole numbers between 1,000 and 100,000 in terms of ten thousands, thousands, hundreds, tens and ones.
3.1.1.3—Find 10,000 more or 10,000 less than a given five-digit number. Find 1,000 more or 1,000 less than a given four- or five-digit number. Find 100 more or 100 less than a given four- or five-digit number.
3.1.1.4—Round numbers to the nearest 10,000, 1,000, 100 and 10. Round up and round down to estimate sums and differences.
3.1.1.5—Compare and order whole numbers up to 100,000.

Source for standard: Minnesota Department of Education, 2007.

Figure 2.4: Grade 3 standard and benchmarks.

Learning Goals Ladders

In *Design in Five: Essential Phases to Create Engaging Assessment Practice*, Nicole Dimich Vagle (2014) organizes *I can* statements into learning goals ladders to show learning progression, from the emerging stages to standard fulfillment. Teachers benefit from paying special attention to the verbs in the ladder. (See Vagle, 2014, for verbs you can easily adapt to your own framework.)

Figure 2.5 (page 42) is a learning ladder that breaks reading standards into scaled targets (or goals).

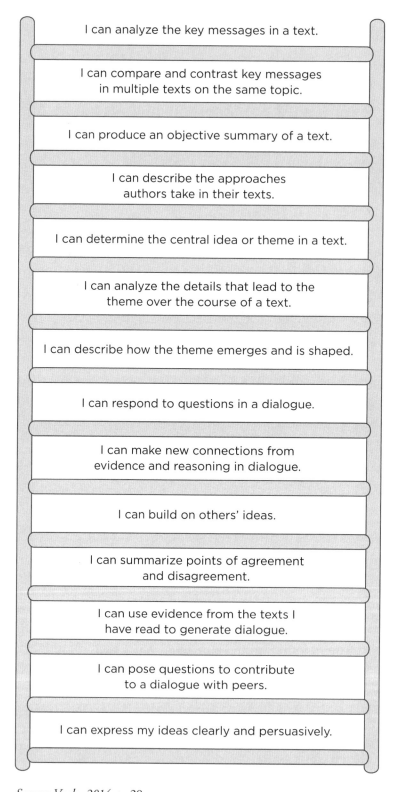

I can analyze the key messages in a text.

I can compare and contrast key messages
in multiple texts on the same topic.

I can produce an objective summary of a text.

I can describe the approaches
authors take in their texts.

I can determine the central idea or theme in a text.

I can analyze the details that lead to the
theme over the course of a text.

I can describe how the theme emerges and is shaped.

I can respond to questions in a dialogue.

I can make new connections from
evidence and reasoning in dialogue.

I can build on others' ideas.

I can summarize points of agreement
and disagreement.

I can use evidence from the texts I
have read to generate dialogue.

I can pose questions to contribute
to a dialogue with peers.

I can express my ideas clearly and persuasively.

Source: Vagle, 2014, p. 29.

Figure 2.5: Learning goals ladder example.

The standard's initial targets appear at the bottom of the ladder and increase in complexity as students climb. The advantage of taking the learning targets and creating a ladder is the power it has with students and teachers. Progressive learning targets guide a teacher's instruction and practice. For students, the learning goals ladder becomes a self-assessment tool.

Communicating Standards and Learning Targets

Teachers best serve students and themselves when they explain what they expect at a unit's outset. Again, there are many effective ways to communicate this information, but involving students in the discussion is essential for developing their confidence and investment. Examples of how to introduce students to the idea of standards and learning targets follow.

- Explain the idea of learning progressions by having them think about how they would teach a friend to ride a bicycle, throw a baseball, or swim. This gets them thinking about the idea of unpacking a skill and leading someone toward proficiency.

- Provide a standard and challenge them to figure out the steps that would build toward proficiency. Have students determine a few learning targets. Follow up with a discussion to provide clarity and guidance for the students and make a decision about the final learning targets.

- Provide the standard and the learning targets. Have them write *I can* or KUD statements or other student-friendly terms.

Aligning Units to Standards

Teachers can begin with the end in mind by reflecting on the applicable standards, determining what they demand of students, deciding how to assess those standards, choosing what formative experiences will lead to proficiency, and creating an instructional process that will be most efficient and effective for students.

Figure 2.6 (page 44) is a process that teachers can use when either auditing a previously constructed unit or creating something new.

Teachers can ask themselves these questions while planning. Notice that each step consistently searches for alignment from the summative and formative assessment experiences down to the instructional level. When analyzing older units, it is easy to see if any activities or assessments need modification or elimination for lack of alignment. Over time, this process becomes second nature and the search for alignment becomes a natural part of planning.

Standards-Based Unit Planning

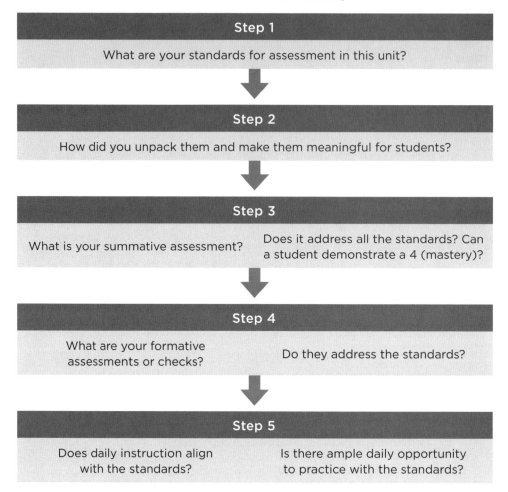

Figure 2.6: Standards-based unit-planning flowchart.

Ensuring Vertical Articulation

The final piece of academic standards alignment is *vertical articulation*, that is, ensuring continuity of learning from grade level to grade level within a given content area. Looking at the standards for one grade level *only* means alignment work is incomplete. Diving into the grade-level standards for students one grade above and below will provide a much more robust understanding of the standards teachers work with throughout the academic year.

When teachers know where students are coming from and where they are headed in relation to the current grade-level standards, their instructional decisions are more informed and contextually relevant. For example, a second grader would be working with a standard such as "Compare and contrast two or more versions of the same story . . . by different authors or from different cultures" (RL.2.9; NGA & CCSSO, 2010a). Looking at the first-grade standard that corresponds, "Compare and contrast the adventures and experiences of characters in stories" (RL.K.9; NGA & CCSSO, 2010a), helps the teacher understand the background knowledge students in second grade will have coming in. Reviewing the third-grade standard, "Compare and contrast the themes, settings, and plots of stories written by the same author about the same or similar characters" (RL.3.9; NGA & CCSSO, 2010a), gives a glimpse of the skill that students will acquire the next school year.

Teachers serve students well and increase their standards knowledge when they consider the following questions while looking at standards vertically.

- How does the cognitive complexity become more demanding as the grade level increases? See figure 7.4 (page 134) for DOK levels and characteristics.

- Does the content in the standard change or require a more in-depth understanding from one grade level to the next?

- How can I ensure student success with current grade-level standards in a way that will translate seamlessly to what their teachers will expect of them next year?

Many standards are *banded*, meaning that more than one grade level connects to a single standard or group of standards. Vertical articulation is a little more challenging in these cases, but still important. With standards for a grades 3–5 band, the standards at the K–2 and 6–8 levels can reveal valuable information about previous expectations for students and the path forward. Within the grade bands, vertical articulation allows teachers to fully explore standards that students practice throughout the grade levels. Teachers who have banded standards may need to create a learning progression that scaffolds the experiences within each standard, even though the standards themselves remain constant for multiple grade levels.

Aligning Behavioral Expectations

Behavioral attributes and characteristics play a significant role in learning and closely link with academic progress and success. It is imperative for schools to place behavioral attributes on equal footing with academic proficiency; if teachers take them seriously, so will their students. Educators can teach these important behavioral attributes in alignment with how they teach academic skills in five steps: (1) identify the important attributes and characteristics, (2) clearly define and contextualize what those attributes look like in action, (3) proactively teach what is expected of students, (4) regularly assess (not necessarily *test*) to determine the discrepancy between the desirable characteristics and what the students are currently demonstrating, and (5) provide feedback about the attributes moving forward.

These behaviors must align with academic standards as teachers move through their instruction and assessment in a unit or marking period. Behaviors are exhibited in different ways depending on the academic skills students are acquiring and the learning environment. Sometimes a simple behavior such as *follows directions* will look different from class to class and activity to activity. Just as with academic standards, teachers must break down behavioral expectations for students to best understand what they are to do and how they are to behave in the classroom.

Learners become self-aware when teachers are explicit about nonacademic expectations. This way, students can see the different ways certain behaviors will manifest when the class, content area, or activity varies. Figure 2.7 provides an example of behavioral expectations broken into specific learning targets.

The teacher aligns each behavior with several learning targets and then shares them with students at the beginning of the year, or he or she can unpack these expectations along with the students.

Just as with the academic side, each classroom experience will not address every behavioral target. However, with a breakdown such as this, students can see how the different behavioral aspects fit together and understand teacher expectations. It is key for teachers to model the expected behaviors because what adults pay attention to is what students eventually believe is important. Assessing these behaviors is a process that happens via teacher observation during class time with feedback loops to keep the learning moving forward.

Talking to Learners

Once learners know that academic achievement, behaviors, and growth are separate from assessment and reporting, developing clarity surrounding both the academic standards and behavioral expectations is the next step. For learning to be relevant, teachers need to clearly communicate standards. Students buy in to the standards-based approach when they know they are important; teachers do this by making standards the focal point of learning.

When preparing to talk with learners about standards and alignment, consider whether they know where they are headed and whether the end goals and benchmarks are clear to them. A teacher's experience with the standards will exceed a student's. Learners need support while making sense of academic and behavioral standards and require examples of what success looks like for each. For many

Behavioral Expectation	Behavioral Targets
Exhibits independence, initiative, and responsibility for own behavior	• Is punctual • Follows routines • Accepts responsibility for own actions • Obtains information independently • Completes retakes • Reflects on formative assessment
Completes assignments with attention to quality and timeliness and seeks assistance when necessary	• Follows directions and completes assignments in class • Completes homework with care • Uses time efficiently • Seeks assistance when needed • Works well without supervision • Manages time efficiently
Participates in and contributes to class and group activities	• Participates regularly • Accepts responsibility in class and in groups • Shows respect for others' ideas • Listens without interrupting • Follows rules • Helps others
Shows respect for others' rights, feelings, and belongings; seeks positive solutions to conflicts	• Respects feelings of others • Demonstrates positivity • Respects property of others • Works to resolve conflict

Source: © 2016 by Thomas Metcalf Middle School.

Figure 2.7: Behavioral expectations.

students, behavioral expectations are clearer than academic ones. Learners often know how to act when they enter the classroom and what repercussions there are for not fulfilling those expectations; however, academic standards, especially in a more traditional setting, can be less clear.

Teachers achieve clarity with students through much more than simply posting standards on the classroom wall or writing them at the top of an assignment. Make academic standards a continual topic of discussion throughout units, marking periods, and the school year. These discussions need to be student centered; this facilitates student ownership of the standards and, in turn, the learning. Allowing students to make sense of the standards, rather than simply being told what they are, plays a huge role in student investment in the learning process.

Equally important is that students understand what the criteria for success look like with behavioral standards and expectations. Teachers play an active role in communicating what behaviors are expected and their importance in relation to academic student learning; teachers know these two are explicitly linked, a concept they must explain directly to students. Discussing behavioral standards as they relate to the future successes in life can be effective, but relating them to more immediate successes is most relevant. In other words, helping students understand that *behaving* today will lead to *success* today is how teachers establish behavioral priorities.

Students will have a variety of questions throughout units about standards alignment, even if they use different terminology to address it. Figure 2.8 highlights some common student questions and how teachers might answer them.

Student Question	Teacher Response
Why is breaking down standards important?	Once you clearly understand what I expect of you and your learning, I can let you take ownership.
How do I know what will be on the assessment?	There will be no surprises on the assessment; you will have to show your learning with the standards.
Why doesn't my effort count?	Effort does count! It will show up in your academic achievement and the behaviors you demonstrate in class.
How many times do I need to show good behavior to get the highest level?	No one is perfect. I am looking for consistency.

Figure 2.8: Student questions and teacher responses about standards alignment.

Talking to Parents

When talking with parents about standards alignment, teachers must address academics and behaviors. On the academic side, parents want to know what their children are learning and what evidence they will need to show. So many parents want to help their children maximize learning, but are unsure of how to go about it. There is a big difference between parents knowing that a teacher has assigned the child a *task* and knowing what the child is supposed to be *learning*. Even if a workbook page supports this learning, students, parents, and educators can work together toward the same outcome when parents are on the same page with their children's learning goals.

Communicating clearly about learning goals and expectations greatly supports parents in this endeavor. Parents need teachers to break the standards down much in the same way as the learners, especially as their children get older and the standards become more complex. If parents see a standard or two in a teacher communication, they may not be able to easily interpret what the expectations are nor how they directly relate to the daily classroom activities and assignments.

When teachers communicate the standards and learning targets to parents, they can more readily facilitate conversations with their children about their learning (rather than their points or grades). Teachers can give parents some questions to replace, *What did you do at school today?* Parents can easily reframe these questions by changing the word *do* to the word *learn*. When parents are clear about the targets, they can ask pointed questions about the topics and skills the students are working on.

With behavioral expectations, teachers can let parents know which behaviors they will report as well as what those look like in the classroom. This, again, facilitates productive conversations between parents and their children about behaviors at school, specifically about successes and areas for growth. When teachers effectively communicate the alignment of academic standards and behavioral expectations for students, a common language develops among all parties.

Getting Started With Standards Alignment

At first glance, curricular standards and the work of aligning them to instruction can be intimidating. Though curricular standards are not new, this process feels new to many teachers. We provide these suggestions to make it more palatable.

- Discuss the academic standards in learning teams. Focus on the verb and the applicable DOK level to deepen understanding as a group.

- Deconstruct the academic standards into student-friendly learning targets.

- Organize the learning targets in a meaningful way for students and parents.

- Plan the assessment process (both summative and formative) based on the standards, the targets, and what they demand.

- Align units of study to the learning targets, building up to the standards in sum.

- Communicate the standards and learning targets to all stakeholders.

Questions for Learning Teams

Pose these questions during teacher team meetings, planning meetings, or book study.

- What quote or passage encapsulates your biggest takeaway from this chapter? What immediate action (large or small) will you take as a result of this takeaway? Explain both to your team.

- What are some strategies to support teachers in continually deepening their understanding of the standards?

- What are some ways in which you currently make standards and targets transparent in order to foster more student ownership of learning?

- How can you best unpack your standards into learning targets that align to the standards?

- How can vertical articulation become an integral part of your collaborative process to ensure consistency and reduce overlap?

- What are some ways that you clearly communicate and explain behavioral expectations (standards) to students?

Formative Assessment in Action

Assessment functions formatively to the extent that evidence about student achievement is elicited, interpreted, and used by teachers, learners, or their peers to make decisions about the next steps in instruction that are likely to be better, or better founded, than the decisions they would have made in absence of that evidence.

—Dylan Wiliam

Assessment in the service of learning continues to be an area of emphasis for teachers striving to optimize student achievement. Classroom assessment is nuanced and contextually sensitive, which makes it a continual part of a teacher's professional journey, and while reaching a level of expertise is certainly possible for all educators, the journey with classroom assessment practices is never complete.

At its best, teachers use formative assessment to make instructional decisions rather than evaluative ones. The balance between the formative and summative purposes of assessment is akin to the relationship between practice and games, and while *doing* formative assessment is an essential first step, teachers in a standards-based learning classroom emphasize *using* assessment results to advance a positive learning trajectory for all students.

Moving From Rationale to Action

The research on the effectiveness of formative assessment is robust, well known, and indisputable in its foundational concepts; however, the development of effective, efficient, relevant, and sustainable practices is why formative assessment has yet to reach both a habitual and ubiquitous presence in classrooms around the world. Teachers know formative assessment is essential to maximizing student achievement, but becoming habitually fluent in and capable of utilizing formative assessment is an ongoing cycle of implement, react, revise, repeat; teachers know what to do, but *doing* it is complex.

The Research

The research we explore in the following sections focuses on eliciting formative evidence, using formative assessment evidence, and tapping into the power of *yet* by students acknowledging that they may not currently have mastered something.

Eliciting Formative Evidence

Because every assessment can serve both a formative and summative purpose, there are no separate design issues between the two per se. Whether teachers employ selected-response questions, constructed-response tasks, or performance assessments, the same care and design finesse applies regardless of the use they intend. That said, being *aware* of the intended purpose is paramount to eliciting assessment evidence at the appropriate level of specificity; formative assessment tends to have an additional focus on specific underpinnings and targets.

Using assessments formatively requires that teachers elicit evidence in the most useful way to allow for easier (though it is not necessarily easy) interpretation and inferences. According to Patrick Griffin (2007), students reveal that evidence through what they say, write, make, or do. He's implying that students provide teachers, through the course of a normal school day, with the necessary indicators that allow them to accurately infer student proficiency. On the other hand, Margaret Heritage (2013), a senior scientist at WestEd, characterizes the interaction between teacher and students as a principal source of evidence in formative assessment, so whether the student is saying, writing, making, or doing, it's the interaction that is most revealing. The takeaway for teachers here is that they must purposefully plan these interactions through the lens of assessment as opposed to simply having activities that students complete. Even with purposeful planning, sometimes these formative moments occur more organically and are as much about student *affect* as they are about proficiency. What students say, do, write, or make can indicate as much about student motivation and self-efficacy as standard proficiency, so while assessment can reveal the next steps in the learning, it can also indicate how willing the student is to engage in these next steps. We assert that any activity can become a formative assessment so long as teachers *teach* through the lens of activities that they intentionally design to elicit evidence of learning and inform them and their students about what comes next.

Teachers commonly initiate formative assessment interactions by posing questions. Ideally, they design these questions to expose the gap between what students know and what they need to know to generate teachable moments, allowing them to introduce interventions that then lead to further learning (Black & Wiliam, 2005; Chappuis, 2015; Hattie, 2009; Sadler, 1989; Shavelson et al., 2008). In *Essential Questions: Opening Doors to Student Understanding*, Jay McTighe and Grant Wiggins (2013) submit that the most effective questions "are not answerable with finality in a single lesson or a brief sentence" but rather are designed "to stimulate thought, to provoke inquiry, and to spark more questions, including thoughtful student questions, not just pat answers" (p. 3). Even in cases with one correct answer, questions can include incorrect answer options that reveal a specific gap or misunderstanding in the learning (Wiliam, 2017).

Certainly, teachers must be keenly aware of potential validity and reliability issues, something that researchers have not yet fully developed and explored in the literature (Brookhart, 2003; Marzano, 2017; Ploegh, Tillema, & Segers, 2009). Again, *validity* refers to whether an assessment measures what teachers intend it to measure, and any assessment's validity hinges not on the task or tool itself, but on the teacher's accurate inferences and interpretation (Heritage, 2010). This speaks to the importance of developing clear success criteria for students while developing assessment experiences. *Reliability* is the consistency with which an assessment measures what teachers intend it to measure (Heritage, 2010), so the consistent inferences and interpretation that teachers draw when using the same assessment activity are paramount. Agreement on the criteria and alignment with the scoring inferences teachers draw between the criteria and what students produce are essential for meaningful, accurate instructional responses.

Using Formative Assessment Evidence

A significant body of research and professional literature has confirmed formative assessment as an essential process to raising student achievement for each and every student (Black & Wiliam, 1998; Chappuis, 2015; Chappuis et al., 2012; Heritage, 2008; Popham, 2008; Shepard, 2000; Wiliam, 2017). John A. C. Hattie (2009) reports that formative evaluation has a significantly high effect size (0.90). *Effect size* is simply a determination of the relative strength of a strategy or approach and the *effect* it has. In this case, the effect is on students who might not otherwise receive the strategy or intervention; the larger the effect size, the greater the strategy's or approach's likely impact. According to Hattie (2009), an effect size of at least 0.40 is the *hinge point* for determining what interventions will bring about at least an average gain; at 0.90, clearly formative assessment yields above-average improvements when implemented with fidelity. Hattie (2009) urges teachers to "pay attention to the formative effects of their teaching, as it is these attributes of seeking formative evaluation of the effects (intended or unintended) of their programs that makes for excellence in teaching" (p. 181).

Every assessment can serve both formative and summative purposes, but limiting the formative assessment process to one that runs parallel to the summative process fails to capture the depth and breadth of the impact formative assessment can have on students' learning trajectories. Assessment does not interfere with instruction in standards-based learning. Instead, the processes are fluid. The fusion of assessment, instruction, and feedback creates the opportunity for teachers to be instructionally agile by making seamless transitions and real-time maneuvers (Erkens, Schimmer, & Vagle, 2018). When teachers embed formative assessment within the instructional sequence, they elicit evidence in rapid, accurate interpretations and their instructional responses aren't necessarily contingent on the quantification and documentation of learning (Wiliam, 2017).

It is important to emphasize that this is not an either-or proposition; there is most certainly a place for more formal formative assessments as *nouns* (assessments that are *things* and take on a more traditional look of something tangible the students fill in), especially when it comes to gathering evidence through collaborative common assessment (Erkens, 2016). The essential point is to find a balance so that teachers use the elicited evidence optimally. In either case, when they view formative assessment as a fluid, actionable process, teachers come to see that instruction and assessment are almost synonymous in the sense that effective teaching without effective formative assessment is next to impossible—the latter informs teachers of their instructional design and execution efficacy.

The key to *using* formative assessment is what D. Royce Sadler (1989) calls the *feedback loop*. Sadler (1989) says students must come to know—either via the teacher or themselves—three things: (1) where they are going, (2) where they are now, and (3) how to close the gap. Gathering evidence allows teachers and students to identify the discrepancy (Heritage, 2013). The resulting feedback articulates what aspects of a student's performance require strengthening and how best to approach that work. *Using* formative assessment evidence is crucial if it is to produce its most desirable results, which are enhanced teaching and learning.

Tapping Into *Yet*

Formative assessment can significantly contribute to building student confidence and self-efficacy (Brookhart, 2013a). Confidence rises when students achieve success. Confidence also rises when teachers allow and encourage students to take risks and do not penalize them for the mistakes that may accompany risks. Confidence rises when teachers use the word *yet* in the context of learning and formative assessment. *Yet* is a powerful and hopeful word (Dweck, 2006). *Yet* tells students they can, even if not right now.

Changing the mindset regarding formative assessment from "I can't do this, and I won't be able to" to "Just because this is difficult doesn't mean I won't be able to achieve it" makes a huge difference in classroom culture. When the focus is on growth, students and teachers tend to see misunderstandings and setbacks as a natural part of learning (Heritage, 2008; Shepard, 2000). How students recover from those setbacks is much more important than getting it right the first time. In a culture of learning and growth, students are more likely to support and help one another because they know everyone will struggle at some point and they will need support as well.

In Action

Teachers cannot know when students will achieve proficiency, even if they have taught the same class, topic, or lesson before. As Dylan Wiliam (2017) writes, "Teaching is a *contingent* activity. We cannot predict what students will learn as a result of any particular sequence of instruction" (p. 56). Some teachers may have an idea of what to expect based on previous experience, but each class and each student within it brings unique combinations of strengths, areas for growth, paths to proficiency, and processes to learn. When in action, meaningful formative assessment methods partner learners with their teachers. Assessment is no longer teacher centered with students waiting to know their grades. It is *assessment* treated as an active verb, indicating progress and movement. Assessment *for* learning is the goal of formative assessment, whereas assessment *of* learning happens with summative assessment (Chappuis, 2009).

After shifting to a standards-based environment, teachers may realize how often they are already formatively assessing students in a given class period or school day. Educators often feel that for it to be called an *assessment*, it has to be something more formalized. Nothing could be further from the truth. For example, teachers and students conversing about student work is formative assessment. Reviewing exit tickets and revising the next day's lesson accordingly is formative assessment. The less educators see assessment as something separate from teaching, the more effective it becomes.

What makes an assessment formative is the action the teacher takes based on the results. It is in these unobtrusive moments, where teachers employ instructional agility based off their observations, that they make a significant impact. This chapter highlights the connection between learning targets and formative assessment, the balance between formative and summative assessment, various assessment methods, and data collection.

Connecting Learning Targets to Formative Assessment

After teachers clearly outline, organize, and communicate learning targets, their connection to the assessment process (through a clear learning progression) should be direct. Developing a plan for various assessments to gather reliable information about student learning throughout a unit of study is important. Figure 3.1 provides a sample formative assessment plan. This is one way to map formative assessment aligned to the targets. A plan such as this works for a single standard or for a cluster of standards, depending on the unit's construction.

Figure 3.2 (page 58) is an example of a third-grade English language arts standard and its benchmarks. This is a robust standard and will require some time before students can produce mastery of the standard in its totality. The formative process is indispensable with a standard that encompasses so much for the learners.

To connect these learning targets with a formative assessment process, teachers need to evaluate each of them to determine both a learning progression and specific instructional steps. All the targets will need to be practiced and formatively assessed to support learners in achieving the standard. This may seem daunting with such a broad standard and high number of learning targets, but some standards require a yearlong process with targets spread out throughout the course of the school year. The first few benchmarks (explain the functions of nouns, verbs, and so on; form and use regular and irregular plural nouns) may be achieved toward the beginning of the year while the last ones (use coordinating and subordinating conjunctions; produce simple, compound, and complex sentences) would not be assessed until later on.

Creating an (Un)balanced Assessment System

Formative and summative assessment work together to create a balanced, accurate picture of what students know, understand, and are able to do. The distribution between formative and summative assessment, however, is unequal. The road to proficiency through assessment is frontloaded, that is, the number and frequency of formative assessments far outweigh those of summative assessments. When the students do the heavy lifting of learning through formative practice, assessment,

Standard: K.CC.B.4—Understand the relationship between numbers and quantities; connect counting to cardinality.	
Benchmarks	**Formative Assessment Ideas**
When counting objects, say the number names in the standard order, pairing each object with one and only one number name and each number name with one and only one object.	• Have a station activity in the classroom with different numbers of objects requiring students to write the number. A teacher runs this station to give immediate feedback. • The teacher provides a given number of items for the whole class and has students lift up a card with the correct number. He or she can be agile based on responses.
Understand that the last number name said tells the number of objects counted. The number of objects is the same regardless of their arrangement or the order in which they were counted.	• As the teacher counts, students collect items and stop when the teacher stops, understanding that the last number spoken is the total amount. • Explore regrouping. With three different types of objects, have students count in different ways. Example: three cotton balls, two pencils, and four erasers is still nine objects, no matter how a student counts them.
Understand that each successive number name refers to a quantity that is one larger.	• Given the same number of popsicle sticks, have students count them. Provide one additional popsicle stick to each student and have them recount to show the change in the quantity and name of the number. • Hold a question-and-answer session with students (whole or small group) asking what happens when the teacher adds one item to a group and having students identify the number. The teacher could model and provide feedback based on a ten frame and modeling quantities.

Source for standard and benchmarks: NGA & CCSSO, 2010b.

Figure 3.1: Standard, benchmarks, and formative assessment ideas.

and feedback, the summative assessment should not feel burdensome. Rather, it is an opportunity to celebrate learning.

Teachers often pose the question of how many formative assessments they should conduct before a summative assessment. The number is contingent on when students are ready to show proficiency. If most students are showing preparedness with three formative checkpoints but some are not, the formative process may take a little longer for those who need more time. The student and teacher must have confidence that the student is ready for the summative assessment. The process of practice and formative assessment should serve as a guide to make decisions about the quantity.

Standard: L.3.1—Demonstrate command of the conventions of standard English grammar and usage when writing or speaking

Benchmarks (Learning Targets)

- Explain the functions of nouns, pronouns, verbs, adjectives, and adverbs in general and their functions in particular sentences.
- Form and use regular and irregular plural nouns.
- Use abstract nouns.
- Form and use regular and irregular nouns.
- Form and use the simple verb tenses.
- Ensure subject-verb and pronoun-antecedent agreement.
- Form and use comparative and superlative adjectives and adverbs, and choose between them depending on what is to be modified.
- Use coordinating and subordinating conjunctions.
- Produce simple, compound, and complex sentences.

Source for standard and benchmarks: NGA & CCSSO, 2010a.

Figure 3.2: Third-grade English language arts standard and benchmarks.

*Visit **go.SolutionTree.com/assessment** for a free reproducible version of this figure.*

Eliciting Accurate Information

Any method of gathering information to fuel student learning and achievement can be valuable. However, teachers should choose the method intentionally. Some assessment methods and tools are better suited to certain classroom situations. Teachers must make informed decisions about which assessment method or tool will elicit results they can most effectively and efficiently use. Once the teacher considers the demands of the standard, determining an effective method for data gathering becomes much easier. Table 3.1 provides potential formative assessment types within the various classroom settings.

Formative assessment methods vary from informal to more formal. Unobtrusive formative assessment is not discernible from what usually happens in the classroom. More obtrusive formative assessment may feel like a pause in the daily happenings, but teachers must treat it as such—a pause. Although more obtrusive methods of formative assessment tend to be common in the classroom (quizzes, drafts of projects and writing assignments, conferencing, journaling, and labs), table 3.2 offers several unobtrusive methods.

Table 3.1: Formative Assessment Types by Classroom Setting

Setting	Assessment Types
Large-group formative assessment	• Question-and-answer sessions • Whole-group exit tickets • Whole-group quizzes (paper and pencil or digital)
Small-group formative assessment	• Question-and-answer sessions • Targeted discussions based on student need • Differentiated practice
Individual formative assessment	• Student conferencing • Differentiated practice • Individual conversations during class time

*Visit **go.SolutionTree.com/assessment** for a free reproducible version of this table.*

Table 3.2: Informal, Unobtrusive Formative Assessment Methods

Method	Examples	Rationale
Observations, in-class conversations, and discussions	Informal one-on-one conversations, whole-group discussions, and literature circles	Teachers can take anecdotal notes and make on-the-spot decisions.
Rapid-response digital quizzing tools (where students use a device like a smartphone, tablet, or laptop to respond to questions)	Selected-response assessments and constructed-response items such as Kahoot! (https://kahoot.com), Socrative (www.socrative.com), or Quizlet (https://quizlet.com)	Teachers and students get instant results.
Whole-group, small-group, or individual questioning sessions	Socratic seminars; popcorn questions and answers (teacher calls on first student to answer a question, student chooses a peer to answer it and then asks a question)	Teachers can easily find out the needs of students to plan instructional response.
Back channel (a [usually] digital discussion forum during instruction or work time where students can question or comment to the teacher)	Edmodo (www.edmodo.com) and TodaysMeet (https://todaysmeet.com)	Students have an easy way to access the teacher and peers with a running record of the communication.

continued →

Method	Examples	Rationale
Student proficiency self-assessment	Thumbs up, sideways, down; I've got it, I need more practice, I do not understand yet	Students can reflect on their learning and communicate that thinking.
Exit tickets	One to three questions about the day's focus	These are quick and focused on a single learning target.
Parking lot (where students can write or type questions or comments that they would like the teacher to address)	Chart paper hung in the room and Padlet (https://padlet.com)	Students may be more open if they can ask questions privately or anonymously.
Graphic organizers	Venn diagrams, step-by-step procedures, T-charts, two-column notes, flowcharts, hierarchy charts, and story maps	They provide a visual means for students to brainstorm or organize ideas.

While not an exhaustive list, the aforementioned assessment strategies illustrate the varied ways teachers can unobtrusively elicit evidence of learning from their students. For example, if a teacher simply needs to know the progress of vocabulary acquisition for later application, a quick check using a digital quizzing tool such as Kahoot! is effective. Teachers can easily access data for the whole group and individual students in a short amount of time. If they require more robust evidence, perhaps as students move toward putting a standard together in sum, a more formal quiz may be a better choice.

PERSONAL NARRATIVE

Rik Rowe

High School Mathematics Teacher,
Marlborough High School, Marlborough, Massachusetts

When we use frequent and ungraded formative assessments to move from "You are here" to our learning targets, learning environments can become rich, collaborative, and engaging opportunities to enjoy the learning process. I liken frequent formative assessments to the way we intuitively correct our steering as we drive along a road. That constant and iterative adjusting becomes natural as we aim for our destination. Teachers and students benefit from regular, ungraded, and feedback-centered formative assessments that often yield *aha moments* as we strategically align with our targets. Engagement heightens as learning moves closer and closer to the learning goal. I often see and hear our learners recognize their efforts on their recent successes ("I knew I finally got that step right") along with becoming more aware of their areas for improvement ("Oh, that's what I'm missing . . .") through frequent formative assessments. Let's use varied ways to formatively assess to bring about exciting learning for retention.

Some ways we formatively assess include: red, yellow, and green cups on the desks of our learners, collaborative questioning, and frequent exit tickets. Each of our learners has a stack of three cups on his or her desk. The cup on the top of the stack indicates the student's current confidence aligning to the learning at hand. A green cup signifies the learner is in sync with the learning and on pace toward our goal. When a yellow cup is on the top of the stack, the learner is indicating that he or she needs more practice, or some question or confusion, but is still with the learning. A red cup on top shouts, "I need help," "I'm lost," or "I'm frustrated with the learning." Our learners have become honest in their selections.

In addition to the cups, our learning environment is a place where questioning has become a natural part of our collaborative growth. We constantly ask questions of each other and often answer questions with other questions. This type of environment develops listening skills along with inquisitive thinking or question formulation. One of our favorite assessing tools is to ask "Why?" We've seen that questioning and thinking that we build around *why* focuses the mind on the task at hand and creates an engaging, robust, learner-centered environment.

Providing frequent and quick check-ins in the form of exit tickets creates a natural way for learners to convey their current state of learning along with what questions they still have related to the current learning targets. These ungraded formative assessments occur as often as every three days. They offer learners a chance to demonstrate their proficiency and give learning facilitators an opportunity to provide specific, timely, and meaningful feedback. Our learners look forward to a colored sticker affixed to their exit ticket when the teacher returns it during the next class. A blue dot sticker signifies "Nailed it." A green dot indicates "Proficient." When learners see a yellow dot, they know their skills are "Approaching proficiency, but not yet there." They find more feedback written on their assessments explaining areas of improvement. A red dot conveys that the learner is in his or her "Beginning stages" of learning for our target. Our learners strive for that blue sticker, but are happy with

continued →

the green one indicating proficiency with the assessed learning goal. Our learners appreciate the colored stickers conveying where I believe their learning is related to our targets without being graded. The colored stickers do not appear to stop the learning like a graded assignment often can. Our learners appreciate the stickers giving them a ballpark assessment of their learning. They remind me if I return their exit tickets without their colored stickers.

We've seen our learners request more frequent formative assessments as they've learned to see them as communication about where they are related to our learning targets. Our learners have welcomed extra practice specific to their areas of improvement in order to demonstrate an even higher level of proficiency on their next attempts. Our learning continues to reach for subsequent learning targets each day, though many learners may be seeking deeper learning associated with prior targets. We welcome and encourage learning that fosters a desire to relate and connect learning targets in an integrated way. This integration often brings about more aha moments and even more questions about the *why*.

Collecting Evidence and Data

Throughout the process of formative assessment, the collected data support both teachers and students in making informed decisions about next steps with their learning. If teachers reserve data collection for themselves, they leave students uncertain of and disconnected from their proficiency levels.

Student portfolios are a powerful way to gather evidence of learning, monitor progress, and reveal the formative process with assessment and feedback for students and parents alike. Portfolios do not have to include every bit of work students do in a unit of study, but they can incorporate several artifacts to show progression. A portfolio works to increase self-efficacy and motivation for students by making growth visual and tangible.

An additional way to gather evidence of learning and progress throughout the process is to chart it visually. No matter who gathers these data and how they display them, both teacher and student must use the information to plan next steps. Formative assessment data should reveal areas of strength as well as areas for growth that lay the foundation for future instruction and practice. Various methods can show student data, but a line graph such as the one in figure 3.3 gives a clear picture of the learning with this particular standard or learning target. It is important to note that learning is not linear; the process includes progress, stagnation, regression, and celebration.

Key Ideas and Details

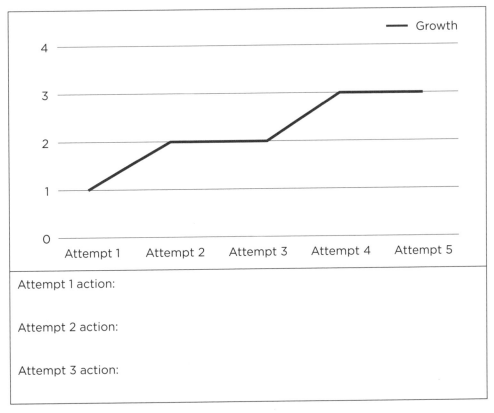

Figure 3.3: Data chart example.

Visit go.SolutionTree.com/assessment for a free reproducible version of this figure.

A step backward in proficiency is normal for students, but how teachers respond to that step back is of utmost importance. For example, when student proficiency drops with a standard, it is a call to action for the teacher to provide additional instruction and practice to the student. Figure 3.4 (page 64) provides a different visual of student achievement in bar graph form; it does include 0.5 levels, which some schools use. When schools use 0.5 levels, they require their own unique description of the learning at that level.

No matter whether the student is gathering the data or the teacher is taking the lead, students seeing their progress provides clarity and transparency with their learning. Using formative assessment to know where learners are throughout the journey to proficiency leads to precision moving forward.

Academic Data Chart

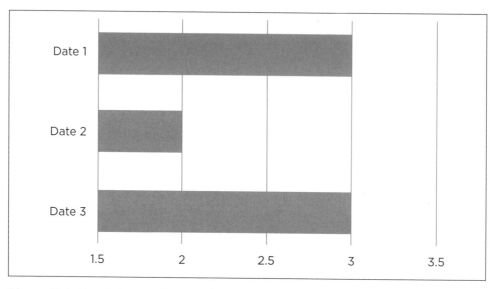

Figure 3.4: Graph to monitor student achievement.

Grading Formative Assessment

The distinction between formative and summative assessment is not simply a determination of whether a teacher assigns a grade. The distinction lies in the idea of whether the mark will be used to guide future learning as a checkpoint or as a determination of proficiency. Because formative assessment simply informs next steps, teachers need not grade it. However, we must acknowledge that policy requires some teachers to grade formative assessment in order to meet requirements for entries into online gradebooks. Regardless of whether a teacher assigns a score, he or she should not use formative assessment data as part of a summative grade for reporting. If a grade or score accompanies feedback, it is incumbent on the teacher to ensure the students' focus is squarely on *using* the feedback. (See chapter 4, page 69, for help making feedback actionable.) At times, teachers will give a completion grade for a formative assessment because they do not want to penalize a student for a proficiency level during the learning. If these scores for completion contribute to the final grade, there is potential for grade inflation. Rather than giving a completion grade, teachers can keep track of formative data (completion or proficiency level) without including them as part of the grade; *completion* can contribute to an overall behavioral rating.

Talking to Learners

Formative assessment goes hand in hand with the learning targets to ensure students are on the right track with their journey toward proficiency. Discussions with students about formative assessment need to be open and ongoing to maximize their impact.

Students will have a variety of questions about formative assessment, and how teachers use it in the classroom. Figure 3.5 offers possible student questions and teacher responses.

Student Question	Teacher Response
If my formative assessment isn't being graded, why should I try?	Your formative assessments let me know when you are ready to move to the summative. If I don't know where you are with your learning, we are not ready to move forward.
How will I know how I'm doing throughout the unit?	Through feedback and conversations with me you will always know where you are with your learning. If you ever feel that you don't know, it is time to ask!
Why does my assessment look different from what other students are working on?	There will be times when I will assess some students in different ways. This happens because I may need to vary my assessment practices to truly find out about progress with learning. It is my way of making sure I am meeting your needs.
How will I know when a formative assessment is happening?	There should be many times when you don't know or feel like a formative assessment is happening and that is OK. Formative assessment and the use of its data is how we learn.
What if I don't get everything right on my assessment?	There is no need to worry about being perfect on formative assessments. The purpose is to pinpoint your needs and plan next steps. These do not count toward a final grade.

Figure 3.5: Student questions and teacher responses about formative assessment.

Teachers should remind students that they are always checking for understanding, trying to best serve students' needs, and figuring out next steps. If students express anxiety or fear of judgment, teachers can calm them by providing simple examples of what formative assessment will look like in action. Teachers should communicate that assessment is not punitive, but is an ongoing conversation. It is not something that teachers do *to* students but rather *with* them.

When students feel like formative assessment is being done to them, it has implications that should give teachers pause. Student engagement drops when learners feel sidelined from the assessment process. Also, teachers overburden themselves when they take on the full workload of formative assessment, rather than sharing it with learners. For example, if a student can just as easily check a piece of formative practice, allow the learner to check work, reflect, and make decisions about future practice.

Talk with students about the fact that assessment happens in so many different ways, from informal conversations to peer editing, from self-reflection to quizzes and assignments, and from digital assessments to classroom discussion and questions.

Because assessment should not overwhelm students, teachers should create a culture where it's safe to make mistakes and where everyone can succeed, making it clear that they are fostering that culture and that students should as well. Ask students, "Do you need to take a risk to learn?" After students talk for a bit, the idea that no one learns without taking some type of risk begins to emerge. Learners need to know that risks are worth it, and that their teacher is there to support them every step of the way. Pairing the risk taking of learning with a supportive formative assessment environment will help learners become comfortable and available to learn.

Talking to Parents

The idea of formative assessment will not be a new one to parents once teachers explain it. They will be able to reference times throughout their schooling that involved questioning, practice, quizzing, and the like. However, the use of this formative practice may look very different for their children, and teachers must make sure parents understand this so they can appreciate the true purpose of formative assessment and its impact on student learning.

Explain that although formative assessment in the classroom may look very similar to their school experiences, it may not have been used to guide student learning, but rather for a summative judgment. Help parents move beyond asking the question of

"What did you do in school today?" only to meet a response of "Nothing" by using prompts such as the following.

- What did you learn today?
- How do you know that you learned it?
- Tell me about an activity you did during reading.
- Do you have any work to show me?
- Tell me one example of something your teacher said that helped you learn more about the topic.

It may take students some practice to answer these kinds of questions with substance, but ask parents to be persistent. An ongoing portfolio of work may also provide some talking points for students and parents. With it, parents can see their children's work, feedback, and progress and contribute to the conversation.

Getting Started With Formative Assessment

Getting started with formative assessment does not mean starting from scratch. It does mean that educators can critically review what it looks like, what evidence it produces, and how that evidence relates to the standards.

- Assess often, and make it unobtrusive when possible. Allow those assessments to shape learning in the classroom. Use the results to communicate with students and plan future instruction.
- Identify your current formative assessment practices individually and in teams.
- Analyze formative assessments for alignment to learning targets, efficiency, and effectiveness.
- Talk to learners about how the formative assessment process supports risk taking and learning.
- Use the power of the word *yet*.
- Determine which formative assessments, if any, you will grade.
- Design each formative assessment to elicit an instructional response.

Questions for Learning Teams

Pose these questions during teacher team meetings, planning meetings, or book study.

- What quote or passage encapsulates your biggest takeaway from this chapter? What immediate action (large or small) will you take as a result of this takeaway? Explain both to your team.

- How can you communicate to students that formative assessment is assessment *for* learning, not assessment *of* learning?

- How are learning targets and formative assessment connected in your classroom? Can you make the connection stronger?

- How can you strengthen the role of the learner in formative assessment?

- What are some important factors to consider when deciding whether to grade formative assessment or give feedback alone?

- How can you better infuse formative assessment into your daily practices to make it less obtrusive or a more sustained practice? How do you already do this?

4

Effective Feedback in Action

Feedback is what happens second, is one of the most powerful influences on learning, occurs too rarely, and needs to be more fully researched by qualitatively and quantitatively investigating how feedback works in the classroom and learning process.

—John A. C. Hattie

Using assessment data is fundamental to closing the gap between where students are and where they need to be. The unpredictability of learning makes feedback essential to effective learning and improvement (Wiliam, 2013). Despite deep and wide research, there is no definitive answer to the question, What's the most effective feedback strategy?

Everything about assessment is contextually sensitive and nuanced; a strategy that is effective in one class might be ineffective in another. Although it is a more favorable practice to utilize formative feedback in the absence of grades or scores, the definitiveness with which some reference the research on feedback minimizes the complexity of the feedback process. Almost everything teachers do in responding to assessment can, on some level, be classified as feedback (grades, for example); however, the real question is how *effective* the feedback was in producing the desired result of advancing proficiency.

Moving From Rationale to Action

Learning is deeply personal, nuanced, and contextually sensitive. In fact, it is impossible to separate learning from its social context (Ruiz-Primo & Li, 2013). Therefore, the culture (and the relationships within) will greatly influence how—or even if—students receive, process, and respond to feedback. What works in one class may not work in another. If feedback were simply about delivery, then the same strategies would have the same impact on all students; just give it and improvement will occur. All teachers know that's not how feedback works.

The Research

Like formative assessment, the research on feedback since the late 1980s is robust, which prevents a thorough literature review in the first section. Rather, we've chosen to focus on a few seminal studies that have had considerable influence on how educators shape their feedback routines.

The research we explore in the following sections focuses on providing effective feedback by measuring student responses to given feedback; answering the question of what happens next; targeting feedback to the learner; prompting thinking; including motive, opportunity, and means; and involving awareness.

Measuring Student Responses

Arguably the biggest lesson one can learn is that teachers should measure effective feedback by the kinds of responses it triggers in the learner (Hattie & Timperley, 2007; Kluger & DeNisi, 1996; Ruiz-Primo & Li, 2013). Feedback that triggers positive and productive responses from learners is, by this definition, *effective*, even when the particular strategy the teacher has used doesn't fully align with what the research says is the most favorable course of action. Every strategy has the potential to elicit both productive and counterproductive responses and filters through student perception (Brookhart, 2017). So while the giving of feedback matters, observing how students respond matters more; it is alluring to speak of feedback in absolutes, but there are no universal strategies that *always* work.

The challenge facing teachers is that they are likely to see mixed results with any strategy. It is possible—even likely—that the same strategy will elicit both productive and counterproductive responses within the same classroom. For example, one of the longest-standing lessons from the research is that grades and scores can interfere with learning and the willingness of learners to use feedback for improvement (Hattie & Timperley, 2007; Wiggins, 2012; Wiliam, 2017). However, it is not inconceivable to imagine *some* students using feedback to improve their achievement despite the existence of a formative score. If, for example, a teacher grades formative work and provides feedback on the next steps for improvement, and the students re-immerse themselves in their work, then no harm, no foul. If all this occurs but students don't act on the feedback, then there's a problem. Even more likely is a combination in which some students act on the feedback while others don't. In this case, the teacher may consider withholding the formative score until those students commit to continual improvement.

Answering the Question of What Happens Next

Despite the inconsistency in results, research does tell us the more favorable practices for advancing student learning and eliciting productive action (Chappuis, 2015; Wiggins, 2012). Because feedback needs to be actionable, the most effective feedback answers the question, What's next? In their seminal meta-analysis, John A. C. Hattie and Helen Timperley (2007) submit that feedback should answer three questions: (1) Where am I going? (2) How am I going? and (3) Where next? Aligned with D. Royce Sadler's (1989) three questions (Where am I going? Where am I now? How do I close the gap?), the question of where to go next or how to close the gap is the teacher's response to the information he or she gleaned from formative assessment work. The identification of the gap is incomplete and the existence of feedback is not enough; students must *use* the feedback to advance their understanding or refine their skill development.

Eliciting a productive response from feedback recipients is more likely when feedback transparently describes *what's next* instead of *what was*, and when students see their current status as merely a starting place for future growth rather than a fixed commodity (Dweck, 2006). Monique Boekaerts (2006) writes that students will appraise each task to determine whether to invest time, energy, and attention along the *growth* pathway toward proficiency or the *well-being* pathway, which is about avoiding emotional threat or harm. Clearly, attention to growth leads to students acting on feedback to increase proficiency, while well-being is designed to reduce risk or harm. While the differences are subtle, these subtle differences often shape a culture of learning.

Targeting Feedback to the Learner

In *Visible Learning*, Hattie (2009) highlights the importance of feedback as a key part of learning. Like formative assessment, feedback has a high effect size (0.73). The most effective feedback provides the learner with cues (areas in need of strengthening) and reinforcement (areas of strength) and relates to the intended learning goals by drawing attention to the performance rather than the person (feedback that focuses on the *learning* rather than the learner).

Formative assessment identifies the gap while feedback provides the next steps for closing the gap. To effectively and efficiently close the gap, teachers must know precisely where students are along their learning continua so they can target feedback at, or just slightly above, current student performance levels.

Hattie (2009, 2012) submits that feedback works at the following four levels.

1. **Task:** Feedback focuses on the specific *task* whether it is correct or incorrect; feedback is typically related to the content.

2. **Process:** Feedback aims at the *process* the student used to complete the task; feedback is typically related to strategies.

3. **Self-regulation:** Feedback focuses on furthering *self-evaluation* skills and how learners can monitor their own actions; feedback is related to the student's self-directed actions.

4. **Self:** Feedback focuses on the *learner* and not the learning; feedback is related to personal characteristics; feedback comes in the form of praise.

Regarding focusing on the learner instead of the learning, feedback to oneself is rarely effective because it provides no information related to improvement and can lead to avoiding risks and choosing the well-being pathway (Boekaerts, 2006). Praise gets in the way of students fully receiving the feedback about their performance (Skipper & Douglas, 2011). The issue is not praise in and of itself, but mixing praise and other feedback. Praise dilutes the remaining information's power (Hattie, 2012).

While implementing these four levels, keep in mind that feedback that is too sophisticated is not helpful; feedback that is too simplistic isn't either. Ultimately, feedback is most effective when it addresses a partial understanding (Chappuis et al., 2012), which means students who have full understanding or no understanding are unlikely to benefit.

Prompting Thinking

Another essential element of effective feedback is that it stimulates thinking (Chappuis, 2012; Wiliam, 2013). Rather than correcting student mistakes, teachers should seek to prompt a response (Vagle, 2014). While teachers must take into account the four levels of feedback (novice learners may need more explicit direction), feedback in the form of cues, questions, or prompts will cause students to *think* rather than just follow directions. As students advance in their proficiency, making them think—even giving them the space to think prior to a prompt or cue—becomes even more critical.

Although teachers know the merits of immediate, timely feedback, others make the case for delayed feedback that allows for metacognitive reflection prior to any teacher intervention (Wiliam, 2013). If feedback is always immediate, there is no space for students to think for themselves and self-reflect on what comes next; delayed feedback can be advantageous for more proficient learners.

Including Motive, Opportunity, and Means

In her report *Focus on Formative Feedback*, Valerie J. Shute (2007) highlights that effective feedback is contingent on three things: (1) the motive, (2) the opportunity, and (3) the means. *Motive* relates to whether the feedback is necessary. Teachers would not give feedback they did not believe was necessary. However, it's important that students believe the feedback is necessary as well. The *opportunity* relates to students receiving feedback at a time when they're most able to use it and whether they are afforded the time to act. The *means* relates to whether students are willing and able to act. Even when all three are in place, there is considerable variability in the effects feedback has on performance and learning (Kluger & DeNisi, 1996). Nevertheless, the motive, opportunity, and means are good places for teachers to audit their own feedback practices for the most basic fundamentals.

What's interesting for teachers is to reflect on the three potential scenarios where only two of three aspects are in place. For example, what if the student has the motive and opportunity, but not the means? What if the student has the motive and means, but no opportunity? What about a lack of motive? Table 4.1 outlines the three potential combinations and their likely ramifications for learning.

Table 4.1: Motive, Opportunity, and Means

Combination	Explanation
Motive and opportunity	Without the means, feedback is essentially useless. There is a belief that the feedback is necessary, there is time to act on the feedback, but there is no willingness or capacity to productively respond to what is supposed to come next in the learning.
Motive and means	Without the opportunity, there is no time to act. There is a belief that the feedback is necessary and there is both the willingness and capacity to act, but there is no chance for the student to make the necessary corrections.
Opportunity and means	No motive renders the feedback, again, useless. Even when students have the space to improve and the willingness and capacity to make those improvements, the lack of motive will stall any improvement efforts.

Source: Adapted from Shute, 2007.

Again, there is no guarantee of improvement, even when all three elements are present. The lack of motive may be the most difficult to overcome, as there is no singular reason for a lack of motivation and there is no single remedy. That said, the lack of motive could be the result of students settling for an initial score or level, which is why feedback in the absence of scores, grades, or levels is a more favorable course of action (Wiliam, 2013).

Providing Feedback With Awareness

Feedback is complicated. Strategies are not transferable to every context; nuance and contextual sensitivity matter most since strategies can have a varying degree of success from classroom to classroom. Most critical is for teachers to provide feedback with a level of awareness that allows them to ascertain a productive (uses feedback to advance proficiency) versus counterproductive (ignores feedback) response. What teachers can't say is, "I give my students effective feedback, but they don't do anything with it." It's the *doing something* that defines effective feedback. If students aren't using it, teachers need to revise their approach.

Feedback is not just about the students; it is also powerful when it comes from students to the teacher (Hattie, 2009). Being open to or seeking feedback allows teachers to measure instructional efficacy and be more instructionally agile (Erkens et al., 2018).

In Action

Effective coaches understand that practice or training is not designed to place a value judgment on the participant's ability level. They understand that the purpose of practice is just that: *practice*. Practice is something that is necessary to *prepare* participants to be successful at the game or performance; it is designed for learning and improvement. This type of practice and feedback is universally accepted as good coaching. Effective coaches focus on *what's next*. This focus on growth allows learners to concentrate on what comes next to improve their practice.

The word *assessment* comes from the Latin *assidire*, which means *to sit beside*. Placing the focus on feedback allows students to become reflective in their practices, develop a growth mindset, and establish the habits of a lifelong learner. Sitting beside learners allows teachers to coach them through the process of learning.

Because defining effective feedback is necessary, the following section does just that. Doing so will help teachers avoid ineffective feedback. Formalizing feedback methods and making feedback manageable are also discussed.

Defining Effective Feedback

Effective feedback might look different in each classroom. There are certainly many forms—conversations, written comments, oral feedback, digital feedback, peer feedback, well-written standards-aligned rubrics, self-assessment, and more. But several key attributes are non-negotiable. All these qualities in isolation have value, but in conjunction with one another, they truly impact and inspire learning. They include the following.

- **Goal referenced:** When providing feedback, keep the standard or learning target in the forefront of thinking and conversations. It is easy to get sidetracked, but teachers need to stay centered on the intended learning and how they can narrow the target for learners.

- **Actionable:** *Actionable feedback* means that the provided feedback gives students next steps that they can use to improve. Feedback comments such as "Good job!" or "You made a mistake here," or even "86 percent," are not feedback at all. Actionable feedback is concrete and specific, and looks forward.

- **Personal:** Mentioning the learner's name goes a long way when providing feedback. The learner should know that the teacher read his or her work and that the feedback is for him or her.

- **Timely:** Time is definitely the hardest part of providing effective feedback. If students misunderstand a learning target but don't receive feedback for four days, feedback isn't as effective. Build in time for students to reflect and act on the feedback when the learning is fresh and they can correct any misconceptions promptly. Feedback doesn't always have to be in written form. Have conversations with the learners on the spot and address misconceptions as they arise. It's important to recognize that *timely* doesn't always mean immediate when providing feedback. Sometimes delaying feedback so learners have a chance to review their own work and self-assess is beneficial. The teacher is responsible for deciding when feedback would be best received and acted on.

- **User friendly:** Although students should be comfortable and familiar with the standards, try not to overwhelm them with technical jargon. Ask learners questions about their work that inspire thinking—why did you make the choice to solve it this way? Can you think of another way to present this information? Most important, make sure that communication is digestible for that student. That is, the student can independently act on the feedback provided.

- **Ongoing:** Learners need to understand that assessment is a conversation between teacher and student. They will make mistakes in the formative process and teacher feedback provides support to learners and continually guides them toward proficiency. A critical step of the feedback loop (Sadler, 1989) is *resubmission*, or students showing that they acted on the teacher-provided feedback. Once they do, teachers provide feedback again. Making students aware that they play a vital role in the feedback loop starts with teachers saying something like, "Remember that assessments are a chance for us to have a conversation. I will respond to your work and you will reply to me."

- **Manageable:** Feedback must be manageable for students to act on. Prioritize learning for them. Look at their work holistically and determine the next right-sized step. Because the feedback loop by definition is ongoing, there will be time to address other misunderstandings in the future (Wiggins, 2012).

Feedback has the potential to help students develop a growth mindset when teachers implement it well. When delivering feedback to students and determining whether it is effective, keep these key questions in mind.

- **How does this feedback impact student confidence?** How does the feedback make students *feel*? When feedback focuses on deficiencies, students' confidence might be hurt when they may only need to address a simple misconception. Are learners overwhelmed by the feedback provided or is it comprehensible? Do students believe the learning is attainable? Do they have the tools to reach proficiency based on the provided feedback?

- **What action can the student take based on this feedback?** Do students understand the next step in their learning? They must have the tools to act on the feedback independently. If students are able to ignore it, they will not take the next step. Some will seek out those missing points and look to improve their understanding, but most will not. Using phrases such as *now let's work on* or *now you can* helps them focus forward. This gives learners an action.

When providing meaningful, effective feedback, teachers redirect student attention to what they did well and what comes next.

PERSONAL NARRATIVE

Starr Sackstein

Director of Humanities, Union Free School District,
West Hempstead, New York

"Good job" is just not good enough. How many times have we offered students "feedback" that looks like that? While teaching high school English, I make it a point to de-emphasize grades on writing and teach students to ask for specific feedback. It begins with vocabulary and really modeling for students how to effectively elicit meaningful direction to grow as a writer.

For example, if we're working in class on developing literature analysis essays, students will review the standards and first self-assess where they are in terms of mastery against each of the main standards. After a draft is complete, a student might ask, "Does this thesis statement adequately convey an argument that organizes my essay and if no, where can I improve it?"

After reading the introductory paragraph, I can specifically provide feedback where I summarize, in my own words, what I think the essay will be about based on the thesis. The student can then tell me how well it aligns with what they meant. This conversation can happen in person, one on one in class, in a conference if the student requires more than five minutes of my time, or via a digital medium (Voxer or Google Docs) if we can't be in the same place at the same time. In a case where the thesis isn't effective, I may tell the student that he or she needs to be clear about the specific theme. Often, it's a matter of rewording or reorganizing the order so that the sequence of the essay follows the road map they have created in the introductory paragraph.

The more adept students become strong at recognizing areas of need; they are better able to ask for the feedback they are really looking for. It's too easy for a teacher to give generic feedback all the time, especially if we aren't really personalizing what each student is working on. But some students may have mastered introductory paragraphs and may need to focus on development or appropriate evidence and they would be looking for different feedback. Even if a student is doing something well, it is in our best interest to use the language of the standards when identifying characteristics that student is already doing proficiently or with mastery.

continued →

The best part is once the teacher models the feedback loop and students practice it, students can do it with each other before they come to the teacher. Using standards or rubrics, students can provide very specific feedback in the same way teachers can, and can even offer specific strategies for improvement based on feedback they have received in the past.

Avoiding Ineffective Feedback

Some feedback delivery methods can both hurt confidence and hinder learning. Deficiency-based and corrective feedback tend to stifle learning.

Deficiency-Based Feedback

Deficiency-based feedback focuses on what the student did wrong and is commonly paired with a numerical or letter grade. This feedback tends to diminish student confidence by placing a value judgment on a student's work, and does not disclose how to improve. Deficiency-based feedback focuses on *what was* instead of *what's next*. For example, assume that a student works on patterns, such as counting by 2s and 3s. For the pattern 22, 24, 26, ____, ____, ____, she writes *30, 32, 34*. She has shown proficiency at pattern identification on the rest of the assessment and through formative practice, but simply made a small error. A deficiency-based way of grading this assessment is to put a red line through the wrong answers, take off three points, and report a score of 23 out of 26. To help the student look forward, the teacher might say, "I was looking at your work with number sequences. I really like how you were able to count by 2s and 3s! I noticed that there was one problem where you made a small error. I want you to find it and correct it. Call me over when you are done, and we can talk about ways to prevent making that small error again."

Corrective Feedback

Corrective feedback refers to the teacher correcting mistakes or misconceptions and requiring little (or no) effort or thought from the student. For example, if a student consistently misspells words that have an *ie* by placing the *e* first, corrective feedback points out all the misspelled words in the student's work and replaces them with the correct spelling. The student does not learn anything. Corrective feedback does not encourage students to actively reflect because someone else is correcting their misunderstandings. Instead, a teacher might identify a couple of errors, point out the pattern to the student, and identify a strategy to prevent these errors from occurring again in future work. The teacher could also direct the student back to his or her notes to make corrections and require submission when the errors are corrected.

Formalizing Feedback Methods

Effective feedback requires a system that ensures each learner receives the necessary amount of support. It is easy to give struggling learners a lot of feedback, but they need help prioritizing what is most important or what step to take first. At the same time, it is challenging to provide inspiring feedback to students who excel (and who might have already shown proficiency with the standard). Teachers would like to avoid capping their learning.

Regardless of method, all types of effective feedback should include a step for resubmission. This crucial step holds both the teacher and learner accountable for participating in the feedback loop (Sadler, 1989). Being mindful about building in time for silent reflection, peer discussions, and goal setting will ensure that students not only read feedback but also act on it. Consider the following three feedback methods.

SE2R

Summarize, explain, redirect, and resubmit (SE2R; Barnes, 2015) is one feedback method that teachers can use.

- **S:** *Summarize* what the student accomplishes.
- **E:** *Explain* exactly what the student needs to demonstrate having met the objective.
- **R:** *Redirect* the student to further instruction.
- **R:** *Resubmit* once the student has reworked the assignment or assessment.

Figure 4.1 (page 80) shows SE2R in use. Educators can use SE2R in written feedback or in discussions with students about their work.

Here's What. So What? Now What?

Figure 4.2 (page 80) illustrates another method in which the teacher (or another person responsible for feedback) structures his or her feedback by summarizing what he or she observed in the student's work and possible suggestions, and explains why those suggestions are important to the body of work and what should happen next. Again, teachers can use this feedback method in many scenarios—teacher-to-student written feedback, peer feedback, or discussions about student work.

TAG—You're It!

TAG—You're it! is effective with teacher-student interactions but also works well for teaching students to provide effective peer feedback because it gives learners an outline that requires them to look for what they like and what comes next. It also helps students question and look for ways to improve work.

Student: *Beth*
Standard: *7.EE.B.4—Use variables to represent quantities in a real-world or mathematical problem, and construct simple equations and inequalities to solve problems by reasoning about the quantities.*
Summarize: *Beth, on this assignment you wrote inequalities from word problems and then solved them to make sense of the problem.* **Explain:** *I really like the way you identified and underlined details in the story problems and looked for keywords to set up your inequalities. This shows me you have a good understanding of how to model relationships. It does look like there is some confusion with the less than and greater than symbols, which was a focus on our learning this week.* **Redirect:** *Please return to our notes on inequality symbols and what they represent and go back through your work and try to identify errors.* **Resubmit:** *Resubmit when you have made those changes so I can re-evaluate your work.*

Source: © 2015 by M. Barnes. Source for standard: NGA & CCSSO, 2010b.

Figure 4.1: Feedback method—SE2R.

*Visit **go.SolutionTree.com/assessment** for a free reproducible version of this figure.*

Student: Jabarri
Standard: RL.1.3—Describe characters, settings, and major events in a story, using key details.
Here's what: When you were writing about the plot of the story, you did an effective job describing the main events, but provided little information about the characters or the setting. **So what?** Describing the characters within the context of the setting and main events provides more clarity as to why the story unfolded the way it did. **Now what?** Now let's work on improving your writing. As you revise your work I want to see you add details about the characters' personality traits and various settings. Please let me know when you have updated your response and we can look through your work again.

Source for standard: NGA & CCSSO, 2010a.

Figure 4.2: Feedback method—Here's what. So what? Now what?

*Visit **go.SolutionTree.com/assessment** for a free reproducible version of this figure.*

- **T:** *Tell* what you like.

- **A:** *Ask* a question about the work.

- **G:** *Give* the writer an actionable suggestion.

- **You're it!:** *Self-assess* what comes next.

An example of how this strategy might play out appears in figure 4.3.

Student: Kendrick
T—Reader: *I enjoyed reading about your opinion piece on schools needing to provide healthy lunches. I liked how clear you were with your position that schools should teach students how to eat healthy.* **A—Reader:** *Where did you get your information? I couldn't tell if some of the pieces were opinions or if they came from a source.* **G—Reader:** *Next, I would make sure to work on your citations. Sometimes I wasn't sure if you were giving your opinion or citing an article you had read.* **You're it!—Writer:** Thank you. To improve, I will work on being clear with what is opinion and what is a citation from an article I read or a video I watched.

Figure 4.3: Feedback method—TAG! You're it!

*Visit **go.SolutionTree.com/assessment** for a free reproducible version of this figure.*

All three methods we show here focus on the future and tell students what they should do next to improve.

Activating Students

If students view the potential outcomes of risk taking to be emotionally harmful, they won't respond productively to feedback. There are students who will respond productively to *what was* feedback, but it is more judgmental than supportive; those who lack self-efficacy may be vulnerable. The place for judgment is during summative assessment, but even still, feedback can always center on what's next.

Consider the following examples. This is the same feedback offered two different ways.

1. "You should have developed a concluding paragraph that reconnects and synthesizes the individual ideas in each of your body paragraphs." (Focuses on *what was*)

2. "Now let's work on developing a concluding paragraph that reconnects and synthesizes the individual ideas in each of your body paragraphs." (Focuses on *what's next*)

If teachers want to deliver effective feedback, they must build in time for students to act on it. Figure 4.4 offers a reflection piece for learners to fill out after receiving feedback. This not only ensures that they read the feedback provided to develop a plan, but also serves as a meaningful communication piece with parents since they can read what the teacher suggested and how the students plan to improve.

Practice Attempt	Feedback I Received	Action Plan
Write a short essay on the major events of World War II, explaining why each event is meaningful.	"What event are you referencing? You keep saying 'when it happened' but you aren't clear about what the 'it' is."	I will revise and clarify what event I was referencing.
Present on a controversial public policy issue.	"Evidence! This standard wants support from research. What evidence did you find for this statement?"	I will clearly identify and cite what research can support my claims.

Figure 4.4: Student feedback collection.

*Visit **go.SolutionTree.com/assessment** for a free reproducible version of this figure.*

Another way to compel students to act is through portfolios. Including a feedback and student reflection page in a student portfolio becomes a strong communication and study tool. Figure 4.5 is an example of a portfolio from a middle school mathematics class.

Make certain students know that replying to the question, What are your next steps for learning? with "I will study more" isn't specific enough. They should be planning for what comes next using concrete and actionable steps.

Managing Feedback

Feedback can seem like a daunting task whether faced with 25 students and a variety of content areas or 150 students in one. No method of feedback is best in every situation. It is the role of the teacher to determine the most practical method of feedback to coach learners forward in their learning.

Teachers can deliver feedback in a variety of ways, such as conversations, written comments, oral feedback, digital feedback, peer feedback, well-written standards-aligned rubrics, self-assessment, and so many more. It is by these means that feedback becomes manageable. Feedback does not always have to be a time-consuming endeavor.

Name:	
Practice Assignments	
What was the practice called? What assignment did I choose for my level of understanding?	What were you practicing? How well did you understand it? Do you need more practice?
In-Class Assignments	
Name: Reflection on my understanding:	
Name: Reflection on my understanding:	
Assessments	
What was the assessment called? What feedback did I get?	What are your next steps for learning?

Figure 4.5: Feedback-focused portfolio.

*Visit **go.SolutionTree.com/assessment** for a free reproducible version of this figure.*

Feedback is about rethinking and reworking the way teachers communicate with students. By placing the focus on where learners currently are and what they should do next to improve their understanding of the standard, the focus is always on growth.

Teachers have the autonomy to determine the most effective method of feedback for a given set of learners. When a class holds a common misconception, whole-group feedback is often best. When a smaller percentage of students in a class misconceive a standard, strategic grouping with different sets of feedback for each misconception can help best meet learners' needs and make feedback more manageable.

In cases like this, it is often best to *think*, *sort*, and *plan*.

- **Think:** Identify common misconceptions that the class will have. Anticipate these before administering the assessment, and look for those misconceptions in the student responses.

- **Sort:** After collecting formative assessment data, such as exit tickets or independent work, sort the papers into piles based on error type or misconception. Make sure to also make a pile for students who need enrichment.

- **Plan:** Make a plan for each misconception or error type. Write feedback and develop a plan for each group. Keeping the number of groups small helps make time more readily available to have meaningful conversations with each group of students centered on the areas of learning that need feedback for improvement.

Figure 4.6 provides a template that aids in strategically planning for common misconceptions.

Standard:		
Misconception:	Misconception:	Misconception:
Plan:	Plan:	Plan:

Figure 4.6: Template to plan for common misconceptions.

*Visit **go.SolutionTree.com/assessment** for a free reproducible version of this figure.*

Making feedback manageable requires teachers to know their standards, what student proficiency of those standards looks like, and what misconceptions students might have along the way.

Talking to Learners

Effective feedback has the ability to increase hope, efficacy, and achievement in learners (Erkens et al., 2018). When well implemented, it also has the potential to help students develop a growth mindset. When communicating with learners about feedback, a primary point to keep in mind is *feedback drives learning*. Feedback provides a path for improvement. Talking with students about a sport or activity that they are passionate about serves as a great springboard for this conversation. For example, ask a basketball player how she improved her layup over the years. She will normally credit practice and a coach who provided feedback and mentorship. When talking to an aspiring artist in the classroom, ask how he improved his drawing over the years. The answer will be practice and feedback.

Some teachers model a desired skill and have students repeat it. Others introduce a new strategy and have students try and try again. Learners must know that their role in the feedback loop (Sadler, 1989) is to *act* on the feedback provided. Most important, students benefit from knowing that they don't learn from making mistakes—they learn from reflecting on those mistakes. When students receive feedback, it narrows the target and makes learning more manageable. The feedback loop requires active engagement from the learner and the teacher. After all, assessment is communication.

Figure 4.7 provides some possible questions students might ask when it comes to feedback and possible teacher responses.

Student Question	Teacher Response
I read all your feedback, but what grade did I get?	Right now I am not focused on your grade. I am focused on your learning and helping you reach proficiency. When I am confident that you are ready for a summative assessment, I will report a grade. The purpose right now is reflection and growth.
Your feedback made sense, so I don't need to do anything else.	Again, we don't learn from an experience; we learn from reflecting and acting upon that experience. I need to see you take action. I need you to participate in the feedback loop as much as I do.
How do I know what my next step is?	Read my feedback and look for the next steps I provide for you. Refer to the success criteria and then plan how you will get there and what resources you have to use.

Figure 4.7: Student questions and teacher responses about feedback.

Talking to Parents

As teachers work to successfully implement effective feedback in their assessment practices, it is critical to find a way to involve parents and other education stakeholders in the feedback process. Many online gradebooks allow teachers to attach anecdotal notes and feedback to an assignment. Other educators implement a portfolio, as readers see in figure 4.5 (page 83), or communication log. They share not only feedback they provide in the classroom but also the student's action plan.

When discussing feedback with parents, explain that although the numerical scores that might have been provided in the past are familiar, they lack meaning and don't provide enough information to help their children at home. A score of 73 percent on a quiz or formative work shows that their learner has improvements to make, but it doesn't communicate what he or she is struggling with or how he or she can improve. It also doesn't help confidence to provide a value judgment while learning is in progress. Feedback should allow the parent into the conversation between teacher and student. With effective feedback, parents don't just see a score. Parents see a story of learning including teacher feedback, student plans, and next steps. They are involved in the conversation of learning.

As teachers focus on feedback in the classroom, they will acknowledge the student's place in learning and provide a path for him or her to improve. The feedback that the teacher provides should help the student, as well as the parent, identify strengths, areas that need improvement, and next steps in learning. Through this feedback, parents gain a clear picture of their learners' progress toward achievement of the standards.

It is also crucial to communicate to parents how and where they can locate the feedback and student reflections. Although parents can view some feedback online, they might also be able to check take-home folders or student portfolios.

Getting Started With Effective Feedback

As long as teachers know standards, are clear about students' destinations, avoid punitive marks, and encourage reflection by looking forward, they can utilize effective feedback in the classroom. Following are suggestions to get started with effective feedback.

- When analyzing student work, focus on where they are in relation to the standard and what advice or next steps they need to get there. Stop focusing on what students did wrong or didn't understand. Make this simple mindset change and you will become the effective coach they need.

- Make the word *next* a staple in your conversations with students, whether those conversations are oral or written. Always focus on next steps to instill that growth mindset in learners.

- Choose a method of feedback that ensures every student has a next step when acting on the feedback. Don't overwhelm struggling students or underwhelm students meeting proficiency on the standard.

- Make sure that you have built time in to have students *act* on the feedback. Be there to facilitate and help answer questions, but let them act on feedback and resubmit. Encourage collaboration and conversation about their learning.

- Talk with learners about feedback and why it is so important to them as they learn and grow. Show them the value in it.

Questions for Learning Teams

Pose these questions during teacher team meetings, planning meetings, or book study.

- What quote or passage encapsulates your biggest takeaway from this chapter? What immediate action (large or small) will you take as a result of this takeaway? Explain both to your team.

- Is the feedback you currently provide to students deficiency based, corrective, or effective in nature? Explain.

- How can you guarantee that your feedback promotes hope, efficacy, and achievement in your learners?

- What are your most effective feedback routines? What do you find most challenging with consistently providing students with feedback?

- How do you or will you share feedback with parents so that they can provide supplemental support at home?

- How do you or will you ensure that students act on the feedback you provide?

Meaningful Homework in Action

The range of complaints about homework is enormous, and the complaints tend . . . toward extreme, angry, often contradictory views.

—Brian Gill and Steven Schlossman

Few aspects of schooling rival homework in terms of multiple perspectives and definitive opinions. While some lament the very idea, others believe there is a place to extend learning beyond the school day. This chapter's purpose is not to stake out a position on one side. Rather, we present a more productive, meaningful approach to homework should teachers decide it is a necessary part of the standards-based learning experience. Students' age and stage of development undoubtedly play an essential role in teachers' decisions about the role of homework, which means they must contextualize the ideas we put forth in this chapter to determine the applicability for each teacher's classroom.

Moving From Rationale to Action

Because homework practices, strategies, tasks, and responses can vary so widely, homework is essentially a neutral practice that will either contribute to or take away from students' learning experiences based on how teachers utilize it. The latest research about homework lays the foundation so teachers can put the subsequent strategies into action to make it meaningful. Because there are many diverse perspectives, it is important for teachers to be mindful of context and nuance. Like most things in assessment, what works in one classroom or school may not work seamlessly in another.

The Research

Like so much in education, there is no definitive right answer. Homework can be a "spur to student achievement or student alienation" (Gill & Schlossman, 2004, p. 174). At its best, homework can be the necessary practice to keep students on their learning trajectories; at its worst, it is a primary source of student disenfranchisement. The research we explore in the following sections focuses on acknowledging homework's upsides and downsides; letting research guide practice; and making homework's purpose clear.

Acknowledging Upsides and Downsides

For students who take longer to learn, homework assignments early in the learning process can be disadvantageous because their initial poor results can reinforce their belief that they cannot learn (Hattie, 2009). For parents, homework is an obvious way to gain access to what their children learn at school. This access, and the subsequent opportunity to provide some assistance, can form an essential, seamless relationship between home and school (Walker, Hoover-Dempsey, Whetsel, & Green, 2004).

That said, the intrusion into family life and the tension surrounding homework completion could have a detrimental effect on the parent-child relationship in two ways. First, the residual effect of repeated conflict over homework could potentially take its toll on the personal relationship (Kralovec & Buell, 2000), while overly involved parents can inadvertently undermine student motivation and autonomy (Patall, Cooper, & Robinson, 2008). Second, parents can mistakenly equate lots of homework with rigor and high-quality education. Rigor is about cognitive complexity, not volume.

For teachers, homework can be the vehicle through which students practice and improve their skills. Having students complete work outside the school day allows both students and teachers the opportunity to keep pace or refine skills and understandings. The opportunity to work outside the classroom also gives teachers the chance to provide more authentic opportunities for students to learn in more real-world, reflective situations and circumstances. As project-based learning becomes more the norm, work completed *off-site* will become more essential. On the other hand, teachers can fall prey to the same rigor-equals-volume trap.

The teacher can, with homework, assess student behaviors (in terms of responsibility and work ethic, for example), though compliance is not necessarily a measure of work ethic. Also, homework may not provide an accurate picture of where students are because their access to parental and peer support can skew the results. Even when the results don't contribute to student grade determination, they contribute to instructional decisions that may run astray of what's truly necessary for students.

Letting Research Guide Practice

While the *always* or *never* positions on homework are the easiest to stake out, neither allows the kind of contextual sensitivity (what is relevant for our context) and nuance required for most aspects of teaching and learning. The research on homework is inconsistent and often contradictory, which means teachers would be well advised to let the research *guide* them, but not let any singular finding *rule* them (Vatterott, 2009).

Many studies find that there is a link between homework and increased achievement (Cooper, Robinson, & Patall, 2006; Epstein & Van Voorhis, 2001). However, the positive outcomes have more to do with the work's nature than with the amount students complete (Hattie, 2009). In fact, the time students spend on homework has little impact on achievement at all (Trautwein, Koller, Schmitz, & Baumert, 2002). Prior to the 21st century, professor of psychology and neuroscience Harris Cooper (1989) finds that, overall, homework at the high school level has twice the impact as homework at the middle school (junior high) level; homework at the middle school (junior high) level has twice the impact as homework at the elementary level.

Even without research, most teachers would agree that homework is increasingly more impactful—even increasingly more necessary—as students grow. Cooper et al. (2006) suggest that homework at the early elementary level (if teachers use it at all) focus on developing the habits, attributes, and traits that surround homework, while at the upper-elementary level, teachers focus on homework geared to improve student achievement; they suggest that from sixth grade on, teachers use homework to increase both in-school and out-of-school (external testing) outcomes.

Contrarian voices suggest that homework is an unnecessary intrusion into family life that, especially for elementary students, has little impact on their overall achievement levels (Kalish & Bennett, 2007; Kohn, 2006). In fact, Kohn (2006) goes so far as to challenge the merit of the positive outcome findings. Poor results on homework—especially the work that comes early in a learning progression—can reinforce for some students that they can't learn, making what should be positive practice the opposite (Hattie, 2009). Homework that teachers assign on principle or as policy can result in students completing what amounts to busywork, with quantity overriding quality. Policies and practices that prioritize quantity (such as thirty mathematics problems per night) over quality (cognitively demanding and learning centered) are clues of potential misuse. An emphasis on completion and compliance can lead to point accumulation, subverting learning and healthy risk taking.

In "The Case for and Against Homework," Robert J. Marzano and Debra J. Pickering (2007) suggest the following ways that research can guide homework policies and practices that are more likely to be productive, learning-focused activities:

- Assign purposeful homework. Legitimate purposes for homework include introducing new content, practicing a skill or process that students can do independently but not fluently, elaborating on information that has been addressed in class to deepen students' knowledge, and providing opportunities for students to explore topics of their own interest.

- Design homework to maximize the chances that students will complete it. For example, ensure that homework is at the appropriate level of difficulty. Students should be able to complete homework assignments independently with relatively high success rates, but they should still find the assignments challenging enough to be interesting.

- Involve parents in appropriate ways (for example, as a sounding board to help students summarize what they learned from the homework) without requiring parents to act as teachers or to police students' homework completion.

- Carefully monitor the amount of homework assigned so that it is appropriate to the students' age levels and does not take too much time away from other home activities. (p. 78)

A teacher's thoughtful, balanced approach to homework can ensure that students are able to practice and deepen what they need to practice and deepen, without homework devolving into an exercise in simple task completion or becoming an intrusion on family life.

Making Purpose Clear

The conventional purpose of homework, and the primary point of emphasis within this chapter, is that teachers use homework as practice, which dictates a *formative* purpose. Assessment expert Eileen Depka (2015) offers the following to guide the decisions teachers make about how to use homework results:

The question is not whether to grade work completed outside of the classroom but instead what type of work is it. Is the work formative and intended to provide further experiences for students to apply to content or skills? Is the work summative and assigned after students have had ample opportunity to practice? (p. 71)

Teachers can send mixed messages to students about the intent of any homework assignment by referring to it as *practice* the day they assign it, but then *scoring* it (and recording that score) the next day. If the purpose is formative, leave it there and focus on Marzano and Pickering's (2007) guidelines.

While the primary focus of this chapter is on homework as practice, it is worth mentioning that homework can have a summative purpose as well. While educators do not typically refer to research papers and projects as *homework*, students commonly work on these assignments at home. It is an overreach to suggest that students—especially middle and high school students—produce all their evidence of learning at school. Some work offers students more authentic opportunities to demonstrate and verify their learning. It is appropriate for teachers to grade this extension work as long as they feel assured that students completed the work independently (O'Connor, 2011; Schimmer, 2016). The validity of these summative assignments is essential, so teachers should not use assignments that students could easily replicate to verify learning. Generally speaking, assignments that require a certain depth of knowledge or original thinking are a superior option.

Another parallel purpose that teachers often cite is a focus on *responsibility* in that they use homework as a way of teaching students about being responsible for their own learning. In other words, the completion of the homework provides teachers with evidence that the student is (or is not) responsible. While this is a noble and worthy goal, it should not distract teachers from focusing on meaningful, learning-centered, *just-right* work. Of course, teachers can accomplish both simultaneously; teachers can assign meaningful practice and observe the level of responsibility. However, merely completing the work is almost always insufficient to reveal a student's level of responsibility.

We cannot stress enough the importance of criteria and intent. If teachers are using homework as a way of developing responsibility, which is a behavioral attribute and not academic comprehension, then they must make that clear prior to the assignment, and students must know the criteria (such as *completed the assignment to the best of his or her ability, identified areas in need of strengthening,* and *seeks extra help and support*). Success criteria, regardless of assessment content, describe the qualities of excellent work and can be expressed in a variety of ways (Andrade, 2013), making it critical that homework success criteria be substantive, rather than trivial (Brookhart, 2007).

In Action

Homework in action can look like many things to many people. This chapter approaches numerous aspects of this sometimes-contentious topic. For example, changing the language with which we talk about homework can help create a different, more hospitable culture surrounding it. Aligning homework with learning targets and differentiating practice with it can help teachers meet students where they are. Considering the impact of homework on families helps guide approaches as well.

If the focus remains on learning, not on compliance, the integrity of a classroom's standards-based learning approach will remain intact, ensuring the separation of behaviors from academics. Supporting students' choices, making practice relevant to them, and providing feedback with assignments instead of grades will go a long way toward engaging them.

The remainder of this chapter focuses on the ways in which teachers can create enhanced, learning-centered homework routines. Again, we do not advocate for or against the use of homework; we do advocate for meaningful homework experiences, should teachers decide it is a valuable part of the learning experience.

Changing the Language

Because of previous experiences and traditional views, the perception surrounding homework is often a negative one. Learning is the goal, and if the nomenclature is going to get in the way, then removing it from the language teachers and students use in the classroom is transformative. Replacing the word *homework* with *practice* provides a new lens with which learners can view assignments. Students have traditionally used practice as a progression that leads to success, such as in sports, where practice is essential and is put into place to ensure success. Practice is key to any learning experience, and the word *homework* may not provide the same feeling for students. This connection to experiences outside of school reiterates that learning happens everywhere, not just in the classroom or at their desks or kitchen tables at home.

The word *homework* itself tells students that the work is reserved for home. But as we know, practice happens on the bus to sporting and other extracurricular events. Practice happens in the classroom. Practice happens at home, as well as at a friend's house. We cannot let a word limit where students practice with the knowledge, skills, and understandings that they develop throughout a school year.

On the other hand, a change in language alone will not change how the students feel about practicing outside the classroom. Teachers must accompany the change in language with a change in the explanation. When they assign homework, teachers must also explain how it contributes to students' success as learners—for example,

"We are at a place where practice would be beneficial. This assignment will provide a chance for you to practice, build your confidence, and receive feedback. Remember that it is OK to make mistakes at this point; mistakes are how we learn."

With the change in language and explanation, the word *practice* seems more appropriate for the explanations and examples in the following text. While changing the language may play a large part in how students respond, what teachers *do* when using that language plays a more significant role.

Aligning to Learning Targets

Practice, as with everything teachers do in the classroom, must align tightly to learning standards and targets. Formative assessment, as we stated previously, should provide evidence to both teachers and students of current proficiency levels and how to take the next steps in learning, and practice should do the same. Teachers deconstruct targets, place them in order of complexity (like the learning ladder in figure 2.5, page 42), and then tie them to practice. With alignment, the decisions about further practice become strikingly clear. Practice that clearly leads to progression with student learning creates a meaningful experience. Although a strong connection to the learning targets makes practice straightforward and purposeful, it does not make the learning or practice easier.

Differentiating Practice

Traditional practice tends to be a one-size-fits-all assignment, but the obstacle here is that students are not one size fits all. They have different needs at different points in their learning and they work at different paces. They have different home lives. When teachers do not consider the readiness of their students, frustration or boredom can leave them feeling that teachers are not meeting their needs. When teachers pay careful attention to the results of formative assessments, they can make informed decisions about what types of practice are appropriate for the students.

Will students object if some have different assignments? The argument of fairness and what it means in the classroom comes up from time to time. In reality, the focus must reside with meeting each student's needs. Fairness isn't equity. Equity is a goal, and it means giving each student what is needed at that time rather than assigning the same practice to all. Preparing students for this cultural shift once again starts with language. Start the year discussing with students their strengths and areas of growth. Can they identify areas in their lives that require more practice? Explain that their teachers can and should individualize learning to meet each student where he or she is. Allow choice in practice when appropriate and talk with students about their needs.

Without a doubt, there are students who simply do not need as much practice as others to develop proficiency. Teachers have had students over the years who were ready for their summative assessments earlier than others. They should allow these students to assess at that point in time or move on to different practice. Additional practice that does not increase proficiency is not necessary. When teachers allow learners to summatively assess early or move on with practice that more deeply addresses the standards, learners engage and invest in their learning.

How might teachers differentiate assignments to meet the needs of learners? Assume a standard requires students to "add and subtract fractions with unlike denominators (including mixed numbers) by replacing given fractions with equivalent fractions in such a way as to produce an equivalent sum or difference of fractions with like denominators" (5.NF.A.1; NGA & CCSSO, 2010b). The following options provide an example of how practice might be differentiated for this standard in a way that builds in student choice. Once instruction and some formative practice or assessment have taken place, students can self-assess and determine the appropriate option.

- **Option A:** Students might choose this level if they still need practice with finding common denominators or equivalent fractions. Teachers might pair this assignment with guided notes or step-by-step directions, and they might not yet address mixed numbers because the learner is still gaining confidence with some learning targets.

- **Option B:** This level addresses more of the rote understanding. Students who choose this practice assignment feel confident with the skill and are ready to practice at the level of complexity of the standard.

- **Option C:** These students have mastered the standard and are ready to make connections and apply their understanding. These students might be able to start exploring complex fractions or evaluating expressions with multiple fractions using the order of operations to extend their understanding.

Many digital resources help teachers differentiate practice. These tools are ever evolving, and the tool itself is irrelevant—it is the action that the teacher and students take that enhances learning. Programs such as TenMarks (www.tenmarks .com; Common Core–aligned mathematics practice) give teachers the ability to create and assign differentiated practice, provide student choice, and allow progression at a pace that is appropriate for the individual student. Within such a program, teachers can assign specific standards-based practices to small groups of students whenever necessary to target their individual needs. In addition, these programs allow students to select which concepts they would like to practice.

Considering the Quantity

Some educators feel that the amount of time a learner spends on practice outside the school should correlate to his or her grade level. A common guideline is ten minutes of practice outside the school day per grade level of the student. Consider the amount of homework a sophomore in high school would have according to this model. Tenth grade equals one hundred minutes of homework for a student. With all the other obligations high school students have outside of school, this student's teachers presume he or she spends an hour and forty minutes after the end of the school day on daily assignments for class. Commonly, students will be involved in after-school activities of some variety. Some at this age level have part-time jobs. These same students need to eat dinner. They need to sleep—around nine hours each night. They need downtime with family and friends.

When exploring homework in action, there is a solution for the issue of assignment length and the individuality of students. Teachers may decide to give a specific time parameter for an assignment. For example, the teacher assigns students to practice for fifteen minutes on a particular skill no matter how many items they complete. Learners understand that while practicing the skill is important, the teacher respects that there are many things requiring their time after they arrive home. This practice honors that students take different amounts of time on practice items. The focus is not on how long it takes to complete each or how many problems they complete, but rather that they spend time practicing.

If the role of homework is to help students practice a skill outside the normal school day that will nurture learning, teachers must assign it with this purpose in mind. They can ask themselves a few questions when moving forward.

- "Is the practice something that they cannot accomplish in the time they spend at school?"

- "Is this additional practice essential to the student's success with the standards?"

- "Is the amount of time required to complete this practice reasonable?"

- "Is this practice meeting the needs of that particular student?"

Once teachers consider and answer these questions, the choice of whether to assign students additional practice outside the classroom becomes clear.

Focusing on Learning, Not Compliance

It is crucial not to penalize learners as they make mistakes in their practice. Solely asking for completion does not develop the deep reflection students need to progress. For effective practice in action, completion of that practice must be for learning while maintaining a constant loop of gathering evidence and communicating actionable feedback.

If assignments are simply looked at for completion, without any additional feedback or interaction, it only serves as an exercise in compliance. Teachers spend a lot of time working to create quality assignments and do themselves a disservice by invalidating the care taken in crafting the assignment when completion is the goal. The purpose is for learners to get as much as possible out of their practice so the assignment is more about the process rather than the end product.

With practice, less is more. High-quality assignments that align to standards do not have to be long to be impactful. When teachers ask students to practice with higher-order thinking skills, cognitive complexity becomes more important than quantity. When considering length of practice, teachers should think about the attention span of their students and how many items are necessary to get a gauge on their learning thus far.

PERSONAL NARRATIVE

Andy Goveia

*Middle School Social Studies Teacher,
Thomas Metcalf School, Normal, Illinois*

As a student teacher, I gave homework as preparation work for the next class. I would have students read complex articles, complete minor assignments, and do pieces of that learning at home so I could have a grand discussion or brilliant activity that made me look like a teacher extraordinaire. But what did I find as I assigned the homework that required more learning on their part than teaching on my part? That I still had to give time for them to catch up, reread, and in turn for me, reteach what I had expected them to learn. Some days, this worked for my class; others, it did not. What did I do? I pressed on.

Then, I reached my first teaching job. Having learned from my errors during student teaching, I decided that homework would be basic learning: simple readings, basic exercises, and other "easy" tasks that students could do to prepare for my brilliant teaching the next day. What did this change do? Believe it or not—nothing different from what I had found before. Students still had questions about what I had asked them to prepare and learn on their own. They needed me to review, work with them, and get them through their misconceptions and challenges before I could move on. I chalked it up to everything except my own practices.

Eventually, the team I teach with (who I am continually learning from) started seriously talking about our assessment and homework practices. I found out that I was giving homework for new learning, and my teammates were either giving homework for reinforcement and practice from what they had done in class or to continue the work from class.

So what did I do? I changed my homework practices. I sometimes give basic readings for preparation, but the first thing we do in class the next day is go through it, in detail, and I answer any questions my students have. Other homework includes students finishing up work they didn't finish in class, or doing another activity or assignment that reinforces, supports, and continues the learning from in class. I don't ask my students to learn without me fully available as a resource in the room. I didn't stop giving homework; I stopped making homework the vehicle for learning.

Giving Students Choice

Student self-selected practice is very effective once they have a clear picture of their target and current level of proficiency. Open communication and feedback paired with ongoing self-assessment create this picture and support the learner in making effective and accurate choices. However, even when the teacher clearly communicates the current proficiency level, students do not always make the appropriate choice. At that moment, the teacher must step in and support the learner as he or she chooses practice that best meets current needs.

Figure 5.1 (page 100) shows students making choices within a specific assignment that has them form groups of three and complete one of the activities by selecting a role and moving across the chart to know their audience, format, and topic.

Figure 5.2 (page 100) affords learners the opportunity to select which practice activities they will complete within a unit of study. Learners choose from a variety of practice activities in the document to develop their proficiency.

Standard: D2.His.4.3–5—Explain why individuals and groups during the same historical period differed in their perspectives.

Role	Audience	Format	Topic
Pioneer moving his family west to the Great Plains	Settlers already living in the location where the family is moving	Dialogue	Perspective on westward expansion
Explorer charting new territory in the Rocky Mountains	The explorer's family that is home in Virginia	Letter	Perspective on westward expansion
City dweller in Boston	Residents of New England	Newspaper article	Perspective on westward expansion

Source for standard: NGSS Lead States, 2013.

Figure 5.1: Student practice choices.

Tema 1—La cháchara

By the end of the chapter, you should be able to know, understand, and do the following.

Know

- Vocabulary pertaining to feelings, introductions, origins, numbers, day, date, and time
- Subject pronouns
- Conjugations of the verb *ser*

Understand

- There are different ways to express *you* in Spanish.
- The alphabet as well as punctuation in Spanish differ from English.

Do

- Ask someone's name and say yours.
- Ask how someone is and say how you are.
- Introduce people and say where they are from.
- Give phone numbers, the time, the date, and the day.
- Spell words and give email addresses.

Learning Standards for Assessment

- Ask for and give personal information in written form.
- Ask for and give personal information in spoken form.
- Read and respond appropriately concerning personal information.
- Listen and respond appropriately concerning personal information.

Summative Assessments (All Completed by September 20)

- Listening Assessment (Avaluación de escuchar)—See review in resource folder.
- Reading Assessment (Avaluación de leer)—See review in resource folder.
- Writing Assessment (Avaluación escrita)—Write a dialogue between two or three people who are meeting for the first time.
- Speaking Assessment (Avaluación oral)—With a partner, create and perform a dialogue in Spanish where you meet for the first time and exchange personal information.

Resources

- Vocabulario (Haiku, Quizlet)
- Videos y apuntes—pronombres personales, verbos regulares, formal versus informal, el verbo ser

Formative Assessment and Practice	
Práctica de Escribir (Writing)	**Práctica de Hablar (Speaking)**
• Picture vocabulary practice	• Quizlet (Haiku)
• Exprésate practice	• Partner dialogue cards—See resource folder.
• Cuaderno de vocabulario y gramática	• Additional speaking practice—See resource folder.
• Grammar tutor activities	• Practice speaking samples—Make sure to get feedback from Sra!
• Practice writing samples—Make sure to get feedback from Sra!	
• Additional writing practice—See resource folder.	
Práctica de Leer (Reading)	**Práctica de Escuchar (Listening)**
• Quizlet	• Quizlet
• Page 7, act. 23	• University of Texas activities (website)
• Page 20, act. 25	• Expresavisión 1 y 2 (online textbook)
• Page 26, act. 36	• Page 7, act. 1
• Page 27, act. 37	• Page 9, act. 5
• Additional reading handouts—See resource folder.	• Page 11, act. 10
	• Page 15, act. 17 (textbook)
	• Page 19, act. 22
	• Page 23, act. 29

Figure 5.2: Unit-length student practice choices.

These examples provide students with choices while maintaining teacher-set parameters. Student ownership of learning through choice leads to engagement and self-efficacy.

Grading . . . or Not?

With practice, the reality is that students don't need a grade to know if they made mistakes. Whether they are getting feedback or comments from the teacher, or simply checking it themselves, a number or letter at the top of the assignment doesn't add anything to the experience. Practice should cultivate a culture of vulnerability and willingness to make mistakes without fear of being penalized with a grade. Scores on practice can lead students to focus on the number or letter rather than on reading or listening to the feedback and taking steps forward.

The question then becomes, Will students do the practice if teachers do not grade it? Although it seems counterintuitive, the answer is yes—as long as the work is meaningful and the language has evolved so students understand that the practice is beneficial. When students see the relevancy of the practice and connection to their success, assigning points or grades to encourage completion is not necessary. Some students will push back to see what happens if they choose not to complete practice. If this happens, have a conversation with the student to find out why he or she did not do the assignment. Was it too easy? Too difficult? Was the connection of the practice being essential to the learning not clear? Depending on the reason, work with the learner to solve the problem. For students who are showing signs of apathy, explain why this work is imperative to their learning. If the situation requires different practice, assign different practice.

Keeping Track of Practice

Many teachers want to track which practice assignments students complete. They can accomplish this in a variety of ways. Teachers could keep a list of assignments and check them off when completed (and completed well). It's easy to indicate whether a student has completed an assignment and is ready to move on, has completed an assignment but needs to do some revision, or has not yet completed an assignment. Figure 5.3 provides an example of how this record keeping could look. This chart is applicable at any grade level.

If the teacher has differentiated the practice and students are not necessarily doing the same activities, a checklist is still useful. However, there will be some blank spaces for students. These spaces do not indicate that the student is missing practice—rather, that he or she is working in the area that needs development. The chart could look similar to figure 5.3, but there may not be such a linear progression of marks. Figure 5.4 is an example of this.

Yet other teachers choose not to track assignments. They simply give feedback as students work through the process. Although this may seem frightening to many

Key C = Complete; ready to move on CR = Complete; needs to revise Blank = Incomplete				
Standard: K.L.4—Determine and clarify the meaning of unknown words.	**Practice 1**	**Practice 2**	**Practice 3**	**Practice 4**
Student 1	C	C	C	CR
Student 2	C	CR		
Student 3	C			

Source for standard: NGA & CCSSO, 2010a.

Figure 5.3: Elementary assignment checklist.

Key C = Complete; ready to move on CR = Complete; needs to revise Blank = Continuing practice				
Standard: HSA.REI.B.4—Solve quadratic equations in one variable.	**Practice 1**	**Practice 2**	**Practice 3**	**Practice 4**
Student 1	C		C	CR
Student 2	C	C	C	C
Student 3		C	C	

Source for standard: NGA & CCSSO, 2010b.

Figure 5.4: Differentiated assignment checklist.

teachers, the accountability in this situation falls to the conversation and feedback loops between learner and teacher. In this situation, teachers rely on their professional judgment and student interactions to determine next steps and monitor student engagement and investment in their work.

Another option is student self-assessment and record keeping of their practice. They can keep track of their assignments just as well as the teacher can. Checklists are useful here as well, as we show in figure 5.5 (page 104).

Learning Target	Suggested Practice	Done	Reflection on Understanding and Modifications
Solve quadratic equations by factoring.	p. 79, 1–13 odds	Done	These problems were too easy for me, so I chose to do 15–20.
Solve quadratic equations by completing the square.	p. 85, 7–13 all	Done	This was an appropriate challenge for me.

Figure 5.5: Self-assessment chart for student use.

Grading practice may seem like a great way to communicate with students and parents about proficiency, but return to the idea of grades as feedback; if parents only see a score, they do not have enough information to support their children at home. The same is true for students—a letter or number is not enough for them to plan next steps. If teachers are going to grade practice, actionable feedback must accompany it. Without feedback, that score or grade is meaningless.

Holding Students Accountable

If teachers don't grade practice, how do they hold students accountable for their work? When a student comes to class without the necessary practice, have him or her complete the work. Students could move to a different part of the classroom or go to an alternate place (such as the media center) to do the work and then rejoin the class when they have completed it. This honors the time and effort teachers put into creating a quality assignment and the necessity of prerequisite knowledge.

If students feel that the practice is optional, they will treat it as such. On the other hand, if teachers demand that learners do the work, they communicate a different message. This message reinforces the fact that practice is vital to learning. As an example, some teachers require students to hand in all formative work prior to the summative assessment. When each assignment has value and relevancy, teachers communicate the message that learning is not optional.

Talking to Learners

When teachers talk with learners about practice, a sense of uneasiness can permeate the classroom environment. The word *homework* has developed a bad reputation over the years with students. They often adopt the overarching sentiment that getting it done is more important than doing it well. Educators can work to change learners' mindsets by assuring them that practice will become something that occurs only when appropriate and necessary to support learning; teachers will assign it in a meaningful way that respects not only students' proficiency levels but their time. While it is still important that students complete the work, teachers focus largely on the purpose of the practice and the evidence that students demonstrate.

The intent is not to communicate to learners that they will not do schoolwork outside the walls of the classroom, but instead to communicate that practice will be meaningful and relevant. Let them know why an assignment is important for their progress and how it fits into the bigger picture of the learning progression toward proficiency.

Figure 5.6 provides possible questions students might ask when it comes to homework and possible teacher responses.

Student Question	Teacher Response
If you're not going to grade my homework or practice, why do I need to do it?	As with any learning, practice is essential to developing proficiency. Because of this, all practice counts because it supports your growth.
If I get to choose my practice, how will I know what to select?	I will work with you to choose appropriate practice in the beginning, before you decide on your own. If you don't know what to choose, just talk to me.
What should I do if the practice is too easy and I feel bored?	If you feel bored, there is no need to complete that practice work. Please see me so we can choose something appropriate.
What should I do if the practice is too hard and I get frustrated?	If you are getting frustrated with a practice assignment, stop. Come talk with me so I can support you. From there, I will decide whether you should keep going or do something different.

Figure 5.6: Student questions and teacher responses about homework.

Talking to Parents

For some parents, leaving the term *homework* behind can be difficult. As much as some parents welcome the idea of their children having more free time in the evening, others will be concerned about whether their learners will achieve academically. This is again something different from their school experiences and can be uncomfortable. Help parents understand that just because a change in terminology is happening doesn't mean that their children will not be practicing at home. Switching the term to *practice* actually opens up the locations where their children work on assignments. Use music (rehearsal and performance) or sports (practice and games) analogies to help parents understand.

Parents need the reassurance that teachers are not sacrificing any learning by changing their language and practices. Taking the time to explain the changes (what will be the same and what will be different) will ease fears. Parents may also struggle with the idea of differentiated assignments. The following language could appear in a syllabus to communicate the idea of practice in the classroom and then be shared with parents.

> *I will assign homework or practice work with each new topic I teach and will check it in, but I will not be grading it as correct or incorrect—this is often your responsibility. I will take some practice as formative work, allowing me a chance to provide feedback. Students must turn in all homework or practice work from the unit by the day of a summative assessment or else they cannot take the assessment.*

Getting Started With Meaningful Homework

When traditional homework practices are so ingrained in school culture and historical context, making changes can be an arduous process. However, when grounded in the purpose of improving student learning, meaningful homework and practice build a platform for growth.

- Analyze and reflect on current homework practices to check for alignment with standards, the option of student choice, and opportunities for differentiation.

- Consider the language surrounding homework or practice. How can you improve or modify it?

- Change any negative language to positively encourage the idea of practice and its essential connection to learning.

- Repurpose your homework or practice. Assign it when students are ready to practice a skill and you are confident that their efforts will not be counterproductive.

- Acknowledge and share with students the difference between *fair* and *equitable*.

- Remove grades from practice to allow students to do just that— practice—without the fear of penalty.

Questions for Learning Teams

Pose these questions during teacher team meetings, planning meetings, or book study.

- What quote or passage encapsulates your biggest takeaway from this chapter? What immediate action (large or small) will you take as a result of this takeaway? Explain both to your team.

- What is the purpose of homework in your classroom, and do students and parents understand that purpose?

- How do you communicate the purpose of homework to your students, and how can you improve?

- How can students become involved in planning and selecting practice activities?

- Think about a typical homework or practice assignment in your classroom. How can you better align it to standards and build relevancy?

- How do you hold students accountable for completing their work?

- What are your next steps for moving your homework or practice methods forward?

Self-Assessment in Action

Perhaps the most powerful promise of self-assessment is that it can raise student academic performance by teaching pupils self-regulatory processes, allowing them to compare their own work with socially defined goals and revise accordingly.

—Gavin T. L. Brown and Lois R. Harris

Ultimately, a culture of learning places the *learner* at the center of the assessment experience. Because assessment is the process determining the discrepancy between where students are versus where they need to be, self-assessment means the students are doing this for themselves. Self- and peer assessment ultimately result in active learners who are invested in their learning to the point of self-direction, rather than being passive recipients to what teachers have to say about what comes next in the learning.

Moving From Rationale to Action

The latest research about self- and peer assessment lays the foundation so teachers can put the subsequent strategies into action. Most teachers recognize the importance of developing students' self- and peer assessment skills—that through self- and peer assessment, students become more intimately involved and more invested in their learning. That said, the process of developing students' skills at recognizing the discrepancies between where they are and where they need to be may take some time.

The Research

The bottom line is that self-assessment leads to increased student achievement and is the epitome of students investing in their own learning (Vagle, 2014). The research we explore in the following sections focuses on proving self-assessment's efficacy; fostering a self-assessment culture; and employing peer assessment.

Proving Self-Assessment's Efficacy

According to Hattie (2009), "Students have a reasonably accurate understanding of their levels of achievement" (p. 43). The good news, according to Hattie, is that this shows that students have a remarkably high predictability of achievement. Students are the definitive source of formative feedback because they have continual access to their own thoughts about their own work (Andrade, 2010). Student self-assessment results in increased achievement because students can, for themselves, determine *what's next* on their road to proficiency (Andrade, 2013; Brown & Harris, 2013; Butler & Winne, 1995; Hattie & Timperley, 2007; Ramdass & Zimmerman, 2008). While teacher-sourced feedback may be more valid and reliable, students can learn to sharpen their own assessment skills to a point where improvement can occur independent of the teacher.

Not only does regular self-assessment increase achievement, but there is evidence of a link between self-assessment and self-regulation skills (Brown & Harris, 2013; Schunk, 2003). As long as teachers link the self-assessment process to essential self-regulatory practices (for example, setting goals, following clear criteria, or self-monitoring progress against standards), the self-assessment process allows for greater self-awareness and *metacognition*—thinking about their thinking (Pintrich, 2002; Zimmerman, 2011). With self-assessment as the anchor, students can set goals, examine their motivation beliefs, exercise self-control, engage in self-observation, evaluate the quality of their own work, and then react to the end results (Zimmerman, 2011). Additionally, the move to standards-based grading allows the summative assessment process to align with the goals of self-regulation. In other words, if students are going to use their grades as part of their overall learning picture that allows them to regulate more learning, then grades need to be evidence of learning (Brookhart, 2013b).

Fostering a Self-Assessment Culture

Self-assessment has tremendous potential for improving achievement (Andrade, 2010; Ramdass & Zimmerman, 2008), but teachers only reach that potential when they intentionally establish the necessary condition—an assessment foundation that makes learning transparent. It is impossible for students to assess themselves if they are not aware of learning criteria. Established learning goals and success criteria help students not only master standards, but *assess* that mastery.

To do that well, students need a clear sense of how to infer quality, especially when the teacher has articulated the success criteria as a general description of quality (typically in a rubric) where the students must match their performance to a level of quality. We know that teacher judgment continues to be generally inconsistent and is something that takes practice (Parkes, 2013), so it stands to reason that students, having no specific qualifications or experience, will need explicit instruction. This takes practice, so teachers invest time and energy into developing student interpretation skills. Finally, creating the habit of receiving and responding to feedback will send a clear signal that every assessment is an opportunity to learn more, whether feedback comes from a teacher, a peer, or the self.

That habit—of receiving and responding to feedback—is part of a specific culture that is necessary to maximize student self-assessment results. This foundation begins with the overarching premise that it's OK to be wrong. Assessment is about determining the discrepancy between where students are and where they need to be (regardless of who is doing the assessing—student, peer, or teacher). This understanding of assessment implies that a discrepancy is likely and that it's desirable to recognize it. When students understand that growth is both possible and necessary, they are more likely to respond productively to their gaps in performance (Dweck, 2006).

Whether during the forethought phase (where students set goals and reflect on their level of efficacy), the performance phase (where students engage in both self-control and self-observation), or the reflection phase (where students engage in self-evaluation and self-reaction), the cultural routines of any classroom must insist that students participate throughout all stages (Zimmerman, 2011).

The *cognitive foundation* is essential because feedback is most effective when it builds on partial understanding (Hattie, 2009). Therefore, it stands to reason that self-assessment requires some cognitive foundation for students to recognize the discrepancy between where they are now and where they are going. Without *some* foundation of understanding, students will struggle to assess themselves.

A common frustration that teachers often share is that while some students fully participate in the self-assessment process, others' participation is minimal (if present at all). One reason for inconsistent participation could be some students' minimal proficiency. Although this is not the only reason students don't participate in self-assessment, it is a significant factor since a large number of studies have indicated that accuracy in self-assessment is linked to academic ability (Brown & Harris, 2013). When students *don't know what they don't know*, it can result in students opting out of the process altogether. There could be times when a teacher allows some students to self-assess while guiding others more directly through a process that makes up for the lack of proficiency. It is essential that students have enough proficiency to make the self-assessment process worthwhile and productive.

In addition to that proficiency, it is important that teachers recognize self-assessment's limitations. We do not mean for these limitations to curb teacher enthusiasm for the process. Rather, they are a reminder that teachers must remain an integral part of the process, especially when it comes to verifying self-assessment results. While Hattie (2009) points out the upside of the accurate predictability, he also suggests that student predictability could result in students only performing to the level of their predetermined expectations.

While Val Brooks (2002) asserts that reliability only matters for external summative assessments, Gavin T. L. Brown and Lois R. Harris (2013) argue that accuracy is important for any assessment. Along the lines of reliability, David Dunning, Chip Heath, and Jerry Suls (2004) identify four potential flaws or limitations to the self-assessment process, proposing that humans (not just students) have a tendency to (1) be unrealistically optimistic, (2) believe they are above average, (3) neglect crucial information, or (4) have deficits in their information. Each of these aspects has the potential to contribute to a skewed or inaccurate self-assessment result. As well, Dunning et al. (2004) point out that issues related to accuracy can double because those not competent within a subject area are likely not aware of their lack of competency.

Two further contributing factors to the accuracy of self-assessment are age and proficiency. As students get older (or as they gain proficiency within any given subject area), their self-assessments become more accurate, which means younger (or beginning) learners tend to be overly optimistic about their abilities. The probability that as students gain proficiency, they become less optimistic about their proficiency, however, should be of little concern to teachers since their self-assessments are likely indicating an improved level of proficiency (Brown & Harris, 2013).

Employing Peer Assessment

There is real value in allowing students to be sources of learning information and feedback in a cooperative setting (Wiliam, 2013). While not without its challenges and implementation complexities, peer assessment is one of the most important education constructs to emerge in the modern era (Slavin, Hurley, & Chamberlain, 2003). Unlike self-assessment, which only involves one person, the addition of one or more other students means peer assessment has a greater number of contributing variables (that is, structure, processes, protocol, and purpose) that can contribute to or take away from the overall impact on learning. These variables are important because the impact of peer assessment depends on how teachers approach it with students, how students perceive its value, what the intended outcome is, and what the end user does with the information (Topping, 2013).

When taught well, peer assessment can contribute greatly to student achievement in ways self-assessment cannot. Unlike self-assessment, peer assessment includes a social and collaborative process that fuses learning and its social context. Training students in peer assessment matters significantly, which makes it essential that students learn both its social and academic aspects (Van Zundert, Sluijsmans, & van Merriënboer, 2010), neutralizing its inherent vulnerability; students must believe they can trust the others assessing their work (van Gennip, Segers, & Tillema, 2009).

The upside is that peer-based feedback is more readily available than teacher-based feedback since there are more students than teachers; the potential downside is that it may not be as reliable because teachers' assessment expertise exceeds that of the students. That said, investing heavily in the front-end training will make it more plausible that peer assessment accurately contributes to student learning (Tsivitanidou, Zacharia, & Hovardas, 2011). Self-based feedback is most available, while teacher-based feedback is least available; when teachers have prepared students well, peer-based feedback finds the sweet spot between the two by offering students yet another source for how they can reach proficiency.

In Action

If teachers want students to be strong, independent learners who drive their own journey, they need to teach students to engage in self-assessment in a meaningful way on a regular basis. When students continually participate in this kind of metacognitive work, the culture of the classroom changes as they are more aware of their journey and the tools necessary to get there. Students can verbalize their understanding and work to communicate their next steps to reach proficiency. While the teacher remains active, self-assessment brings students to a level of authentic and meaningful participation throughout the learning.

Student awareness and understanding of learning targets is the first step toward effective self-assessment. Creating the culture of vulnerability is imperative as well. Beyond that, subsequent sections describe how to model vulnerability and teach the process of self-assessment. Approaching peer assessment carefully, to maintain the culture of vulnerability, is discussed next, and finally, employing self-assessment tools is explained.

Communicating Learning Targets

As always, standards-based learning requires clear communication about what students are learning, transparency about the standards and learning targets, and clear expectations about what proficiency looks like. Be explicit. Say to the class, "This is the standard, and this is how you know when you've met it."

Teachers can use learning targets—when they create and clearly communicate them with a sense of the parts and the whole—to teach and encourage students to engage in ongoing self-assessment. Teachers can ask, "What were our targets for today? How do we know if we have met them?"

Students can track their progress toward those targets. For example, students who know that they are proficient after viewing a video of themselves dribbling a soccer ball might say, "I see that I do dribble in the space with both my dominant and nondominant foot while increasing and decreasing speed." This student knows the specific criteria on which a teacher would judge his or her performance, because the teachers and learners have outlined learning targets and discussed success criteria. Having clear criteria also allows students to generate evidence more independently to demonstrate progress toward proficiency of the standard.

Figure 6.1 provides a rubric (created in advance of instruction or created with students) that not only outlines the standard for the student but also success criteria and levels of proficiency.

Standard: SL.6.1—Engage effectively in a range of collaborative discussions (one-on-one, in groups, and teacher-led) with diverse partners on grade 6 topics, texts, and issues, building on others' ideas and expressing their own clearly.			
Standard Not Met	**Approaching Standard**	**Standard Met**	**Excels With Standard**
Was not prepared, did not participate in the discussion, or did not acknowledge ideas presented by others	Was somewhat prepared for discussions and referred to the text; followed guidelines set for the discussion and followed goals and roles; asked and responded to ideas contributed by others	Was prepared for discussions and referred to evidence in the text; followed guidelines set for the discussion and helped set goals and roles; asked, responded to, and reviewed ideas contributed by others	Was very well prepared for discussions and referred to specific evidence in the text; followed guidelines set for the discussion and helped set and track goals and roles; asked, responded to, and reviewed ideas contributed by others
My next steps:			

Source: SL.6.1 by Schimmer, Hillman, and Stalets was made with ThemeSpark.net and is licensed under CC BY-NC-SA 4.0. Source for standard: NGA & CCSSO, 2010a.

Figure 6.1: Criteria and proficiency levels rubric example.

When self-assessing, this rubric becomes a guide that learners can reference to know what the standard expects of them. When asked to self-assess, students could refer to this rubric and might respond, "I know I haven't met the standard yet because although I referred to the text in my response, I didn't really use evidence from the text. I need to do a better job of having concrete evidence to support my discussion points." As teachers ask students to self-assess against the rubric, they can also ask them to plan next steps for their own learning.

Creating a Culture of Vulnerability

In a culture of vulnerability, one where learners constantly look to grow, self-assessment is part of everyday classroom life. Teachers infuse it into instruction whereby they encourage learners to pause and reflect on their work by referring to success criteria and planning their personal next steps. Again, students must understand that making mistakes in learning is unavoidable. It's reflection and action that gets them to the next step.

Modeling the Behavior

Creating students who are active self-assessors requires explicitly inviting them to join in the process, as well as teaching them how to do it. Unfortunately, most learners don't naturally self-assess their academic proficiency, despite the fact that most have some self-assessment experiences outside of school. Whether in sports, dance, video games, or a whole host of other activities, students are self-assessors; they simply haven't made the connection to what's possible with their in-school experiences.

Here are some ways to begin teaching learners to engage in self-assessment.

- **Invite students to talk about their learning:** Encourage them to not only speak about what they are learning but about what mistakes they made and what they did when they made the mistake. Ask questions such as, "Can you share with me what you would do differently if you were to design this experiment again?"

- **Let students set their own goals:** When they set goals, they know what success looks like. Encourage them to self-assess often by asking, "What is your next step in reaching that goal? How will you know when you have achieved it?"

- **Celebrate mistakes:** Encourage students to be vulnerable when they get something wrong or struggle. Ask them to identify what learning target they don't yet understand and what you can do to support them.

- **Engage in one-on-one conversations with learners often:** Conversations about personal growth and challenging goals are most meaningful when there is mutual trust. Students need to trust that it is acceptable to be vulnerable or wrong. Make sure to build in time for this practice.

- **Make mistakes and be vulnerable in teaching:** Model anticipated misconceptions and engage in self-assessment for students to see. Ask yourself (and the students) questions such as, "What was the error in my work? How can my work improve? What should I do differently next time?"

- **Provide success criteria for students:** When appropriate, provide the answer key and let students figure out mistakes or misconceptions. This is not providing a crutch; it is showing them the target and asking them to get there.

- **Celebrate successes often:** Do so especially when a learner self-assesses, acts on his or her own assessment, and shows success. Learners need to see the value in the process of self-assessment.

- **Encourage learners to engage in peer feedback:** Models such as Here's what. So what? Now what? and TAG—You're it! (see figure 4.2, page 80, and figure 4.3, page 81) teach learners how to successfully peer assess and provide feedback against standards.

Approaching Peer Assessment Carefully

Peer assessment can have power in the classroom, but teachers must use it correctly when learners are ready to engage in the process. When used incorrectly, peer assessment can harm the culture of safe vulnerability and risk taking teachers worked to create. Like most things with assessment, when done well, peer assessment can be a powerful contributor to student growth and achievement; when done poorly, it's just the opposite. Before asking students to assess each other, teachers need to provide instruction about and guided practice in self-assessing. Carefully group students when peer assessment occurs, and, as always, have students practice.

Trying Self-Assessment First

While peer assessment has the potential to be a powerful tool in the classroom, it is more important that students engage successfully in self-assessment first. Learners must gain confidence in their own work and be responsible for the planning of their own next steps before they can provide any feedback to peers. When encouraging students to engage in peer assessment, it is important to consider whether each learner is proficient enough to gauge another student's understanding and offer next steps.

Additionally, asking students to be vulnerable enough to share their early work with others in the classroom is a difficult hurdle to overcome. Often, students are not ready to admit mistakes and are not willing to openly accept feedback from a peer. Teachers must respect those feelings.

Pairing Students

Decisions about pairings and groupings are nuanced and require some thought about what is the most productive configuration. The question is always about whether one student is proficient enough to assess the other students' proficiency. For example, if one takes longer to reach proficiency, it might not work to pair him or her with a student who is approaching or has reached proficiency. The student who is substantially further from proficiency might be unable to offer an accurate assessment of the other's achievement and struggle to suggest how his or her work can improve. In other situations, it might not work to pair one struggling student with another novice because both need direct, meaningful feedback.

It is necessary that each learner acquires new knowledge and advances his or her proficiency of the standard in the process of peer assessment.

Practicing Peer Assessment

If a teacher desires to have students assess not only their own work, but their peers', he or she can begin with teacher-created peer assessment. The teacher can take a blank assessment and complete it, but be sure to make mistakes and leave room for improvement. By anticipating misconceptions and common mistakes, teachers can complete a hypothetical assessment in advance of instruction to allow students to practice peer assessment. This has some clear advantages for both the students and the teacher.

For instance, students practice in a low-stakes situation with no consequences for inaccuracy; also, they can practice *how* to provide feedback. Accuracy suffers when communication between students is unsupportive or counterproductive. Students need instruction regarding how to give one another feedback in the most productive manner; this practice allows for a safe place to critique work. Finally, teachers can use this peer assessment practice as formative assessment because it reveals (or at least partially reveals) student proficiency through their ability to recognize strengths and that which needs strengthening in other students' work. Knowing that the teacher is the student allows learners to talk about errors and how to correct them without hurting confidence or providing wrong next steps to peers.

Employing Self-Assessment Tools

Outside of modeling the behavior and teaching students to engage in self-assessment, teachers will find there are many tools they can incorporate into instruction and assessment to have students be active in the process. Figure 6.2 is one such tool that can help students identify areas of strength and areas that need more instruction throughout a unit or after an assessment.

I am really strong at these.
Standards:
I know this because:
I am pretty strong at these, but need some practice and review.
Standards:
What I can do to strengthen my understanding:
I need help with these.
Standards:
Support I need and what my plan is:

Figure 6.2: Self-assessment tool.

*Visit **go.SolutionTree.com/assessment** for a free reproducible version of this figure.*

Not only does this involve students in the process of assessment, it also provides meaningful feedback to the teacher for how to plan next steps for each learner in the classroom. For example, if several students identify that they need more instruction on understanding cells and how particles move, teachers can plan small-group work to meet those needs during the next class period. Templates such as this also provide a powerful communication piece to include parents in the learning process.

Figure 6.3 provides an example from a high school mathematics class studying functions. The form asks students to reflect after practice or an assessment to understand more than simply what they got right and wrong but also why they got it wrong, what their overall understanding is, and what they learned from those mistakes. In the first two columns, students will check whether they got a question right or wrong. In the next two columns, ask students (if wrong), "Was it a simple mistake or do you need more teaching?" The last column asks learners what they learned about their understanding and what they plan to do to improve it.

Standard:					
	I Got It Right	I Made a Mistake	If I Was Wrong, It Was a Simple Mistake or . . .	I Need More Teaching	Here Is My Mistake and What I Learned From It
Question 1					
Question 2					
Question 3					
Question 4					
My next steps:					

Figure 6.3: Self-assessment tool.

*Visit **go.SolutionTree.com/assessment** for a free reproducible version of this figure.*

Again, this example provides classroom teachers with an abundance of information as they view the self-assessments and see what topics students identify as topics needing more attention. It also requires students to reflect on their understanding as they analyze their work.

Figure 6.4 (page 120) provides another example of self-assessment and using the feedback loop (Sadler, 1989). Students can self-assess based on the standard and the school's four-level grading scale. Learners can use the box to describe the evidence for why they scored themselves the way they did. Having students not only talk about their progress but also where they believe their scores to be at that moment in time gets them thinking about their scores and draws them to the rubric as they describe what evidence put them there. The teacher can use the right side to score and compare. The bottom boxes allow the conversation to continue as learners discuss additions to their work and how they are getting close to proficiency and as the teacher responds.

Standard: RL.4.2a—Determine a theme of a story, drama, or poem from details in the text.	
Student assessment:	Teacher assessment:
Score:	Score:
Student comments:	
Teacher comments:	

Source for standard: Louisiana Department of Education, n.d.

Figure 6.4: Self-assessment tool.

Visit **go.SolutionTree.com/assessment** for a free reproducible version of this figure.

Self-assessment can and should start at an early age. Even in kindergarten, as shown in figure 6.5, learners can tell teachers where they are in relation to the target.

Standard	I've Got It!	I'm Still Working	I Need to Work on This	Teacher or Parent Notes
	☺	😐	☹	
	☺	😐	☹	

Figure 6.5: Self-assessment tool.

Visit **go.SolutionTree.com/assessment** for a free reproducible version of this figure.

Asking students how they feel about a task is often a good indicator about their success with that target. This again becomes a strong communication tool between home and school.

Figure 6.6 offers an example of how teachers can tie self-assessment to student choice.

Remember that you have the right to modify your assignment if it becomes too easy or too challenging. We have one goal—growth! Make your practice meaningful. Based on your work over the last ten minutes, how are you feeling?
3—I feel great. In fact, that practice might have been a little too easy for me. I need a challenge. Your practice assignment: Grab the extension activity off the back table and give it a try.
2—I did well, but I was challenged. I feel like I just need more practice to be successful. Your practice assignment: Try page 56, numbers 11–19.
1—I am a bit overwhelmed and need some help. That practice was challenging for me. Your practice assignment: View the video on the class website and the practice attached.

Figure 6.6: Example of offering choice based on self-assessment.

Visit **go.SolutionTree.com/assessment** *for a free reproducible version of this figure.*

As students self-assess, teachers can ask them to determine what they feel an appropriate next step to be for their learning. Do they need more practice? Do they need enrichment? Oversight by the teacher will still be necessary to make sure that the choices students make are appropriate and meaningful for their level of understanding. Although students are learning to self-assess, it is important to remember that the teacher plays a key role in accurately determining a student's proficiency.

Talking to Learners

When talking with learners about self-assessment, it is important that teachers help them understand that they learn not only from experiences, but more so from reflecting on those experiences. They don't learn from completing a formative assessment. They learn from reading the feedback, reflecting on that feedback, and acting on it. For example, football players don't only learn from playing in the game; they learn from watching video, getting feedback from their coaches, and setting goals for themselves for improvement. Teachers want learners to engage in self-assessment so they can take charge of their learning. Learners should know that their teachers want them to be reflective, analytical, self-aware, and driven, and that self-assessment can get them there.

After a task, assignment, or assessment is complete, it is crucial that learners take the time to stop, consider their efforts, reflect on the feedback they receive, and plan for next steps. Explain to students that mistakes are opportunities to learn and that if they only receive feedback from their teacher (and aren't involved in the process of assessing their own work and planning next steps), then they lose out on the opportunity to make important decisions about what's next. Teachers wish for learners to be the eventual drivers of their own journeys, and self-assessment allows them to take a turn in the driver's seat of assessment.

Explain to learners that teachers will also ask them to engage in the collaborative process of peer assessment. The benefits of this process are abundant. Learners can take responsibility for their own learning, develop lifelong assessment and goal-setting skills, enhance understanding through the exchange of ideas and knowledge, and engage in the standards at a deeper level.

As teachers talk to their learners about engaging in self- and peer assessment, they should be open and vulnerable about how they self-assess every day in their own lives, especially with teaching. Explain that when teachers finish a lesson, they often go through some reflection centered on the following questions: What went right? What could I have improved on? What would I do differently the next time? As teachers work in front of students, they often stop and analyze their own work—and they can do that out loud. They can show students that *teachers* make mistakes and how *they* learn from them.

Figure 6.7 provides some possible questions students might ask when it comes to self-assessment, as well as possible teacher responses.

Student Question	Teacher Response
Why do I need to self-assess?	I need you to take ownership of your learning. I could provide next steps for you, but I see you are in a place to do that for yourself. Looking at the success criteria, what are you going to do to reach that proficiency level?
How do I self-assess?	Refer to the rubric or success criteria. Use this as a checklist for learning. Now look at your own work. What are you missing? What can you add? How can you reach proficiency?

Figure 6.7: Student questions and teacher responses about self-assessment.

Talking to Parents

Parents can support the concept of risk taking and mistake making at home by changing their language and asking questions like these.

- What mistakes did you make today? How did you grow from them?

- What learning targets are you currently struggling with? What support do you need to be successful with those targets?

- What would you do differently if you were to complete that project (or assignment or assessment) again?

- Where are you now? How will you improve?

Parents can support this change by also modeling self-assessment at home. They can talk with their children about how they assess, reflect, set goals, and grow in their daily lives. However, this change will not happen if teachers don't invite parents to be part of the process. Communicate with parents often (via newsletters, emails, a beginning-of-the-year open house, parent-teacher conferences, and so on) about this change, and send self-assessments home so parents can see how their children engage in the process.

Getting Started With Self-Assessment

Students do not intuitively know how to self-assess. In fact, it will challenge them. Instructing them on the process, showing them how on a daily basis, and ensuring they are aware of their destination (the standards) will go a long way.

- Work on clearly communicating standards and their learning targets and showing the relationship between the parts and the whole.

- Model self-assessment for learners. Show them what the process looks like and how they can use it daily.

- Create a culture in which being wrong is OK. Celebrate mistakes and learning. Ask students to share their mistake and ask peers to provide meaningful feedback.

- Build in time for self-assessment. Learners don't grow from completing a task; they learn from reflecting on it.

- Start early and young. Encourage learners of all ages to reflect on their understanding and verbalize what comes next.

Questions for Learning Teams

Pose these questions during teacher team meetings, planning meetings, or book study.

- What quote or passage encapsulates your biggest takeaway from this chapter? What immediate action (large or small) will you take as a result of this takeaway? Explain both to your team.

- How do you currently incorporate self-assessment into your assessment practices? What about peer assessment?

- How can you teach students to be active in the self-assessment process?

- How do you model the self-assessment process using the standards and targets as your guide?

- How aware are students in your classroom of their personal progress toward proficiency on the standards?

Summative Assessment in Action

The accuracy of summative judgments depends on the quality of the assessments and the competence of the assessors.

—Connie M. Moss

An essential part of a balanced approach to classroom assessment is the verification that learning has occurred. The *summative* purpose of assessment is to make an overall judgment of achievement in a specific area of learning at a specific moment in time. The ways in which teachers report achievement and other important aspects can vary and evolve (such as moving away from traditional letter grades), but educators will certainly always need to verify, synthesize, and report student achievement. Standards-based learning environments have teachers refocus grades to be only about achievement, deferring all other aspects—attitude, work ethic, citizenship, responsibility, respect—to separate criteria and processes.

We can divide summative assessment into two somewhat independent processes: grading and reporting. This chapter focuses on the grading piece, which is essentially the act of making an overall determination of achievement; in this sense, *grading* is a verb that doesn't necessarily result in the exclusive use of a letter or symbol to communicate achievement levels.

Moving From Rationale to Action

At its best, summative assessment completes a balanced approach to classroom assessment and makes teaching and reporting seamless; at its worst, it can undermine student optimism and create a schism between how teachers instruct and how they verify learning.

The Research

Research on standards-based grading is very much in its infancy since it is a newer approach to reporting achievement; the variations in implementation also contribute to the difficulty in effectively measuring the approach (Brookhart, 2013b). However, the principles of sound assessment practices are not; summative assessment is still *assessment*, which means the principles—primarily *validity* and *reliability*—still apply. The research we explore in the following sections focuses on keeping summative assessment current; assessing learning instead of task type; distinguishing between standards and standardization; and knowing what's negotiable and non-negotiable.

Keeping Summative Assessments Current

As instruction and formative assessment continue evolving, they will become more disjointed from traditional summative assessment practices. This disconnect creates some issues around accuracy and whether reported grades are valid.

Grade validity is in question when teachers do not exclusively assess achievement and when grades mean different things in different schools, in different classrooms, and for individual students (Brookhart, 2013b). Several studies have found at least some mix between achievement and nonachievement factors (such as work habits, effort, attitude, and responsibility) when teachers determine grades, though achievement is the *primary* influence (Cross & Frary, 1999; McMillan, 2001; Randall & Engelhard, 2010; Waltman & Frisbie, 1994). However, even a slight mix can contribute to misunderstanding. Even when teachers claim that they have based grades solely on achievement, there can be evidence to the contrary (McMunn et al., 2003).

The habits, practices, routines, and processes of traditional grading are not easy to relinquish; it first requires an initial shift in how teachers think about and approach the process of verifying learning. By developing a standards-based mindset, they can begin realigning how they report with how they teach (Schimmer, 2016).

We find most of the information about modernization in the professional literature (Dueck, 2014; Guskey, 2015; Guskey & Bailey, 2010; Marzano, 2010; O'Connor, 2011; Reeves, 2015; Schimmer, 2016; Vatterott, 2015; Wormeli, 2006). While there may be some slight divergence at the most granular levels (such as descriptors or numbers), educators almost unanimously agree that to be meaningful and informative, teachers must base grades—in whatever format—on the most recent and consistent level of performance against the curricular standards, not on points, percentages, or behavioral compliance. This focus on standards requires a shift away from viewing summative assessment through the lens of tasks that students must complete.

Assessing Learning Instead of Task Type

Traditionally, teachers anchored summative assessment around task types (such as tests, quizzes, assignments, and projects) that they weighted based on how much they decided each task should contribute. The move to standards-based learning makes that approach obsolete. It's not that these events can't and don't still occur. They do. But the size, timing, or nature of the event becomes unimportant; students' demonstration of learning is what matters, along with cognitive complexity and consistency of the demonstration. Of course, that transition is still occurring in most classrooms.

Assessments themselves can take on a slightly different form. For example, teachers can revamp a traditional test to better align with a standards-based instructional process. Instead of having each section represent a certain question type, teachers organize test sections by standard. Each section has the appropriate and applicable mix of question formats to assess each standard.

Distinguishing Between Standards and Standardization

One unfortunate byproduct of the standards movement has been the confusion between standards and standardization. They are not the same. Curricular standards are the identified performance outcomes within any discipline or any cross-curricular competency. Having performance standards does not mean every student must demonstrate learning the same way. That is standardization.

Standards are akin to building codes, where there is an expected standard that builders must meet; the same holds true for learning. That said, not every building looks the same, or standardized. Standards need not result in standardized assessments, although standardized assessments are part of most education experiences. For teachers, this means that assessing standards could result in a variety of products or demonstrations, which is why it is so critical that they intimately understand the standards they teach. Most standards do not dictate the assessment method, though each standard's cognitive complexity will lead to the most favorable assessment method. For example, multiple-choice questions do not effectively serve standards that require students to *critique* or *evaluate* because this type of question, at best, limits critique and evaluation. Students can critique or evaluate orally or in written form; they can do it live or by recording. The opportunities for students to be creative within the parameters of critiquing or evaluating are plentiful, so despite the *standard* (to critique or evaluate), the demonstration need not be *standardized*.

This all leads to the overarching need for teachers to have a comprehensive assessment conversation, not just a *grading* one. When teachers begin designing assessments with clarity about learning goals, success criteria, and learning progressions, and then use formative assessment and descriptive feedback on an ongoing basis, the natural outflow is a clarity as to what the summative assessment experience is and is not assessing.

Knowing what they are assessing allows them to develop clear performance criteria, which leads teachers to know where they can employ creative and flexible opportunities without compromising the validity and reliability of summative assessments.

Knowing What's Negotiable and Non-Negotiable

Understanding the negotiable and non-negotiable aspects of summative assessment increases the likelihood that practices will remain aligned with a standards-based learning environment. The purpose is non-negotiable. It is how the teacher uses the learning evidence that distinguishes the formative from the summative; while the formative purpose is to pay close attention to details and specific learning targets, the summative purpose is about an overall judgment or verification of standards (Black, 2013). The use of assessment in the classroom is, of course, non-negotiable. Eliminating it altogether is not an option. However, schools could eliminate grades (including letter grades connected to predetermined percentage increments) while continuing the process of grading (verifying and reporting) through more robust descriptors (proficiency language).

The way teachers conduct and use assessment is very much negotiable. Overall judgments need not result in a ratio, score, or singular symbol. They can use more robust criteria (rubrics and scales) and other more extensive indicators of achievement as instruments of verification (Brookhart, 2013c; Marzano, 2017). There can be multiple scores, descriptions, highlighted criteria, and a whole host of other iterations within the necessary process of summative assessment.

In Action

By recommitting to learning, establishing clear standards of performance, and assessing all sides of every learner, teachers can re-engage with a summative assessment paradigm that aligns with a standards-based instructional reality. The following sections help teachers when they are choosing priority and supporting standards, as well as when they are assessing a standard. We examine cognitive complexity of standards to design summative assessment and grade student work. We also discuss knowing what to avoid and dismissing outliers when employing summative assessment. Again, along the lines of *assessment as verb*, it is the use of the assessment (in this case reporting) that indicates an assessment's primary purpose.

Choosing Priority and Supporting Standards

Before any discussion on grading, it is important to start by *beginning with the end in mind*. By knowing their *end*, teachers can be mindful as they plan their *means*. Throughout the journey, learners may chart their own course by trying out different strategies; teachers may explore new paths through individualized instruction based on student need, but having a common destination keeps us grounded and focused.

Teachers often mistakenly assume that summative assessment is necessary for each learning target. Standards are deconstructed for the purpose of formative assessment, while summative assessment addresses the standards in their entirety.

Also, too many standards on an assessment can overwhelm learners. Selecting, teaching, and assessing priority standards with depth lessens that possibility. These priority standards should have the power and make an impact on future learning. When intentionally planning standards-based units, teachers must start by asking, "What are my priority standards?" Larry Ainsworth (2013) defines priority and supporting standards as follows:

> [Priority Standards are] a carefully selected subset of the total list of the grade-specific and course-specific standards within each content area that students must know and be able to do by the end of each school year in order to be prepared for the standards at the next grade level or course. Priority Standards represent the assured student competencies that each teacher needs to help every student learn, and demonstrate proficiency in, by the end of the current grade or course. (p. xv)

> [Supporting Standards are] those standards that support, connect to, or enhance the Priority Standards. They are taught within the context of the Priority Standards, but do not receive the same degree of instruction and assessment emphasis as do the Priority Standards. The supporting standards often become the instructional scaffolds to help students understand and attain the more rigorous and comprehensive Priority Standards. (p. xv)

Priority standards are what drive and shape the planning of instructional units and assessments. As the saying goes, *if everything is a priority, then nothing is*, which means that deciding a standard is a *supporting standard* does not diminish its importance. Prioritizing focuses a teacher's instruction, assessment, and feedback attention. When looking at a writing piece in an English class, it is possible to assess a large number of standards. For example, teachers will always be looking for correct mechanics and conventions; however, they may not always be the priority for the given unit.

A supporting standard for a given unit might also be a standard that the teacher will not summatively assess *at this time*. In this sense, these standards might be ones that are more ongoing in nature that teachers report later on in the year. Figure 7.1 is a rubric that informs learners what priority standards teachers are assessing. Following the rubric is a checklist of ongoing, supporting standards that learners should be mindful of as they complete their writing. With this, learners clearly understand what teachers are assessing them on and what *other* standards they should be sure to include in their writing. Teachers only report on the unit's priority standards but will always guide learners in developing those supporting, ongoing standards.

Realistic fiction for _____ Date: _____						
		0	1	2	3	4
Priority Standards	Self-Assess	Even with help, I still don't get it.	I'm starting to get it with help, but I am still confused.	I kind of get it, but I still make mistakes.	I get it.	I can teach it. I can even show you more.
W.4.1.a—Introduce a topic or text clearly, state an opinion, and create an organizational structure to support the writer's purpose.						
W.4.3.b—Use dialogue and description to develop experiences and events or show the responses of characters to situations.						
W.4.3.d—Use concrete words and phrases and sensory details to convey experiences and events precisely.						

W.4.3.e—Provide a conclusion that follows from the narrated experiences or events.								
W.4.4—Produce clear and coherent writing in which the development and organization are appropriate to task, purpose, and audience.								
Supporting Standards								
W.4.3.c—Use a variety of transitional words and phrases to manage the sequence of events.								
W.4.5—With guidance and support from peers and adults, develop and strengthen writing as needed by planning, revising, and editing.								
W.4.6—Use technology to produce and publish writing.								
L.4.1.b—Form and use the progressive (such as *I was walking*; *I am walking*; *I will be walking*) verb tenses.								
L.4.1.f—Produce complete sentences, recognizing and correcting inappropriate fragments and run-ons.								
L.4.1.g—Correctly use frequently confused words (such as *to, too, two*).								
L.4.2.a—Use correct capitalization.								
L.4.2.b—Use commas and quotation marks to mark direct speech and quotations from a text.								
L.4.2.c—Use a comma before a conjunction in a compound sentence.								
L.4.2.d—Spell grade-appropriate words correctly, consulting references as needed.								
L.4.3.a—Choose words and phrases to convey ideas precisely.								
L.4.3.b—Choose punctuation for effect.								

Source: 2016, B. Minton, Thomas Metcalf Laboratory School. Source for standard: Adapted from NGA & CCSSO, 2010a.

Figure 7.1: Priority standard rubric.

Assessing the Standard

As teachers design summative assessment, it is also critical to determine what evidence students must produce in order to show proficiency. By determining success criteria in advance of instruction and understanding what summative evidence must be shown by learners, teachers can begin instruction with a clear destination.

Figure 7.2 is an example of a scoring rubric that the teacher has intentionally used at the beginning of the summative assessment (and communicated this in advance of the assessment) to inform learners of the standard's proficiency levels—the progression from simple to sophisticated.

Standard: 7.G.B.4—Know the formulas for the area and circumference of a circle and use them to solve problems; give an informal derivation of the relationship between the circumference and area of a circle.

4	3	2	1
Clearly demonstrated and explained the formulas for the area and circumference of a circle and used them to solve problems; gave an informal derivation of the relationship between the area and circumference of a circle	Knew the formulas for the area and circumference of a circle and used them to solve problems; gave an informal derivation of the relationship between the area and circumference of a circle	Knew the formulas for the area and circumference of a circle	With support, understood the formulas for the area or circumference of a circle

Source: 7.G.B.4 by Schimmer, Hillman, and Stalets was made with ThemeSpark.net and is licensed under CC BY–NC-SA 4.0. Source for standard: NGA & CCSSO, 2010b.

Figure 7.2: Sample scoring rubric.

Teachers can rework even a traditionally written test for greater alignment with a standards-based instructional process as long as they clearly communicate the standard. Instead of having each section represent a certain question type (such as multiple choice or short answer), teachers are now organizing test sections by standards. Figure 7.3 provides an example of the beginning of a summative assessment using a Socratic discussion on the Israeli-Palestinian conflict. As students begin their assessment, their first communication is the standards.

Standard	Proficiency Level
SL.7.1.d—Acknowledge new information expressed by others and, when warranted, modify their own views.	
SL.3.1.a—Come to discussions prepared, having read or researched material under study; explicitly draw on that preparation by referring to evidence on the topic, text, or issue to probe and reflect on ideas under discussion.	
SL.6.1.b—Follow rules for collegial discussions, track progress toward specific goals and deadlines, and define individual roles as needed.	

Source: © 2016 by A. Goveia. Source for standard: NGA & CCSSO, 2010a.

Figure 7.3: Summative assessment introduction.

Examining Cognitive Complexity

When designing summative assessment, teachers should direct their attention to the verb in the standard, and the content on which the verb acts (if applicable). The verb in the standard represents the skill that the teacher is assessing. For example, if the standard is asking learners to *analyze*, teachers should not ask them to *identify*. While identifying might be a supporting learning target that teachers assess through the formative process, its presence on the summative assessment is redundant because every target is already embedded in each standard as an underpinning.

If teachers fail to assess at the correct DOK level that the standard demands, they could ill prepare their students for future assessments or classes because they'll never have needed to demonstrate the prerequisite standard at its cognitive level. Even more, teachers can exacerbate the disconnect between external standardized assessments and classroom assessment when, for example, they summatively assess only targets or assess them to an insufficient DOK (for instance, assessing at Level 2 when the standardized assessment is more demanding at Level 3).

Teachers analyze standards to determine the level of complexity necessary for students to meet proficiency in that standard. We revisit this step as we explore summative assessment because teachers need to recognize and honor the level of complexity of the standard that they are assessing. An overview of Webb's DOK appears in figure 7.4 (page 134) to show the overall description of each level.

DOK Level	Description of Level
Level 1	Recall and reproduction
Level 2	Skills and concepts
Level 3	Strategic thinking
Level 4	Extended thinking

Source: Webb, Alt, Ely, & Vesperman, 2005, p. 37.

Figure 7.4: Webb's Depth of Knowledge levels.

Using the DOK model, it's easy to see that if a standard is written at Level 3 (strategic thinking) but the teacher is assessing with verbs such as *infer* or *interpret* (Level 2), the assessment would not be truly assessing the standard. With a Level 4 standard, verbs such as *analyze, critique, create,* or *prove* would be appropriate question starters on the summative assessment.

Whether using Webb's DOK, Bloom's taxonomy, or another tool, teachers need to understand the full cognitive complexity of the standard and match that during summative assessment in order to provide an accurate evaluation. Educational psychologist Benjamin Bloom (1956) outlines the following to classify education goals (or standards).

- **Knowledge:** Students recall specific information, methods, or structure.

- **Comprehension:** Students understand what teachers communicate and can make use of the material by translating, comprehending, and interpreting information based on prior knowledge.

- **Application:** Students can apply the knowledge to new situations.

- **Analysis:** Students can identify and analyze patterns, as well as break down ideas or concepts into easier parts and find evidence to support generalizations.

- **Synthesis:** Students can put together elements and parts to form a whole. They can use old concepts to create new ideas.

- **Evaluation:** Students can assess theories, compare ideas, and make judgments about the value of material for given purposes.

Questions typically arise as to what question types teachers should use in summative assessment. Identifying the level of complexity of the standard gives teachers critical information as to *how* they should assess that standard. Less complex standards—Level 1 in DOK or knowledge in Bloom's—rely more on memorization, such as teachers asking students to define, label, list, identify, or calculate. These types of questions typically have a single right answer. For this level of complexity, selected response (such as multiple choice) is an appropriate question type.

However, more complex standards—Levels 2 and 3 in DOK and application and analysis in Bloom's—lend themselves to more complex demonstrations and may require extended writing or showing steps. In this case, the teacher needs evidence of thinking that simply selecting an answer cannot reveal. The most complex standards—Level 4 in DOK or synthesis and evaluation in Bloom's—often require the highest complexity via performance assessments. In this case, the standard might ask for something students designed, or something tangible. Teachers often defer to the essay, but limiting summative assessment to extended written responses is an inherent disadvantage for those for whom writing is not an area of strength, but who are otherwise relatively proficient against the standard.

With the switch to standards-based learning and assessment comes freedom and excitement for the possibilities of assessment. Let the standard (and its verb) be the guide for selecting the method of assessment. Examples follow.

- **"Develop models to describe the atomic composition of simple molecules and extended structures" (MS-PS1-1; NGSS Lead States, 2013):** This standard asks students to *develop models*. Thus, teachers need to give them the opportunity to do so.

- **Creates presentations that communicate information to audiences using a variety of digital environments and media (adapted from International Society for Technology in Education, 2016):** This standard requires students to *create* presentations in order to communicate.

Gaining Confidence

This is one of the few chapters in this book in which we explore the process of how to assign grades. Chapter 9 (page 165) explores proficiency scales in detail, but for the purpose of this chapter, we are assuming that readers are grading on a four-level mastery scale through sound or standards-based grading practices. On this proficiency scale, 4 represents mastery, 3 represents proficiency with the standard, 2 represents a basic understanding, and 1 represents a novice understanding.

While grading, it is important to stay true to the standard and the student's proficiency level with *that standard only*. A major goal of standards-based grading is consistency among different teachers, different classrooms, and different schools. This shift is a hard one, especially when coming from a traditional grading system where the norm is to determine one score regardless of how many standards are assessed or to identify what the learner did wrong and reduce points from a total for each misstep. The switch to standards-based grading changes the focus from *What did they do wrong?* to *What level of proficiency does the evidence prove?* Of course, not only will it be necessary to retrain ourselves as assessors to look at students' work holistically to determine their overall level of proficiency with each standard, it will be necessary to retrain students and parents so that the summative assessment process remains transparent.

As teachers look to gain confidence in the realm of standards-based grading, they can explore the following ideas.

- **Examine inter-rater reliability by grading assessments as a team:** Grade independently and compare. Talk to members of the department or team about why the evidence elicits this level.

- **Develop common rubrics:** Discuss what proficiency looks like in action. Establish a common understanding of what evidence students must show in order to reach mastery. An example of a rubric is seen in figure 7.2 (page 132).

- **Revisit the standard:** When in doubt, teachers should look at the work holistically, reread the standard, and trust themselves as the experts to determine the overall proficiency level.

Grading in Action

Through the grading process, teachers should avoid at all costs focusing on how many questions a student incorrectly answered. When they focus on wrong answers, they're not focusing on the standard, and once again it becomes a points game. Grading a student based solely on the number of errors is not standards based. At all points in grading, the standard should be the focus. Many teachers feel that a standards-based grading system is much more subjective than a mathematical computation, but it is not when our focus stays on the standard. Professional judgment trumps numerical calculations when determining proficiency levels. Always go back to the question, Has the student met the standard? The following example where a teacher ties the number of questions wrong to proficiency of the standard on a four-level scale explores more deeply why this practice can be misleading.

- **Four:** No questions wrong or one question wrong

- **Three:** Two or three questions wrong

- **Two:** Four or five questions wrong

- **One:** Six or more questions wrong

As an example of a standard where grading based on the number missed does a disservice to the students, consider the standard "Spell correctly" (L.6.2.B; NGA & CCSSO, 2010b). Revisiting "Three: Two or three questions wrong," the teacher would need to be mindful of which words the students spell incorrectly and the complexity of the writing. One student might have spelled the words *there*, *because*, and *once* wrong, while another might have spelled *juxtaposition*, *exaggerate*, and *descend* incorrectly; those two learners are not the same, yet the limited scale would falsely indicate that they are.

Following are three different scenarios in which learners missed the same number of questions on a summative assessment. The teacher is assessing the following Common Core mathematics standard: "Apply and extend previous understandings of addition and subtraction to add and subtract rational numbers; represent addition and subtraction on a horizontal or vertical number line diagram" (7.NS.A.1; NGA & CCSSO, 2010b). In the standards-based classroom, the teacher asks students to add and subtract rational numbers, as well as represent some problems on a number line. The teacher has included a real-world application problem as well as a problem that asks learners to identify the misunderstanding in a preworked problem, explain what that person did not understand, and describe what his or her next steps should be.

- **Scenario 1:** A student understands and is proficient at the standard. He can fluently add and subtract rational numbers. However, he got two questions wrong—the application problem and the one where the student has to offer advice and next steps.

  Grading: He met the standard. He can add and subtract rational numbers, as the standard asks. In a four-level grading system, this student's proficiency level is a 3. This student would not receive a 4 because he has not met an advanced level of understanding. He performed at the level of proficiency and DOK that the standard demands.

- **Scenario 2:** A student (who is known to rush) completes the assessment with ease. She showed throughout the unit that she had reached proficiency of the standard, understands the application problem, models addition and subtraction on a number line, and gives accurate, thorough next steps on the misunderstanding problem. However, she shows errors on two of the easiest problems on the assessment.

  Grading: This student has mastered the standard; she can even identify next steps and show you more. However, she rushes and doesn't check answers. The teacher and the student have been working on this behavior, and the teacher continues offering time-management and work-checking strategies. This is an opportunity to use reassessment to help the student improve behavior. The conversation might sound something like, "Remember that we have been working on taking our time and checking work. I see that you got two problems wrong. I want you to find those two, correct them, and then let's have a conversation about the errors that you made." After conversation and corrections, in a four-level grading system, this student would demonstrate a Level 4 understanding. The teacher would also note and report behaviors.

- **Scenario 3:** A student completes the assessment, and he got two questions wrong. One was from the first section and dealt with subtracting a negative number and the other was the advice question, which also dealt with subtracting a negative number. However, he was able to add, perform some subtraction, and model on a number line.

  Grading: The teacher is able to conclude that this student is approaching a proficient understanding but is not there yet. How exciting that he understands how to add, perform some subtraction, and model on a number line, but he needs to work on subtracting negative numbers. He has a partial understanding of the standard. On a numerical scale, this student demonstrated a Level 2 understanding. However, it is obvious that this is an error that the teacher can reteach and reassess. The teacher should have a conversation with this learner about next steps in his journey to improve his understanding and undergo reassessment.

Dismissing Outliers

If data that teachers collect on a summative assessment do not align with data they collect through formative assessment, it will be necessary to look for the circumstances interfering with reliability (assessment language, bias, or personal issues for students, for instance). Teachers should explore any outliers in data to resolve inaccuracies. For example, if formative data consistently show a student to be proficient with a standard, and the summative data show that the student only has an emergent understanding, the teacher must explore this discrepancy. Was the student having a bad day? Did the teacher use language on the summative assessment that was too advanced for the learner? What else could have happened to cause this discrepancy? Was it just one student or a group of students? After answering these questions, the teacher can plan his or her next steps accordingly.

Inconsistent data are a teacher's call to action. When sound assessment principles are in place and assessments align to the standards, positive trends should appear. New evidence will either replace old evidence (with knowledge or comprehension) or contribute to the teacher's determination of the most consistent level of performance (more complex standards) to ensure the most accuracy.

Turning Summative Into Formative

Students should understand (and teachers should honor) the truth that even though an assessment may be summative, every moment in learning can be a new starting point. Should a student not reach proficiency on a standard at the date of the summative assessment, the teacher should make available opportunities for reassessment. This process can be formal, in which the student initiates the reassessment and develops a plan of action that he or she shares with the teacher so they can work together toward a better understanding, or informal, in which the teacher reassesses the student in real time.

For example, in a first-grade classroom, at the time of an assessment, a teacher might find that a student only has an emergent understanding of the standard, "Count to 120, starting at any number less than 120. In this range, read and write numerals and represent a number of objects with a written numeral," and reports that progress (1.NBT.A.1; NGA & CCSSO, 2010b). Later in the marking period, when assessing the standard that requests students "compare two two-digit numbers based on meanings of the tens and ones digits, recording the results of comparisons with the symbols >, =, and <," the teacher notices that to support the position, the student is now fluently counting from any number (1.NBT.B.3; NGA & CCSSO, 2010b). The teacher can and should, at this point, reassess that earlier standard to verify that the student has reached proficiency. Because the learner has become proficient at that standard, the teacher updates his or her academic grade to represent the most recent understanding.

In a standards-based classroom the academic grade that teachers deliver should be 100 percent from summative assessment data. The grades they report should represent students' most recent or consistent understanding. While they should never, in theory, factor formative assessment into the summative grade, it is important to honor the fact that some schools must, for the time being, record grades throughout units. As long as teachers replace old evidence with new and students' early attempts at learning do not negatively impact their final grade, teachers can work around this hurdle before the school implements a full standards-based reporting system. Some schools choose to enter formative assessment data in the gradebook weighted at 0 percent. Others choose to routinely update and replace old scores with the most recent evidence (discussed more in chapter 10, page 187). No matter the system, the critical idea is that new evidence should always replace old.

Kirsten Hany

High School Social Sciences Teacher,
University High School, Normal, Illinois

I would qualify my first four years of teaching as traditional in both class-room and grading practices. When I began working at University High School, I was absorbed into a standards-based grading pilot that shifted my entire ideology. The process has been slow and challenging; I have had to re-evaluate my lesson plans, formative assessment, and create new summative assessments that align to standards—all in an attempt to give parents an accurate view of their children's level of achievement.

The first step in creating an accurate vision of achievement for my high school students was removing behavioral elements from the assessment, meaning, if a student turns in a paper late, I do not take points off. While this seems counterintuitive to the traditional educational process, it is necessary to ensure an accurate grade is communicated. This does not mean that students are free of consequences; for example, if an assessment is turned in late they may receive a behavioral consequence, but their grade will remain unchanged in order to reflect an accurate depiction of their abilities. I also went through a period where I altered and discarded numerous formative assessments (traditional busywork and homework) in order to ensure that the work students were doing was aligned with the summative assessment. While this process was tedious it ensured that my students were practicing standards, receiving feedback, and then directly applying that knowledge to a specific standard. With this I was able to create rich and in-depth conversations with students on their strengths and weaknesses and give them meaningful ways to apply that to their assessments.

My biggest challenge came from knowing that students at the high school level still require a traditional grade in order to report out their grade point average for college applications. It often feels like a never-ending circle of assessing proficiency against a standard and then computing what that standard grade looks like in a traditional format (all while asking students to focus only on the standard grade). Creating rubrics with clear guidelines that detail a standard grade as well as a traditional grade has worked well for communication purposes. There has also been a positive shift in the overtone of parent and student conversations; no longer are they asking what can they do to bring up their grade. Now the dialogue surrounds what skills students can practice to enrich their learning.

This process of creating summative assessment that is authentic and directly connected to standards has taken years and much like during my students' retake process, I find myself constantly revisiting and revising my lessons and assessments.

Ensuring Quality Assessment

Even with well-designed assessments that align to the standards, it is important to constantly go through the procedure of analyzing and improving them. Figure 7.5 is an assessment quality checklist adapted from *Classroom Assessment for Student Learning* by Jan Chappuis, Rick Stiggins, Steve Chappuis, and Judith Arter (2012) that teachers can use to guarantee that assessments are high quality.

			Teachers should use the following checklist to evaluate an assessment's quality. 3 = Yes, or clearly present 2 = Partially, or implied 1 = No, or missing
3	**2**	**1**	**Format**
			White space around each problem is adequate so the problems are distinct and separate from one another.
			Work space is large enough for each problem for students to solve problems, show work, or explain steps.
			Quantity of problems per page is appropriate, and not overwhelming to the students.
			Font size is large enough for students to read easily.
3	**2**	**1**	**Standard**
			The assessment clearly states the standards it measures.
			The match between stated standards or learning targets and items or tasks on the test is clear.
			Standards assessed represent what was taught in class.

Figure 7.5: Assessment quality checklist.

continued →

3	2	1	Design
			The assessment method the teacher uses is capable of accurately reflecting achievement on the standards he or she is assessing.
			The assessment includes enough tasks or exercises to support the intended use (to lead to a confident conclusion about student achievement on the stated standard or standards), or it is clear that it is part of a larger overall plan to sample achievement sufficiently for the intended use.
			There is nothing in the assessment itself or in the conditions under which the teacher administers it that could lead to inaccurate estimates of student learning.
			Instructions are clear and concise.
			The teacher allocates sufficient time for students to succeed.
3	**2**	**1**	**Communication**
			The teacher communicates results from the assessment so that the intended users of the information understand how they connect to learning.
			The results clearly show students what they have mastered and what they still need to work on.
			Results provide clear direction for further instruction.
			The teacher communicates results in a timely manner.
3	**2**	**1**	**Student Involvement**
			Students are able to reflect on their learning as a result of the assessment and to identify strengths and areas for further learning.
			There is a mechanism in place for students to track their own progress on learning targets and to participate in communicating their status to others.

Source: Adapted from Chappuis et al., 2012.

*Visit **go.SolutionTree.com/assessment** for a free reproducible version of this figure.*

Talking to Learners

Of course, not only is it necessary for teachers to retrain themselves as assessors to look at students' work holistically and determine their overall level of proficiency with each standard, it will also be necessary to retrain students and parents so that the summative assessment process remains transparent.

Learners must understand that summative assessment is about verification of learning. It occurs in intervals when the teacher has collected enough formative data and evidence to be confident that he or she has taught the standards, the students have met them, and he or she is ready to report on the proficiency level against those standards to parents and students.

Summative assessment should never be a surprise for learners as long as they clearly understand the standards and what success against those standards looks like. As students prepare for summative assessment, they can start by putting *Can I* in front of the standard. For example, "*Can I* 'determine a theme or central idea of a text and how it is conveyed through particular details' (RL.6.2; NGA & CCSSO, 2010a)? If not, *can I* identify the learning targets I am still struggling with to focus my studying?"

Teachers help learners trust the standards and learning targets and let them guide their learning. When discussing summative assessment with them, revisit discussions about formative assessment and self-assessment. To continue the conversation, talk with students about the idea of practice versus games or artistic performances. Athletes invest their hardest work during practice so they can perform well during the game.

Figure 7.6 provides some possible questions students might ask when it comes to summative assessment as well as possible teacher responses.

Student Question	Teacher Response
What if I am a bad test taker?	If you know the standards, you will be just fine. I will make sure that your grades are an accurate reflection of your knowledge, even if we need to reassess in a different format. You will have a chance to show me what you know.
It's not fair that summative assessment is 100 percent of my grade!	Actually, it is the most accurate way to communicate your understanding. Think about homework and formative assessment. Shouldn't you be making mistakes at that point in your learning? I wouldn't want to penalize your overall grade by factoring in early attempts at learning.
We both got two questions wrong. Why do we have different scores?	Let's look at your proficiency with the standards and what questions you got wrong. Your level of understanding is based on the questions you got wrong. Let's discuss it.

Figure 7.6: Student questions and teacher responses about summative assessment.

Talking to Parents

Parents need to understand that they should not think of standards-based summative assessment only as a traditional test. Summative assessment should not be an event that leaves students overwhelmed or stuck. By providing clear standards in the beginning of the unit and teaching to those standards, students should be prepared and confident walking into assessments. Teachers must plan the entire unit with the summative event (or events) in mind. Formative assessment throughout the unit assesses the key component parts of these standards and the teacher delivers feedback with this assessment (and the standards) in mind.

People often think that standards-based assessments have higher stakes because they often represent 100 percent of the academic grade. Let parents know that the decision to transition to standards-based learning stems from wanting to honor the natural learning process; that educators don't want to punish students for early attempts at learning; and that they do not want to falsely inflate or deflate grades based on compliance. Vulnerability is encouraged through the learning process so students can learn from mistakes instead of being punished for them. Because of this, a grade is based on summative assessment data. If a student is proficient at a standard, it will show in his or her assessment. Help parents understand that self-assessment is critical to their children's success and growth. Encourage parents to discuss formative data, feedback, goal setting, and next steps at home leading up to summative assessment. Parents should encourage their children to engage in reassessment whenever they don't reach proficiency.

By assessing standards on a summative assessment, teachers are outlining them as crucial for students to learn; moving forward with an emergent understanding would not be beneficial for the student.

Getting Started With Summative Assessment

Once teachers have adopted standards-based language and mindsets, decided on priority standards, and deconstructed those standards for formative and summative assessment, the process of designing summative assessment begins. This does not always mean starting from scratch. It could mean improving what is already there.

- Know your standards and divide them by unit. Determine your priority standards for each unit (what you will report on).

- Design summative assessment with the standard in mind. What is the verb in the standard? What is the desired level of complexity for that standard?

- Guarantee that you are only assessing the standard, not the underpinnings or learning targets—you should assess those in the formative assessment paradigm.

- Reorganize your assessments *by standard*. Be clear with your standard and how you are assessing it. This makes the process of grading easier as you determine proficiency for each standard.

- Ensure that you have removed all behaviors and nonacademic factors from summative reporting.

Questions for Learning Teams

Pose these questions during teacher team meetings, planning meetings, or book study.

- What quote or passage encapsulates your biggest takeaway from this chapter? What immediate action (large or small) will you take as a result of this takeaway? Explain both to your team.

- Is the level of complexity in your summative assessment the same as the level of complexity the standard outlines? How can you improve in this area?

- How do you know when students are ready to be summatively assessed?

- Do summative assessments currently represent 100 percent of the course's grade? If not, why?

- Do your summative assessments meet the demands of quality design?

- Do your summative assessments address the priority standards for the unit?

Redos, Retakes, and Reassessment in Action

If we really want students to reflect on their mistakes and revise their thinking and/or performances, they have to know their efforts will count. If we want them to heed our feedback on their work, they have to know that it can be used to improve their status.

—Rick Wormeli

Some students take longer to learn. Do grading practices honor or contradict that truth? Redos, retakes, and reassessment are arguably the most critical and most controversial aspects of standards-based learning in action, which is why every teacher should vet the ideas within this chapter through the nuances of his or her own classroom. Even teachers who resoundingly support the notion can feel overwhelmed by the process both in theory and execution. That is why this chapter—and even this first section—focuses heavily on the implementation side of redos, retakes, and reassessment.

We submit that success and failure with redos, retakes, and reassessment are a matter of strong or weak execution, even though this is difficult to admit. This is not to suggest that students have no role in the success of a redo, retake, or reassessment process—they do—but teachers are wise to look first at how they set up and implemented the process before turning to the students. That said, this chapter is not about wagging fingers and blaming teachers; all three of us have experienced resounding success and absolute failure with reassessment.

This chapter will provide some insight into the formative realm with redos, but prioritize two processes for summative assessment: (1) retakes and (2) reassessment. Each has a home in a standards-based environment, and most of this chapter will define those terms and speak to moments when it is appropriate to use each.

Moving From Rationale to Action

Research specific to reassessment practices is limited. Reassessment practices draw primarily, once again, from the assessment principle of validity. Learning is continual, but the moments of verification (summative assessment) are more periodic. Therefore, it is likely that at least some students continue to learn after the moments of verification; if grades are to be accurate, then the reverification of learning is necessary. As well, teaching students to learn from their mistakes is an essential characteristic of a lifelong learner, so the practice of reassessment feeds the process of productively responding to assessment results.

The Research

If teachers treat each assessment as a one-time event with no opportunity to learn and grow, then students will never develop a growth mindset. Summative assessment can disrupt an instructional approach that focuses on this growth mindset (Dweck, 2006) if teachers do not establish and maintain a seamless relationship between teaching and learning. Teachers can't summatively assess students every day, but they can emphasize the most recent and most consistent levels of performance, which will, in the end, produce *more* accurate assessment and reporting of achievement. *If students learn* has to matter more than *when students learn*.

The research we explore in the following sections focuses on understanding when to use each assessment type, giving credit for the student's most recent evidence of mastery, addressing pushback, and disregarding task type.

Understanding When to Use Each

The purpose for separating these practices into three groups is to showcase the varied ways in which teachers incorporate opportunities for additional learning in their classrooms. We can house all these practices under an umbrella term, but the differences between redo, retake, and reassessment are noteworthy and explained next. In any case, teachers should attempt to provide students with reassessment opportunities when the instructional decisions that were based on the initial results were ineffective (Bonner, 2013).

Redo

A redo means doing something a second time—taking what you did, learning from the mistakes, and doing it again. In the educational realm, a *redo* is completing a piece of formative practice again. Teachers should use redos when a learner benefits from starting over. Those occasions include when learners are off base when practicing—by misreading instructions, for example. There are other times when students do not have the prerequisite skills necessary to complete an assignment and a redo would be appropriate following some additional skill building and development.

Retake

The term *retake* refers to a formative or summative assessment that teachers re-administer after additional reteaching, feedback, and practice. Examples include having a student respond to the same short-answer questions an additional time and drafting projects and writing assignments before producing the final product. At first glance, the drafting process may not seem to fit the description of a retake, but consider that the prompt for the writing or project has not changed for the new draft. There has been additional feedback and learning throughout the process, and quite possibly additional practice when the student has identified a gap in his or her skills.

Reassessment

Reassessment is often the act of summatively assessing students in a different way than the original method or using a new assessment tool. The practice transforms the original summative into a formative exercise. It does not have to include all standards that the teacher originally assessed, especially if the student has already demonstrated mastery over some. The nature of reassessment is such that when teachers employ a new method or create a new tool, they can target the standards they are including specifically to the needs of the students. Reassessment candidates have shown deficiencies that the teacher did not expect and that require additional learning. Reassessment takes various forms, including a new test form or conversing with students.

From this point on in the chapter, we focus on retakes and reassessment and how they relate to summative assessment. Teachers often do not formally identify redos in the formative realm as such because they are a natural response from the teacher. When a teacher checks in on a learner and sees that the work is headed in the wrong direction, it usually results in the teacher requesting a redo. In an effort to be concise, we use the word *reassessment* rather than both. It is important to remember that when *reassessment* appears, the words *redo* and *retake* can replace it if the teacher is going to reuse the assessment tool, rather than employing something different.

Giving Credit

Standards-based learning gives students who complete reassessment full credit for what they know. Full credit would mean teachers use the *most recent* evidence when there are few contributing variables to proficiency, while they would use the *most frequent* evidence with more complex standards that have several contributing variables (Schimmer, 2016).

Averaging scores, especially over time, undermines accuracy. Even teachers who embrace the practice of reassessment can inadvertently distort achievement levels by averaging old and new demonstrations of learning. Teachers exacerbate these issues by using the traditional 101-level percentage scale (including zero) along with relying on the mean average. Of the three kinds of averages (mean, median, and mode), the *mean* is vulnerable to extreme scores; using a percentage scale increases the likelihood of a wide variation in grade determination (Guskey, 2015). For example, every 40 percent grade requires a 100 percent just to reach a mean average of 70 percent. That means students who get off to a low or slow start have to exponentially outperform themselves. However, if the original score was 60 percent, then they need only an 80 percent to reach a 70 percent average.

Addressing Pushback

One of the most common pushbacks against reassessment is that allowing students multiple opportunities to demonstrate proficiency does not represent what happens in the real world. Some argue that there are no second chances in life and that the efforts of those who demonstrate proficiency on their second chance are somehow less than the efforts of those who get it right the first time. While it is true that one could pick a handful of professions (pilot, surgeon) where there are no second chances, the truth is that the argument against reassessment is more about convenience.

The truth is that the world in which we all live is filled with second chances. For example, thirty-three states place no restrictions on the number of times someone can take the bar exam (Heidemann, 2016). Another truth is that students are not adults. As educator and educational consultant Rick Wormeli (2006) writes:

> Sure, most adults don't make as many mistakes requiring redos as students do, but that's just it—our students are not adults and, as such, they can be afforded a merciful disposition from their teachers as we move them toward adult competency. (p. 136)

The adult brain doesn't function as such until we reach our early to mid-twenties, which means it's unfair to hold students to adult-like responsibilities or characteristics (Dobbs, 2011). There is nothing inappropriate about wanting students to aspire to adult-like behavior, but falling short shouldn't cost them because those expectations are beyond their stage of development.

And finally, students do live in a very real world. For example, 15.5 million U.S. children live in poverty (DeNavas-Walt & Proctor, 2015), and 40 percent of U.S. children will spend at least one year living in poverty before the age of eighteen (Ratcliffe, 2015). According to the Feeding America (2017) *Poverty and Hunger Fact Sheet*, children in poverty are more likely to experience hunger; households with children report food insecurity at a significantly higher rate than those without children. That said, the fact sheet makes clear that the majority of people who are food insecure do not live in poverty, and the majority of people living in poverty are not food insecure. From an assessment perspective, the point is to realize that students—whether food insecure or poor or both—already live in the real world that some teachers think lies in the future. *Food insecurity*, or not knowing when one will next eat, can lead to lower reading and mathematics scores, physical and mental health issues, emotional and behavioral challenges, and an increased risk of obesity (Cook & Jeng, 2009). Students' worlds are very real indeed.

Disregarding Task Type

Teachers already reassess students (independent of whether they philosophically agree with the practice) because they almost certainly assess every standard more than once. However, teachers who focus on task type instead of standards might not see it this way. Differentiation between assessment results should lean on the discrepancy in cognitive complexity, not the event's title. For example, a *test* shouldn't be worth more than a *quiz* if both assess the same standard with the same cognitive complexity.

The first step toward managing routines around reassessment is to recognize where it's already taking place. By refocusing on the standards instead of the task types, teachers will recognize where they have already built reassessment into their learning progressions and can begin reconciling old and new evidence without overwhelming themselves.

When the cognitive complexity changes (when a quiz is at DOK Level 2, but the test is at Level 3), then the connection is lost, so teachers may need to supplement with duplicate events; it's not an all-or-nothing endeavor, so while most reassessment opportunities are already a natural part of the learning progression, teachers may occasionally need to create duplicate assessments. The key to these supplemental assessments is to ensure they are addressing either an incomplete sample or a discrepancy between a previous result and what the teacher knows about a student's current proficiency status. Again, a thoughtful approach can and will balance the need for accurate verification and teacher workload.

It is not inappropriate to require more learning in advance of any reassessment opportunities; this is always at the teacher's discretion and relates to the assessed standard's complexity level.

In Action

Redo, retake, and reassessment implementation is not an easy undertaking. Considerations include quality, procedure, and how it will work in a classroom with many assessments, many students, and limited time. Managing reassessment is difficult and can cause some educators to lose sight of the ultimate goal—ensuring that students learn. When teachers maintain this at the forefront of their thinking, taking on the task can feel more like a moral imperative than a choice.

PERSONAL NARRATIVE

Garnet Hillman

Author and Educational Consultant, Crest Hill, Illinois

In my junior year of high school, I had to write a rather large research paper. It was the first time I had a writing assignment of this magnitude, and for the previous two years I had watched the eleventh graders toil as they worked through this assignment. I followed the steps my teacher had provided throughout the writing process, finally got to the end, and turned in the paper. When the teacher returned it sometime later, let's just say that the mark was lower than I expected. At this point, there was no recourse for me, no additional draft to take the feedback and improve the writing; there was nothing I could do. I internalized this experience, and for years to come did not believe that I could write. It was well into my adult life before I realized that writing was not only something I could do but also an activity that I truly enjoyed. I learned that the only way to get better at writing is to write. This may have been very different if I had been provided the opportunity to learn and grow from my writing experience in eleventh grade.

Spending Time Prior to Reassessment

The time between assessment attempts varies. One resolute idea is that students must take action to increase their proficiency and provide evidence that this has been accomplished. However, with most situations, there are exceptions to this guideline, such as when the student's formative work has told a story of proficiency and the current evidence shows a lack thereof.

Perhaps the learner has had a tough day and is not in a good frame of mind for the assessment. It is also possible that the student needs a different manner of assessment to show an accurate proficiency level. For example, if the standard is, "Gather and make sense of information to describe that synthetic materials come from natural resources and impact society," the student could accomplish this in a variety of ways (MS-PS1-3; NGSS Lead States, 2013). It would not matter whether students describe these processes in written or spoken form to demonstrate mastery. Employing professional judgment in these situations meets learners' needs.

Here are some ideas for how to spend the interim between the original assessment and the reassessment. They can be used individually or in combination to facilitate the additional learning students need to progress.

- Complete any formative work that is missing.

- Choose additional practice from a bank of activities.

- Meet with the teacher for reteaching.

- Using the feedback provided, make changes to the original work.

Requesting Reassessment

Many teachers find it useful to ask students to submit a form to request a reassessment. This would have the student not only indicate what he or she has done in the interim but also plan out the logistics of the reassessment—when it will happen, which standard requires reassessment, reteaching opportunities, and so on. To be clear, teachers do not design a request-to-reassess form intending that students must *ask* to reassess because continual learning is a pillar of standards-based learning. It is, however, a way they can expect students to meaningfully participate in organizing their thoughts around strengths, areas in need of growth, and other reassessment considerations.

Figures 8.1 and 8.2 (page 154) give two examples of forms that students can fill out prior to reassessment. Both work in paper form, but digital forms may save time and allow for easier data management. Teachers can provide these forms at any grade level and determine what information they need from students prior to reassessment. Figure 8.1 is a basic form that gathers information to assist the teacher in planning when the reassessment will happen and identifying the standards to be reassessed. Figure 8.2 is not only for planning the reassessment but also requires student reflection.

Request to Reassess Form
Name: Class period:
Standards to reassess:
Day or time for reassessment:

Figure 8.1: Reassessment request form.

*Visit **go.SolutionTree.com/assessment** for a free reproducible version of this figure.*

Retake Form
• You need to share this form with your parents. • Please make sure that you take action on the feedback you received prior to our reteaching session.
Name:
Which assessment would you like to retake?
Did you complete and turn in all formative assessments, all assignments, or both?
Did you do your best on the assessment?
On what standards would you like to be reassessed?
What did you struggle with or not fully understand the first time, causing you to submit this retake form?

When would you like to meet with me to receive reteaching?
If you feel that you do not need reteaching, what will you do to improve your understanding? By not completing reteaching, you agree to submit your work to me twenty-four hours before the reassessment.
_____ I have read and understand the process of completing a retake. _____ I have discussed this form with my parents or guardians.

Figure 8.2: Reassessment request form.

*Visit **go.SolutionTree.com/assessment** for a free reproducible version of this figure.*

Managing Reassessment

Teachers understand the value of reassessment, but often struggle with how to manage it. Concerns arise, such as how much time it will take, when the reassessment will happen, and how many times learners can reassess. Teachers feel overwhelmed thinking they have to create many versions of an assessment and keep track of which learners have attempted each one. One way to reduce the number of reassessments is to be honest about when the time is right to summatively assess. If most of a class will be scoring at a Level 2 (working toward standards, basic), it may not be advisable to summatively assess. With sound assessment practices, teachers know along the way where their students are with their proficiency. If most students are not ready, the teacher is setting himself or herself up for quite a reassessment procedure. Waiting may mean that a unit gets extended by a few days, but it is worth the time so learners are prepared for what is coming up next; it is a decision where teachers spend time to save time.

This section outlines ways to ease these fears and make the reassessment process meaningful and manageable. Remember that the student must meet the teacher at least halfway if not more; the brunt of the workload with reassessment should fall on the student. Make the students own the reassessment process with the teacher in a supporting role. The following are guidelines that will support efficient reassessment processes.

- Only reassess the standards for which the learner has not reached proficiency. If the teacher has assessed several standards and the student is only lacking proficiency on one, the teacher should reassess only the one.

- Keep in mind how much evidence is necessary to prove proficiency. If five questions will provide enough evidence to give an accurate picture of proficiency, then a ten-question assessment is unnecessary.

- Consider changing the method. If a conversation with a student can prove additional proficiency, then something more formalized is unnecessary. An anecdotal note as evidence can be maintained for record-keeping purposes.

- Take advantage of class time. There may be opportunities within the classroom setting if the reassessment is not lengthy.

- Prepare for students. Having learners complete a request to reassess allows the teacher time to prepare any necessary materials.

- Have set times of the day or week for reassessment. Provide students with a few options for scheduling (whether within the school day or outside it) and keep track of who will be attending.

- Determine time frames for when students must complete reassessment. Whether it is two weeks after the close of a unit or a week before the end of a marking period, clearly communicate time frames to students.

- Recognize when yearlong standards occur in the curriculum. If a standard returns later in the school year, a reassessment may not be necessary until that time.

Without guidelines for students to follow, the time it takes to reassess can be overwhelming and unmanageable. To be clear, teachers do not have to give up every planning period, homeroom, advisory time, or lunch period to reassess with learners. They do not have to stay after school or arrive early each day to make reassessment a reality. Providing students options while maintaining some parameters is key.

Students must know when and how a reassessment is available to them. Teachers can communicate this information at the beginning of the school year via a syllabus, an informational sheet, a brochure, or a website. It is important that teachers transparently state and universally share policies and procedures. General guideline examples follow.

- Students must give their best effort on the original assessment. Students must take action between the original assessment and the reassessment in order to be eligible.

- Teachers have the discretion on what that action entails (additional practice, reteaching, or completion of all formative work).

- Students must set an appointment to reassess.

- The appointment time will not exceed two weeks after the original assessment.

There may be some pushback on the first requirement related to determining whether a student is giving his or her best effort. Teachers can monitor effort because they will ideally know where the student's proficiency level is before the summative assessment; this is a residual of sound formative assessment strategies. The concept of giving best effort does not have to be in a written policy. In fact, it's better if it's not; teachers can support this behavior with the environment they create without formally stating it. If a student has shown proficiency, but only answers three questions on a fifteen-question assessment and refuses to complete the rest, the teacher may choose to decline a reassessment opportunity.

The following is another example to consider. While they are similar in nature, subtle differences may better align to the needs of a teacher, school, or district.

- Students may only reassess on a standard two times.

- The reassessment, if a test or a quiz, will be on the same standard but include different questions.

- The reassessment, if it is a writing assessment, speaking assessment, or project, will be on the same standard but may have the same or a different prompt.

- Students will have one week after a completed unit to reassess.

- Students are responsible for scheduling the reassessment from the options the teacher has set aside.

- Students must fill out the request-to-reassess form, indicating the action they have taken to increase their proficiency.

- The new score will replace the original score on the assessment.

Record-Keeping

Teachers need effective, efficient record-keeping methods. Two possible approaches are to (1) replace old proficiency levels with new evidence of learning or (2) keep several data points for the same standard. The former recognizes that proficiency levels should change as students grow and improve; the latter reveals where a student begins his or her process. Both have their strengths and challenges, so teachers must use their professional judgment to determine which method will work best for their classrooms.

The advantage of replacing old proficiency levels with new ones is the focus on the current level of learning. For example, if a student takes a summative assessment and demonstrates a Level 2 proficiency, but then reassesses and the proficiency improves to a 3, the teacher would record the new level—a 3. If new information from reassessment will replace the old in records, it may be advisable to keep an archive of the previous levels of proficiency behind the scenes. This way, the teacher has information to provide parents about their children's growth with their skills and understandings. Many gradebooks have the option to include anecdotal notes with grades, such as, "Reassessed on (date) and improved from 2 to 3." Teachers can also keep this information in a simple spreadsheet or paper record.

Keeping several data points from reassessment attempts for the standards has its obvious strengths. Students and parents will feel like they are in the communication loop and can see growth over time. If teachers keep these data points, they should avoid averaging these attempts. When several data points appear in the record, teachers must assign the most weight to the most recent and consistent evidence of learning.

Portfolios are an effective way to support record keeping by capturing evidence of student proficiency and growth. They can be kept in paper form or digitally. Kidblog (https://kidblog.org/home), Seesaw (https://web.seesaw.me), Ed.VoiceThread (https://voicethread.com/products/k12), and Weebly (www.weebly.com) offer different options to create a portfolio of student work (such as blogging exclusively or video and audio content options). (Visit **go.SolutionTree.com/assessment** to access live links to the websites mentioned in this book.) The responsibility for this process does not have to fall solely on the teacher. Students can take on the task of collecting and maintaining portfolios of evidence.

Gaming the System

Many times, traditional grading and assessment systems condition learners to focus on point collection, compliance, and grades. What about students who attempt to game the system? They initially might see reassessment as an opportunity to find out what is on the test the first time around, knowing they will get a second opportunity. However, when sound assessment principles and a balanced assessment architecture are in place, students do not receive this opportunity. With well-crafted assessment tools, students will not be able to do something as simple as memorize answers from the previous assessment to improve their score. From the beginning of the unit of study, the teacher has clearly and transparently communicated the standards, learning targets, and assessment methods. Teachers will choose whether a retake (the same assessment tool as the first attempt) or reassessment (a different tool to assess the same standard) is most appropriate. Assessment tools are created to seek evidence of learning no matter whether it is the first attempt or a reassessment.

Keeping the Focus on Learning

The reassessment process should absolutely not be punitive. Making it so destroys the emphasis on learning. If teachers design the reassessment to be much more difficult than the original, it's counterproductive and not standards based. It will prevent some students from furthering their learning and could potentially make them fearful of the next assessment. Others will give up with the reasoning that if they couldn't show proficiency with the original assessment, how would they do so with something more difficult? Making a reassessment more difficult also skews the evidence of learning that it produces. The integrity of the standard cannot be compromised; the level of complexity is determined by the standard, not how many times a student has reassessed. Persevering to learn complex content, understandings, and skills prepares students for the demands they will face in the next steps of their school careers and beyond. When reassessment becomes punitive, the opposite message is communicated.

Grading Reassessment

Teachers should grade reassessment in the same manner they would grade any other summative assessment. When gathering summative data to make a decision about a proficiency level for a student, they should apply the same scoring mechanisms, rubrics, and guides. Again, reporting does not include averaging reassessment results with previous attempts.

It is important to avoid parameters that restrict how much students can earn (a portion of the original amount) on a reassessment or set a maximum score (less than full credit) for the reassessment. For example, it is common for a teacher to say, "You can correct this, but you will only get half the points for the corrections." This works against student motivation if the score is so low that with half the points back, it is still a failing grade. It is also common to have policies that state, "A student can earn no more than an 80 percent on a reassessment." Both examples support a system in which students will figure out if the reassessment is worth it based on the points they can acquire.

Talking to Learners

The need for reassessment opportunities for students is a critical component of standards-based learning, and helping students clearly understand why it must happen and how it will work is essential. Students, especially at the middle and high school levels, are often not used to the practice of reassessment in their learning experiences.

When talking to learners, explain that learning is not linear; there are predictable progressions and regressions that happen throughout the journey toward proficiency. Because of this, there will be times where students do not show initial proficiency with summative assessment, which means they will need to revisit some of the content and skills they have previously practiced. Every student will develop proficiency at a different rate than his or her peers. Some may inadvertently feel that they are doing something wrong if they don't "get it" at the same time as other learners; anticipating this and proactively communicating this to students can mitigate or at least soften the blow of initial misunderstandings. Offer students a variety of examples of learning at differing paces. Ask students if it would work to set a hard deadline for babies learning how to walk. Students can easily understand situations like these, but do not commonly link them to their thoughts about learning in school.

Learners may falsely claim that the concept of reassessment does not apply to academics in the same way it does in other settings. At this point, have them consider what learning is and what it looks like. Ask how learning outside the classroom walls differs from what happens within. Remind them that learning is learning, regardless of location; that learning is not restricted to schools; and that hands-on learning experiences are definitely not limited to after-school hours.

Learners also need to know that teachers expect their best efforts each time they produce evidence. Teachers should tell students that they need students' best work on any given day and they can help make decisions about how to support students in their learning. Be prepared for some learners to misunderstand the process, asking, "What's the catch?" This feeling comes from previous experiences when a reassessment was either not an option or offered by a teacher for a reduced grade. Reassure learners that there is no catch and that learning is the priority for everyone no matter whether it happens on a first attempt, on a second attempt, or even further down the line.

Figure 8.3 provides some possible questions students might ask when it comes to redos, retakes, and reassessment and possible teacher responses.

Student Question	Teacher Response
Why do I have to fill out a form to reassess? Can't I just stop by?	The reassessment form serves two purposes. It helps me plan so I will have all the materials ready when you come, and gives you the opportunity to reflect on your performance. That's important so you know what you need to practice in the meantime.
I did well on my first assessment, so why is my grade the same as for someone who took three tries?	Learning is not a race. I am going to report your proficiency level when it is time for a grade, not how many tries it took. Just because you did well the first time on this occasion doesn't mean that will happen every time.
Why is there a different test for reassessment?	I do not want to know if you can memorize answers; I want to know if you are proficient with the standards. A different assessment tool will give me good information on whether you can do the skill well or you need more practice.

Figure 8.3: Student questions and teacher responses about redos, retakes, and reassessment.

PERSONAL NARRATIVE

Brian Durst

*High School English and Communication Arts Teacher,
Grafton High School, Grafton, Wisconsin*

Like many educators, I want to create a learning environment centered around a mindset that teaches students to be patient, trust the learning process (and the teacher), and celebrate growth. But there is a powerful force that challenges such conditions. We live in a culture that continues to reward, rank, and emphasize grades over learning, points over progress, and recall over creation. It's time to reassess our culture of learning. By acknowledging and acting on the following truths, educators live up to their professional title and create learning permanence.

1. Learning is a messy process. Consequently, teaching all students to learn is challenging work. Some factors cannot be explained; others

continued →

are beyond our control. What if performance on formative assessments does not match outcomes of the summative assessment? This calls to question the assessment design. Do the expectations match the preparation? In some cases, what educators perceive as understanding is far from mastery; the student has relied on help from a teacher, peers, or notes. Obviously, the learner is not ready for independent proficiency demonstrations. Maybe the summative assessment caught the student on a bad day—external factors such as lack of sleep, trouble at home, multiple tests on the same day, health issues, and relationship drama play into it. All these circumstances are life obstacles; they justify second chances.

2. Learning happens at different times. In fact, learning never ends. While a school calendar may suggest times to report progress, the learning process is not a race, nor a winner-take-all competition. A student may demonstrate early proficiency on one assessment, but show inconsistencies with the standard on a future assessment. When we embed the skill or concept in future assessments, we allow multiple opportunities for students to demonstrate mastery. This also holds all students accountable for learning and retaining, not simply a one-and-done measure of success. Students who consistently show proficiency may elevate their performance to a level of mastery, while late learners earn the opportunity to show new evidence of growth. Making reassessment a natural part of our class time prevents the feeling of being singled out; no one feels exposed or labeled as *behind*.

3. Not all students will learn a concept or skill on the first attempt. In a growth-minded environment, teachers and students are held accountable. If learning is the priority, standards deserve to be assessed multiple times. A teacher's responsibility becomes supporting and rewarding growth. The student is accountable to practice, learn, and retain.

4. Learning evidence appears in many forms. If we remember to teach learners, not curriculum, we honor learning with respectful tasks. Reassessment practices give students a voice in seeking ongoing opportunities to demonstrate new evidence of learning. Allowing learners to reassess shifts the mindset and reinforces our message; it shows how learning is continuous while teaching students to be positive, patient, and resilient. Consequently, students pay closer attention to standards when they know there is still room (and opportunity) for growth.

Talking to Parents

For many parents, reassessment was not a common idea during their time in school, especially at the secondary level. There was teaching, practice, and then a final assessment. The grade on that final assessment was permanent; revisiting the topic or skill would only happen if it arose in a future unit of study. Relying on these experiences to build understanding of a new way of looking at reassessment is critical to get parents on board.

When speaking to parents, explain the role reassessment plays in learning. Ask them to think of a time when they wished that a teacher would have offered them a reassessment. Maybe there was a test they wish they could have tried again or a paper that could have benefited from one more draft. Ask what that felt like for them and if they worked diligently without reassessment to build the skills that were missing or still developing. If parents are uncomfortable sharing their experiences or don't remember, provide one of yours, highlighting the opportunity for learning that students can miss without ample reassessment possibilities. Teachers can share with them that they would never want their own children to feel that learning was out of reach or that there is not enough time to revisit a concept. The potential for each learner is limitless and parents need to hear this about their children.

A common concern with reassessment is the feeling that a student who achieves proficiency before another should receive a higher grade. This sentiment is rooted in the idea that learning is a race and the first one to the finish line deserves a reward. Explain that rather than a reward-punishment paradigm, the classroom supports learning for all and that a standards-based learning environment is where teachers compare students to the standards, not one another. Finally, tell parents that the focus is their children and their learning, so reassessment is a must.

Getting Started With Redos, Retakes, and Reassessment

Reassessment can be difficult to implement. Middle and high school students may see this as another layer in the game of school. Getting started with the following steps will ensure the intended purpose.

- Identify current redo, retake, and reassessment practices in your classroom. What are the strengths? Are there areas for growth?

- Devise a plan for reassessment that is manageable and that students can lead.

- Identify standards that spiral in your curriculum and determine how you could reassess those standards when they return.

- Determine whether a new assessment is necessary or if you will re-administer the same assessment.

- Decide how you will record the scores and data from reassessment.

Questions for Learning Teams

Pose these questions during teacher team meetings, planning meetings, or book study.

- What quote or passage encapsulates your biggest takeaway from this chapter? What immediate action (large or small) will you take as a result of this takeaway? Explain both to your team.

- What are your current reassessment procedures and policies? What are you proud of and what might need some improvement?

- Do your current reassessment policies support and encourage a focus on continual growth?

- What policies and procedures must be in place to improve the practice for both teachers and learners and make the process more manageable?

- How will reassessment be used in the grading process?

- How can learners play an active role in the reassessment process?

- What are some effective ways to get parents on board with the paradigm shift surrounding reassessment?

9

Proficiency Scales and Rubrics in Action

The genius of rubrics is that they are descriptive and not evaluative. Of course, rubrics can be used to evaluate, but the operating principle is you match the performance to the description rather than "judge" it.

—Susan M. Brookhart

In general, success criteria describe qualities of exemplary work; the more direct expression of criteria comes through rubrics and scales, solidifying criteria as a natural progression of sophistication (Andrade, 2013). While teachers can develop scales and rubrics in a variety of formats, the fundamental purpose is to make performance criteria transparent and accessible. Scales and rubrics work together in tandem, with the rubric providing a more narrow and detailed view of success with a particular standard or skill, and the proficiency scale providing a more holistic, overarching view.

Moving From Rationale to Action

Scales and rubrics are similar in that both attempt to create a continuum that articulates distinct levels of knowledge and skill relative to a specific topic (Marzano, 2010). Operationally, however, there are differences that emerge in that *scales* are often number based (from 0 to 4, for example), whereas *rubrics* tend to use a descriptive scale (from novice to exemplary, for example). Both scales and rubrics create a progression of quality (from the simplest to the most sophisticated).

The advantage of both scales and rubrics is that the energy and focus of instruction is on the intended *learning* rather than the specific *task* at hand; this may be the most important aspect of scales and rubrics because they create a cohesive pathway that transforms a series of (what can appear to be) random assignments into a purposeful progression of learning.

The Research

The research we explore in the following sections focuses on making criteria transparent, interpreting accurately, using student-friendly language, moving from simple to sophisticated, choosing a format, and deciding between general and task-specific criteria.

Making Criteria Transparent

When teachers make learning goals and success criteria transparent in an organized, clear, and cohesive way, it is far more possible that students will fully invest in the assessment process (Andrade, 2013; Vagle, 2014). Transparent success criteria in the form of a scale or rubric make it easier for students to see where they are headed and are essential to maximizing the self- and peer assessment processes we discussed in chapter 6 (page 109). Provided the success criteria are not trivial or tangential, transparency pulls back the curtain not only on what teachers expect of students in terms of their performances, but reveals specifically how teachers will judge those performances.

Scales and rubrics are technically the same thing in that both attempt to create a continuum that articulates distinct levels of knowledge and skill relative to a specific topic (Marzano, 2010). David Balch, Robert Blanck, and David Howard Balch (2016) describe a rubric as a "visual narrative of the criteria that defines and describes the important components of an assignment. The criteria are stated in several levels of competence; from not meeting the requirement to mastering it" (p. 20). Operationally, however, there are differences that emerge in that *scales* (also called *holistic* rubrics) are often number based (such as 0 to 4), whereas *rubrics* (also called *analytic* rubrics) tend to use a descriptive scale (such as novice to exemplary). Both scales and rubrics create a progression of quality, from the simplest to the most sophisticated, so students and parents can clearly see what it takes to reach the next level.

Interpreting Accurately

Clearly articulated criteria are also essential for teachers. Within a criterion-referenced, standards-based learning environment, it is necessary that teachers have (or develop) the confidence that the judgments they're making about students' performances are similar to the judgments their colleagues would make (Guskey & Jung, 2016). While this consistency in applying success criteria (*inter-rater reliability*) takes time to develop, it is important because so many standards require teachers to infer quality. There is, for example, no completely objective way to assess argumentative writing. There are aspects of quality, but success is a matter of interpretation in which the teacher has to match the quality of the writing to the specific level of qualities the criteria outline.

The research is mixed on whether teachers in general are skilled at accurately summarizing student achievement. Some claim that teachers are the best sources for judging student performances because they have more experience with their students (Meisels, Bickel, Nicholson, Xue, & Atkins-Burnett, 2001); however, others claim that an inability to distinguish between student achievement and student traits can cloud teacher judgments (Moss, 2013), especially when teachers are assessing students with diverse backgrounds (Martínez & Mastergeorge, 2002; Tiedemann, 2002). If the former is true, rubrics and scales will only strengthen that skill; if the latter is true, then rubrics and scales are necessary to ensure achievement and traits do not intermingle in the assessment process. According to Catherine Welch (2006), reliable scoring rubrics must meet the following five characteristics.

1. Be consistent with the decisions and inferences teachers make with the results.

2. Define the characteristics of the response that teachers will evaluate along a continuum.

3. Convey performance criteria in an understandable way.

4. Use items that elicit a range of performance.

5. Align with the content standards that teachers are assessing.

While rubrics and scales appear in a variety of structural formats, the reliability of the scoring inferences derived from the rubric or scale is a non-negotiable feature (Parkes, 2013).

Using Student-Friendly Language

Rubrics and scales provide learners with a natural progression of quality that runs from the *simplest* to the *most sophisticated*. Teachers can create as many levels as they choose, provided they can describe the differences in quality between the levels. Labeling the levels is the easy part; describing them is much tougher. For example, it's easy to label twelve levels on a scale: 4+, 4, 4–, 3+, 3, 3–, and so on. It's much more challenging to describe the differences between the levels. One would have to make transparent the specific differences between a 3+ and 4– and between a 2 and 2+, and so on.

This is why effective scales and rubrics tend to have a more reasonable number of levels (Balch et al., 2016). We most often see four. When there is a fifth level it is often the *not yet* or *insufficient* category, which allows the four-point scale to become a five-point scale that aligns with an A–F grading construct. Each point should represent a point of proficiency. Again, that runs from the *simplest* to the *most sophisticated*, so each of the descriptions should reflect that.

Exceeds is one descriptor to avoid (Guskey, 2015). There is a big difference between a demonstration of learning at the *most sophisticated* level and one that *exceeds* the standards. The implication with the term *exceeds* is that students must now perform beyond their grade level to reach the highest level on the criteria. It also makes the highest level exponentially more difficult to achieve and could lead to a curving mindset that inadvertently (or intentionally) reserves the top level for only those truly special demonstrations.

When teachers use *meeting* as a level (often the third of four levels), they create a definitive destination that makes it difficult to distinguish between low and high quality. Again, scales and rubrics should describe levels of quality, so in that sense, all levels along a scale or a rubric are *meeting* to one degree or the other; the continuum of *simple* to *sophisticated* is lost when there is a finite destination. There are certainly a number of schools using *meeting* as the third level, but ideally, the top level is not exponentially more difficult to achieve. The issue is resolved when *meeting* is the fourth level, but as the third, schools will most often designate the fourth level as something *beyond* or *exceeding* standards. Schools should not expect students to *exceed* the standard to reach the top level, so while they can implement *meeting* as the third level successfully, it does require some extra thought and finesse.

A finite level may be appropriate for finite standards that have one correct answer (often at grades K–3), but most standards are at a DOK that reaches beyond a binary choice. Those higher DOK levels require teachers to examine a performance's quality or consistency. That means a singular level is, at best, incomplete. Practically speaking, with so many other word labels to choose from that are equally appropriate and applicable, it's unnecessary to arbitrarily add confusion.

Moving From Simple to Sophisticated

Once teachers choose the word labels (assuming the scale is not simply 0–4), the descriptors should be clear and based on the same aspect. If a portion of proficiency asks students to, for example, "support claim(s) with clear reasons and relevant evidence, using credible sources and demonstrating an understanding of the topic or text" (W.6.1.B; NGA & CCSSO, 2010a), then each description should describe the quality with which students are able to do that. Novice writers will support claims at the very basic level, while exemplary writers will do so at the most sophisticated level. Susan M. Brookhart (2013c), educational consultant, professor of education, and author, advises that level descriptions should follow these criteria.

- Be descriptive.

- Be clear.

- Cover the whole range of performance.

- Make relatively easy distinctions between each level.

- Center the target performance at the appropriate level.

- Feature parallel descriptions from level to level.

As well, Brookhart (2013c) submits that effective rubrics and scales avoid listing both *requirements* and *quantities* because requirements only produce a yes-or-no distinction, while quantities are about counting, not quality. She goes on to add:

> The rubric description is the bridge between what you see (the student work, the evidence) and the judgment of learning. If you're not going to take advantage of that main function, you might as well just go back to the old-fashioned way of marking a grade on a paper without explanation. (p. 22)

Choosing a Format

While it is possible to use all rubric or scale formats for either formative or summative assessment, an assessment's function drives the most favorable format to align an assessment with its subsequent action. *Analytic* rubrics provide unique, separate descriptions on multiple aspects of qualities for any given performance (Balch et al., 2016; Brookhart, 2013c). This is advantageous for formative assessment because it asks for a more granular analysis. Describing each criterion separately makes it easier for teachers and students to recognize both strengths and areas in need of strengthening. This can allow teachers to make instructional decisions that help them differentiate what's next.

Holistic rubrics, on the other hand, ask the teacher or student to make a single overall judgment of quality along the performance levels (Balch et al., 2016; Brookhart, 2013c). Rather than describing separately the aspects of quality along each level, teachers would *holistically* describe each level in its totality. This is advantageous for summative assessment because it often requires a single determination despite some specific deficiencies. Teachers do not ignore specific criteria; rather, they synthesize all the criteria into a singular description that outlines what a novice through exemplary demonstration might look like. While most teachers will likely spend the majority of time using analytic rubrics, they optimize the relationship between analytic and holistic rubrics when they use an analytic rubric for instruction, and then synthesize it into a holistic rubric for grading.

Deciding Between General and Task-Specific Criteria

The other decision educators face is whether to develop general or task-specific scales or rubrics. The advantage of general rubrics is that criteria are longitudinally transferable throughout multiple demonstrations of the same outcomes or standards; teachers can use the same general rubric to assess multiple samples of, for example, argumentative writing. The disadvantage of general rubrics is that they inherently require greater skill at inferring quality because the rubric itself does not address the specific task at hand.

Task-specific rubrics offer the opposite. They do not transfer as readily from one assignment to the next, which is a disadvantage (Balch et al., 2016; Brookhart, 2013c). However, they are low-inference tools that often result in greater consistency in application. Teachers have to weigh the short-term advantages of task-specific rubrics with the long-term advantages of general rubrics, and while general rubrics can take more time to develop, apply, and calibrate, they are worth the effort in the long run.

Despite their inherent differences, general and task-specific rubrics can work in harmony. Suzanne Lane (2013), professor of the research methodology program at the University of Pittsburgh, says a "general rubric may be designed that reflects the skills and knowledge underlying the defined domain. The general rubrics can then guide the design of specific rubrics for a particular task" (p. 316). This allows teachers to take advantage of each type of rubric and leads to greater consistency across task-specific rubrics, because each would derive from the rubric the teacher had originally developed (Lane, 2013).

Understanding the strengths and limitations of the different variations of scales and rubrics allows for a more transparent assessment process that anchors instruction (and learning) on the knowledge, skills, and understandings that teachers expect students to attain.

In Action

Teachers employ both proficiency scales and rubrics in standards-based learning environments, but with slightly different definitions and uses. Again, *proficiency scales* in this book are the holistically described levels that teachers use to communicate proficiency across grade levels and content areas. Proficiency scales tend to be applied school- or districtwide to provide consistent language with the descriptors. Descriptor labels are usually one or a few words. Rubrics, on the other hand, have more robust descriptions. Rubrics are for particular assignments, assessments, or specific standards to give feedback about the proficiency level. If a descriptor for a level 3 is *proficient*, then a rubric for that standard or standards would describe what proficiency looks like. This chapter helps teachers understand and develop quality proficiency scales and rubrics. Additional sections are devoted to inter-rater reliability and student involvement.

Defining Success

No matter how many levels a scale or rubric includes, each must have a clear and concise description. These descriptions foster a process for teachers to guide not only their instruction but also practice and assessment for students. They also prompt teachers to reflect, learn, and improve.

The description for a scale or rubric should be succinct. Lengthy text is more difficult for students to consume or comprehend. In addition, long and very detailed descriptors can close the door to the variety of ways a student can show his or her mastery of the standards. When a description gives too many specific details, students will only rise to that description. Clarity versus specificity is an important distinction when writing success criteria.

Creating quality success criteria should move beyond quantifiable requirements and guidelines of compliance to a true description of learning. Requiring a specific number of words or pages in a paper does not ensure proficiency because quantity and quality can be quite different; simply writing seven pages does not mean the student has met the standard. Only a minimal quantity of evidence may be necessary to reach proficiency and receive feedback.

Creating Quality Scales and Rubrics

The following sections include examples of more- and less-effective proficiency scales and rubrics. Quality scales and rubrics provide students with criteria with a language of learning. They describe the characteristics of a successful product in relation to the standards. Quality scales and rubrics leave the door open to multiple ways to show proficiency. They build student self-efficacy so they can adeptly identify where their learning is and how to move forward.

Proficiency Scales

Consider the scale in figure 9.1, which takes the levels and pairs them with percentage-based increments.

Level	Descriptor
4	90–100
3	80–89
2	70–79
1	60–69

Figure 9.1: Low-quality proficiency scale.

This example scale does nothing to communicate about student learning or academic proficiency. Equating the levels to percentages places the focus squarely on grades and feeds into the notion that grades are more important than learning. Using language to describe the learning provides meaning, where a number or letter cannot. That language helps students strive for learning. The purpose of a proficiency scale is to support learning, and the connection to a percentage or letter grade works against that mission.

Now compare it to the proficiency scale in figure 9.2. It also has four levels.

Level	Descriptor
4	Advanced
3	Proficient
2	Basic
1	Emergent

Figure 9.2: High-quality proficiency scale.

*Visit **go.SolutionTree.com/assessment** for a free reproducible version of this figure.*

Figure 9.2 uses a language of learning to describe the four levels. Although short, these descriptors communicate proficiency and function as a starting point for creating rubrics with more substantial language.

Rubrics

Examine the rubric in figure 9.3, which lists requirements in checklist style.

	3	2	1	Not Included
Proper title and heading				
Introductory paragraph				
Three body paragraphs				
Concluding paragraph				
Comprehensibility				
Bibliography				

Figure 9.3: Low-quality rubric.

This rubric has specific requirements but is severely lacking in other areas. The focus is on the inclusion of elements rather than the writing's substance. The teacher can check off the items with a 3, 2, 1, or Not Included. There is no language to describe the difference between those levels and no guidance to help learners know what success looks like.

Now compare it to the rubric in figure 9.4 (page 174). It too has four levels. Which rubric tells a story of learning over a story of compliance?

This rubric provides both learners and teachers with a great deal more information. The different assessed standards appear, as do specific success criteria for each. Language for each level helps students understand the skills and knowledge teachers expect them to have.

Determining the Number of Levels

The number of levels on a scale or rubric depends on the number of accurate and definable success criteria for the learning. Can teachers accurately describe the learning in three or four different levels? Could they break it down further, into six? A range between two and seven levels for scales and rubrics is advisable. Beyond that, it becomes challenging to describe the differences. Remember, teachers must be able to *describe* (not just label) the differences between each level, which is why seven pushes the boundaries of clear distinctions of quality. A four-level scale is most common in a standards-based environment, giving some separate distinction in levels without so many that they become difficult to define. Regardless, they must tie to language that describes a natural progression of quality from the simplest to the most sophisticated.

Standard	4	3	2	1
Produce clear writing with examples.	Writing is clear and understandable to a variety of audiences with examples that explicitly support the thesis.	Writing is clear and understandable. Examples support the thesis.	Writing is mostly clear and understandable. It provides a few examples without clear ties to the thesis.	Writing is unclear at times. It provides insufficient examples.
Conduct a short research project based on focus questions.	Research of the writing topic is extensive and from various sources. There is a clear connection to the focus questions.	Research of the writing topic is from a variety of sources and is based on the focus questions.	Research of the writing topic is from only one source and is based on the focus questions.	Research is present but unrelated to the focus questions.
Demonstrate command of conventions.	Convention use adds to clarity and development.	Convention use, even with minor mistakes, does not interfere with comprehensibility.	Some convention errors interfere with comprehensibility.	Many convention errors interfere with comprehensibility.

Figure 9.4: High-quality rubric.

Visit go.SolutionTree.com/assessment for a free reproducible version of this figure.

If grading on a percentage scale is a requirement, teachers can skip to chapter 10 (page 187) to read how to convert to one from a proficiency scale.

Writing Proficiency Scale Descriptors

Teachers typically generalize the language when writing proficiency scales. The overarching nature of proficiency level descriptors ties together the wide variety of subjects or classes with a common thread. A descriptor such as *proficient* works in first or fifth grade or in a Spanish or physical education class. What *proficient* means for each of those depends on the standard and learning targets specific to each subject. It is up to the teacher to contextualize the scale with more specific language, but the scale itself is universally applicable.

Establishing a common understanding of the terms is crucial; optimally, teachers will collaborate among colleagues to do so. Figure 9.5 includes a bank of ideas for proficiency scale descriptors. Note that the example descriptors for a level 4 do not include *exceeds*, but words that demand a deep understanding without going beyond the grade-level standard.

1	2	3	4
Below basic	Basic	Proficient	Distinguished
Emergent	Working toward standards	Meets standard	Excels
Not meeting standards	Progressing	Meeting expectations	Extending
Beginning	Intermediate	Satisfactory	Deep understanding and application
I do not understand.	I need some help.	I get it.	I could explain it to others.
Novice	Developing	Proficient	Advanced

Figure 9.5: Language example for proficiency scale descriptors.

*Visit **go.SolutionTree.com/assessment** for a free reproducible version of this figure.*

Figure 9.5 does not include descriptors for a 0 level, which many schools and districts will include as a fifth level. This fifth level typically indicates *lack of evidence* or *insufficient evidence*. Both communicate that the teacher (and even the student via self-assessment) does not have enough evidence to make a decision about proficiency. Insufficient evidence could also be indicated as a 1 on a four-level scale. These descriptors can stand alone for reporting or be paired with a number.

Regardless of whether the words or numbers will be used for reporting, clear meaning and consistent application are paramount. Once developed among teachers, a common understanding can be transferred to students and parents. This proficiency scale language also guides rubric development, with scale descriptors providing the overarching ideas for each proficiency level.

Crafting Rubrics

For consistency, rubrics should contain the same number of levels as the proficiency scale. Common sense dictates that having a different number of levels between the scale and the rubric increases the potential for confusion among students and parents.

Well-crafted rubrics, no matter in what content area or skill, have some common characteristics. They use language that is positive (stating what the evidence *should* look like instead of focusing on missing elements or characteristics), as well as student friendly. Some explanation may be necessary with examples of student work, but a rubric's language should not be a barrier to student understanding. When using the rubric, students should be able to identify their current proficiency level and see what it takes to move to the next level.

Teachers can generate two types of rubrics to use in the classroom. Skill-specific rubrics can span multiple assignments, assessments, and units. Teachers can most easily use them with standards that do not have specific content tied to them. A language arts standard that requires students to cite textual evidence can go with a rubric that the teacher uses each time he or she addresses that standard. Other rubrics are specific to a particular content area or unit of study. These provide a more detailed description of the evidence that students produce with the content as a guide for the skill. An example is a rubric that a teacher develops for a mathematics standard, such as knowing the formulas for circumference and area of a circle and using them to solve problems.

When creating a rubric, begin with the proficient level. Considering the standard or standards and their essential verbs, describe what evidence would look like to meet them. For some teachers, a rubric's proficient level is very similar to the standard itself. The next task is to work on the surrounding levels (levels 4, 2, and 1 on a four-level scale). What would evidence look like on a more complex level or if a student delved more deeply? What would the evidence look like when a student is working toward proficiency but has not yet achieved it? What would evidence look like for a student in the beginning stages of learning with the standard?

The most difficult level for many teachers to describe on a rubric is the most sophisticated level (a level 4, for example) of proficiency. *What is a 4?* looms large for some. There are a variety of ways to write the description of a level 4 on a rubric. For example, examine student work on a standard that is very high quality. Consider what characteristics of the work make this so. Determine the level of sophistication given the cognitive complexity and the students' developmental stage. Another approach is to illustrate how a student could transfer the knowledge and skill to a new situation. An important consideration when writing the highest-level descriptions on a rubric is that a larger quantity of work does not mean that the student has shown a more advanced proficiency. Rather than upping the number of requirements, change the demands or sophistication.

Figure 9.6 offers a rubric from a physical education class; it has four proficiency levels and four standards. It is for the entire unit of study related to dance that students will complete over multiple weeks.

Proficiency Level	4 Advanced Application	3 Meets Standard	2 Working Toward Standard	1 Does Not Meet Standard
Standard				
Demonstrates control performing a sequence of locomotor and nonlocomotor movements	• Develops a creative and complete dance sequence • Makes sequence consistent all the time	• Develops a complete dance sequence • Makes sequence consistent most of the time	• Develops an incomplete dance sequence • Makes sequence often inconsistent	• Develops an incomplete dance sequence • Makes sequence different each time
Participates daily in moderate to rigorous physical activities while performing movement patterns	• Actively participates every day • Engages in rigorous activity while performing movement patterns	• Actively participates most days • Engages in physical activity while performing movement patterns	• Actively participates some days • Engages in some physical activity while performing inconsistent movement patterns	• Seldom participates • Seldom engages in physical activity while performing inconsistent movement patterns
Follows teacher's directions and those of peer leader for grade level	• Listens to others and displays patience • Motivates other group members	• Listens to others most of the time and displays impatience occasionally • Displays frustration with others at times	• Listens to others sometimes and displays impatience sometimes • Requires teacher assistance to refocus and remain in the group	• Refuses to listen to others and displays impatience often • Commands others to listen and follow demands
Works cooperatively	• Works very well with others all the time	• Works well with others most of the time	• Works well with others some of the time	• Does not work well with others

Figure 9.6: Four-level rubric.

*Visit **go.SolutionTree.com/assessment** for a free reproducible version of this figure.*

Figure 9.7 is from an ecosystems unit with one standard that the teacher broke down into two skills. There are only three proficiency levels, and the teacher has left the Excels level open for the first skill; the students are to prove how they have created a model that moves beyond the proficient level.

Standard: MS-LS2-3—Develop a model to describe the cycling of matter and flow of energy among living and nonliving parts of our local ecosystem.

Learning Target	Excels	Meets	Working Toward
Develop a model.	Fill in your own description of how the project shows a deeper understanding of the standard:	• Identifies producers, consumers, and decomposers • Shows how energy flows • Shows how matter cycles	• Identifies some producers, consumers, and decomposers • Shows energy, but not how it moves • Shows matter, but not how it cycles
Obtain, evaluate, and communicate information.	• Explains how energy flows and demonstrates what would happen if a piece wasn't there • Explains how matter cycles (between living and nonliving) and demonstrates what would happen if it didn't • Uses detailed text evidence to support ideas • Is detailed and clear (reader makes almost no inferences) • Uses multiple reliable sources in text ("according to")	• Explains how energy flows • Explains how matter cycles among all parts (living and nonliving) of the ecosystem • Uses text evidence to support ideas • Is clear (reader makes few inferences) • Uses multiple reliable sources	• Explains energy but not how it moves • Explains that matter moves but doesn't show a complete cycle • Provides some text evidence but doesn't fully support ideas • Is unclear (reader makes many inferences) • Uses a single source or unreliable sources

Source: © 2016 by K. Budrow. Source for standard: NGSS Lead States, 2013.

Figure 9.7: Three proficiency levels plus student participation.

*Visit **go.SolutionTree.com/assessment** for a free reproducible version of this figure.*

One additional rubric example appears in figure 9.8. This skill-specific rubric is for multiple assignments or assessments. It is not as detailed, but when teachers use it multiple times throughout a school year, students will become more familiar with the demands.

Skill	Advanced	Proficient	Basic	Emergent
Identifies ways that a catastrophic disaster may affect people living in a place	Describes and explains how a catastrophic disaster affects people living in a specific place	Identifies ways that a catastrophic disaster may affect people where they are living	Lists catastrophic disasters that may affect people	Identifies catastrophic disasters that may affect people

Figure 9.8: Skill-specific rubric.

Some digital rubric creation tools such as ThemeSpark.net, and portals such as the Literacy Design Collaborative (https://ldc.org), can be great resources. Teachers can search for standards and automatically generate rubrics. These rubrics are a great starting place with standards for which teachers are struggling to develop language or for teachers who are newer to the process. However, rubric generators are only a starting point. There will likely be some language that makes sense to a teacher or team of teachers and other language that does not align with the instruction. Teachers must use their professional judgment to examine and alter these rubrics if necessary to best meet the needs of assignments, assessments, and standards.

Deciding When to Use Rubrics

As with anything, there is a time and place for rubrics in the classroom. A rubric is not necessary for every assignment and assessment in a standards-based classroom. They are most desirable when student responses are *scalable*, which means responses run from simple to sophisticated; not every assessment lends itself to scalable responses. Teachers can easily give feedback on student work in the formative process without a rubric. Rubrics cannot replace a teacher's personalized feedback, but can gauge progress with a standard.

When using a rubric with summative assessment, teachers should inform students of it and grant them access to it from the unit's beginning. Success criteria should never be unclear to students, regardless of whether there is a rubric for that particular assignment or assessment.

Supporting Inter-Rater Reliability

Both proficiency scales and rubrics, when teachers create them with clarity and use them with fidelity, work to increase inter-rater reliability within groups of teachers. A standards-based learning environment inherently supports inter-rater reliability because of its focus on common standards and targets. This can be enhanced by moving beyond the shared understanding of standards to creating success criteria within scales and rubrics. They hold students to the same challenging demands no matter the class. Common grading scales can give a false impression of consistency, because they can be used differently with no consideration of learning evidence. It is the determination of common learning expectations and the consistent interpretation of elicited evidence that significantly impact and improve consistency among colleagues.

Conversing with colleagues about evidence and where it falls on a rubric or scale is one of the most important discussions teachers can have, although making the time to do so is often easier said than done. Meeting agendas fill with other items, and if teachers use the same rubric, they may assume it will be automatically reliable. Criteria always hold an element of interpretation, so the more teachers converse about their interpretations, the more consistent their usage will be. When having this discussion, teachers bring examples of student work and have everyone in the group use the rubric to assess the work. The debriefing that follows builds consistency with collective decisions about which evidence corresponds to which level on a rubric or scale.

This dialogue serves multiple purposes. It creates a common understanding of the rubric or scale and builds teachers' confidence in their ratings. One reason teachers reduce rubrics to quantifiable and compliance requirements is confidence. It is much easier to count the number of words or pages or make sure students choose the right formula than it is to make and use a rubric that describes the language students are using in their words or how students can effectively apply a formula to solve problems. By working together, teachers can build this confidence by using rubrics and scales based on quality.

Involving Students

Teachers should actively involve students with both proficiency scales and rubrics. Both are created for students and teachers, so if a disconnect exists, the scale or rubric has lost value. The rubric opens the discussion of what is possible with the standard and makes plain the expectations, increasing the opportunity to involve students from the outset.

Students can also help create rubrics. Doing so can increase their understanding of the standards and help them consider what quality evidence looks like. Teachers will still need to remain involved in the process, as there will be times that the student knowledge base and understanding are not developed enough to consider the variances in work levels. Working together, students and the teacher can start the rubric and then revise as student knowledge and understanding grow. Having the students actively involved in writing rubrics will make self-assessment and peer review opportunities more effective and efficient.

PERSONAL NARRATIVE

Katie Budrow

Sixth-Grade Science Teacher,
Charles J. Caruso Middle School, Deerfield, Illinois

In my second year of teaching, one of my amazing mentors suggested that I look into student-created assessment tools. Obviously, I had more than a few concerns as the process got started. As it turns out, my fears were completely unfounded.

We started as a whole group, putting the standard at the top of a page and creating boxes underneath for each level. Students developed the information in small groups, reporting back to the whole class so we could capture it together. They debated over details and fiddled with the wording. They argued over how to format the rubric, suggesting that bullet points would be easier to read but sentences might be clearer. They even asked if we could delete the lowest level, arguing that because they had the opportunity to revise, nobody would end up at the bottom level anyway. They questioned all kinds of things, like whether they should include neatness or if coloring mattered. I would gently step in with a question and coach them back to the verbiage of the standard when necessary, but for the most part, they ran the show. Eventually, they would guide each other to reference the standard, and the healthy debate continued.

After a lengthy conversation, we all came to a consensus. We had a good, solid rubric. Not perfect, but good. We then repeated the process with the other three classes, and I merged all those rubrics together to create a final one. To my surprise, all the classes had a similar process and came up with similar results. I made a few small changes as their four rubrics were bundled into one, but nothing major had to change. Their work didn't need it. When I presented it the next day, the rubric had more clarity and more detail than anything I could have created alone.

However, what we didn't know at the time was that first rubric really just ended up being a rough draft. That was arguably the best part—the rubric wasn't something static. It was a living document, and we could change it at any time. It was ours. Not my rubric full of my expectations, not the students' rubric filled with whatever they wanted, but our rubric that we owned.

Talking to Learners

Students may think that both scales and rubrics are for teacher use only, which means they may not pay attention to their impact on their own learning. Teachers need to help learners change their perception by presenting scales and rubrics as shared tools that support learning. Often, how teachers grade or what teachers are looking for is opaque at best, which leaves students guessing. It is important for students to know that there is no gotcha with the success criteria—what is outlined is what is expected. Teachers reassure students that transparency leading to their success is the goal, and that this is a *we* venture rather than a *teacher versus learner* one.

Learners will ask questions about how the levels and rubrics translate to grades. Share that while proficiency levels are a kind of grade per se, the purpose of proficiency levels is not to equate levels to a percentage-based score or contribute to accumulating points. Students must come to know that a proficiency level is the description of evidence of learning in relation to the standard. Although teachers may use them to determine a final grade, students must know that their purpose is to *describe* what success with the standards looks like.

Students need to know that scales and rubrics provide guidance throughout the learning progression. If success criteria are unclear to students, teachers must provide a means to better communicate them. Whether it is showing quality work exemplars or changing the scale or rubric to more student-friendly language, clarity is the priority. How to progress through the different levels and understanding should be straightforward so students can take ownership of their learning. Knowing where their proficiencies lie and what the next level looks like motivates learners to continue toward the goal.

Teachers who maintain a positive attitude when speaking about proficiency scales and rubrics will transfer that to their students. Talk with learners about the value of knowing success criteria from the beginning to the end of a unit. When students can see that a rubric guides them through the complex demands of the standards, it builds trust and students learn to appreciate their value.

Figure 9.9 offers questions students might ask when it comes to proficiency scales and rubrics and possible teacher responses.

Student Question	Teacher Response
You gave me the rubric at the beginning of the unit. What should I do with it?	The rubric will guide your learning and skill development throughout the unit. When success criteria are clear, you'll know what you need to do.
How does my score on a rubric translate to a grade?	Yes, there will be an overall grade, but I want you to focus on your proficiency level. The rubric's purpose is to describe those levels rather than to provide a grade.
What should I do if I don't understand the rubric?	Please come and speak with me if you are unclear about a rubric. It is a tool I want you to use so you understand how to show proficiency with our standards.

Figure 9.9: Student questions and teacher responses about proficiency scales and rubrics.

Talking to Parents

Once they have developed rubrics and scales, teachers share that common understanding with parents. When talking to parents, it is helpful to bring or show examples. A hands-on example is an effective way to introduce what parents will potentially view as a new use for these tools. Examples such as movie ratings and business ratings on websites like Yelp (www.yelp.com) can show how scales are already present in their daily lives.

Let parents know how they will find the scales and rubrics that teachers will use—online, in a portfolio, or on paper. Sharing scales and rubrics plays a huge role in facilitating effective parent involvement. Provide parents with questions they can ask their children about their work and where it currently falls. Sample questions follow.

- Can you show me what you are working on right now or tell me about it?

- Tell me about the assignment's requirements. What are the assessment's demands?

- Where would you place your work on the scale or rubric right now?

- What can you do to improve your proficiency and show it?

Once the teacher scores the evidence of learning, he or she can share it with parents. This sharing can be facilitated by the student or teacher. For example, a teacher can have students go home and talk with their parents about their learning and proficiency levels, and to hold them accountable, the parents can email the teacher with a quick summary of the discussion. Not everyone will participate, but teachers expect students to go home and talk about their learning.

If teachers will report rubric and scale levels as grades, communicate that process as well. Parents need to know that if their child claims to not know why his or her score is at a certain level, they can counter and facilitate a productive conversation.

Getting Started With Proficiency Scales and Rubrics

While some teachers may have been using scales and rubrics for quite some time, they may be newer tools for others. No matter where teachers are beginning, following these steps will support them as they create or revise their scales and rubrics.

Proficiency scales:

- Decide how many proficiency levels you will use on the scale.

- Write short descriptors for each level.

- Develop a common understanding of those descriptors with colleagues.

- If you will use the scale for reporting to students and parents, communicate the levels, their descriptors, and how you will use them to all involved.

Rubrics:

- Determine which standard or standards you will assess; identify the specific aspects of quality you will assess, especially when developing rubrics for formative assessment.

- Decide how many levels you will use on the rubric.

- Craft rubric language to describe evidence that will elicit the different levels of proficiency (teacher created or teacher and student created).

- Collaborate with colleagues to score student work on the rubric and calibrate and increase inter-rater reliability.

- Use, reflect, and revise!

Questions for Learning Teams

Pose these questions during teacher team meetings, planning meetings, or book study.

- What quote or passage encapsulates your biggest takeaway from this chapter? What immediate action (large or small) will you take as a result of this takeaway? Explain both to your team.

- What aspects of your current rubrics and scales do you see as areas of strength? Which aspects might you need to strengthen?

- How do you clearly communicate your scales and levels to students and parents? Is there anything you could or would do to enhance the effectiveness of your process?

- Do you create and use your rubrics as individual teachers or as a collective grade-level or content-area group? What led to that decision? Is that an approach you should continue?

- How do you envision involving students in the creation and use of rubrics and scales?

- How do scales and rubrics impact self-assessment and peer review activities?

Standards-Based Reporting in Action

A standards-based report card identifies the specific learning goals within the curriculum so that the appropriate rigor can be ensured. It also communicates more detailed information about student learning progress with regard to those goals to bring about higher levels of success.

—Thomas R. Guskey and Jane M. Bailey

The full transformation to standards-based learning in action culminates with reporting by standards. The move to standards-based reporting is fundamentally optional in that schools *could* maintain a more traditional reporting construct (such as grades A to F) while changing everything else related to determining those grades. To be clear, however, we think that the final piece in fully transforming to standards-based learning is a move to a more modern, aligned reporting system.

When educators implement standards-based reporting at the school or district level, it is important that they invest the appropriate amount of time in changing teachers', students', parents', and stakeholders' mindsets first. After establishing those mindsets, then doors to standards-based reporting at the school or district level swing wide open.

Moving From Rationale to Action

The good (and bad) news for teachers and schools is that there is no one way to implement standards-based reporting. This is good news because they have the opportunity to personalize the processes and systems. This is bad news in a sense because teachers and schools *have* to make many choices; it would certainly be more efficient (not necessarily as *effective*) if there were a one-size-fits-all solution.

The ideas, strategies, and suggestions within this chapter are not exhaustive. We will explore the fundamentals that teachers and schools can use to make sound decisions when exploring reporting. Grounding in the fundamentals ensures decisions in the interest of developing a meaningful, transparent reporting system.

The Research

The research we explore in the following sections focuses on reporting three sides (growth, achievement, and student attributes); determining versus calculating grades; and waiting to employ standards reporting.

Reporting Three Sides

Effective standards-based reporting begins with clarity of purpose because it will drive both processes and products. In *Developing Standards-Based Report Cards*, Thomas R. Guskey and Jane M. Bailey (2010) suggest that "teachers and schools be clear on what information the report card communicates, who the primary audience is, and what the intended goal of the communication is or how the audience should use it" (p. 31). A slightly different process drives each of the three sides of standards-based reporting—(1) growth, (2) achievement, and (3) student attributes—so it stands to reason that purpose precedes the development of new, more efficient processes.

The first, and most prominent, side of standards-based reporting is achievement. A standards-based learning environment emerges from the separation of achievement and behavior. This is easier said than done. Research indicates that even teachers who claim to be grading exclusively on achievement still often use grading practices that do not fully align to this ideal (Brookhart, 2013b).

However, to only assess achievement would be to ignore two other equally important sides of summative assessment that paint a complete picture of where learners are in their growth and development. One of the equally important sides of grading and reporting is verifying student attributes (Schimmer, 2016), or process goals (Guskey, 2015), that specify the degree to which students are meeting their behavioral goals. (Growth is the other equally important side.) Teaching students important life skills that will serve them as adults, a common proclamation, rings hollow if there is not a process for establishing, teaching, assessing, and reporting the development of these attributes. What has traditionally been a *hidden curriculum* must emerge from the shadows with honest, transparent expectations and processes. If the goal is to proactively improve student attributes and characteristics, then those attributes and characteristics must be described with clarity and specificity (Guskey, 2015; Reeves, 2015).

The third side to summative assessment is verifying and reporting growth. Assessing growth measures a student against him- or herself, so while this is different from achievement, it can be an equally important aspect of summative assessment—especially for those students who are not yet proficient and those with special needs or circumstances. Students can make tremendous progress without reaching proficiency, so without formal assessment, acknowledgment, and reporting of growth, teachers lose a very real opportunity to contribute to students' continued engagement and confidence (Tomlinson & Moon, 2013).

Determining Versus Calculating Grades

Electronic gradebooks lead many teachers to rely on algorithms to determine student grades; these algorithms most often result in a percentage-based grade that teachers then match to a predetermined increment to produce a letter grade. Relying on an algorithm falls short of accuracy because, according to Thomas R. Guskey and Lee Ann Jung (2016), "computers use only numbers. They know nothing of the individual students who produced those numbers, the learning environment, or the nature and quality of the assessments" (p. 54). In other words, algorithms ignore quality and context. The two challenges with this approach in a standards-based instructional classroom are that (1) teachers cannot ratio all standards because proficiency cannot always be the result of ratioing the number correct over the total, and (2) even for those standards that can be ratioed, the thoughtless manipulation of assessment data results in *old* ratios being combined with newer ratios to arrive at some middle average that can be quite distant from a teacher's professional judgment (Guskey & Jung, 2016); that does not square with a standards-based instructional classroom.

There is both an art and science to grading, so while numbers can help with the initial calculation, the teacher must remain the final decision maker when it comes to grades; this means teachers engage in grade *determination*, not just calculation. This makes it essential that teachers understand how to organize learning evidence in service of communicating the most accurate grades possible. Sometimes the most recent evidence is the most accurate, but sometimes the most frequent is the most accurate.

Teachers most often cite the *most recent evidence* as the most accurate measure of proficiency as it allows students the opportunity to grow past their initial demonstrations. This holds true when assessing standards with few contributing variables in how students demonstrate proficiency and represent a somewhat linear learning trajectory; these standards usually relate to foundational knowledge, skills, and understandings. Using the most recent evidence renders the old evidence invalid.

The *most frequent evidence* is most accurate when teachers are assessing standards with a number of contributing variables. Here, teachers contextually reconsider previous evidence given the most current demonstrations (versus dismissing it). The standard's complexity dictates that one sample is insufficient to generalize about student performance (Parkes, 2013). Assessing argumentative writing, for example, requires multiple samples before teachers can accurately know where students are along their writing trajectory.

We can also make a case for using both the most recent and the most frequent evidence. For example, teachers who use midpoint or interim benchmarks along the path to full grade-level proficiency might use the most recent evidence at each benchmark, then the most frequent once the grade-level standard is in play. Alternatively, teachers who only assess a portion of the grade-level standard early in the progression may choose the most recent until they assess the full scope of the standard, then switch to the most frequent. The line between using the most recent and most frequent is admittedly blurry; the priority is an accurate determination, which requires carefully considering how to determine grades.

Waiting to Employ Standards Reporting

Standards-based learning does not require teachers or schools to develop and use standards-based report cards; that's negotiable. However, reporting by standards is the natural end to standards-based learning and will complete the transition to a standards-based learning environment. We submit that the report card is the last thing teachers should change or develop. They gain efficiency and effectiveness when standards-based *reporting* comes from standards-based *grades*, which teachers determine via standards-based *evidence*, which comes from standards-based *assessments*, which teachers develop through standards-based *learning*.

What is non-negotiable is using summative assessment practices that lead to determining accurate grades; schools might create a hybrid approach to reporting in which teachers determine grades through standards-based grading, even when they use traditional symbols to report them (Schimmer, 2016). For high schools especially, this hybrid approach can have the short-term advantage of not changing yet another thing parents (and other stakeholders) may find aversive; it has the long-term advantage of aligning what external agencies (primarily colleges and universities) require in terms of transcripts.

It is critical to remember that the symbols teachers use to summarize and report learning are not as important as the process they use to determine the symbols and the meaning behind each symbol. Traditional reporting symbols that teachers produce via modern assessment practices and processes are still better than modernized symbols or labels they produce from flawed processes and practices.

In Action

Students all have different beliefs when it comes to education, different support systems at home, and different readiness levels with the academic content. However, when it comes to reporting in a traditional grading system, teachers often lump these students into one of five different overarching categories (A, B, C, D, or F) based on predetermined percentage increments; schools expect learners and parents to decipher the meaning of that one letter to provide a comprehensive view of student achievement.

If schools ensure that grades are only about achievement, they are more likely to convey a clear, consistent, and accurate message. Throughout this chapter, we explore making the change to standards-based reporting by looking at implementation at classroom, school, and district levels. Having a shared vision, creating clear purpose statements, and deciding what to report are all crucial steps in developing standards-based report cards. The following sections explore these tasks.

Making the Change

Whether teachers look to change how they communicate student achievement or to strengthen a standards-based classroom, it is wise to take an analytical look at the grades they are currently delivering and consider these three critical questions.

1. Has growth impacted the academic grade?
2. Have behaviors impacted the academic grade?
3. What portion of the grade is academic achievement?

Consider figure 10.1, which shows a classroom using a 101-level grading scale.

Unit 1—Quiz 1	55
Unit 1—Quiz 2	78
Unit 1—Project	88
Unit 1—Test	96

Figure 10.1: Reporting by event in a 101-level grading scale.

When averaging these scores, the norm in a traditional grading system, the student ends up in the C range (79.25 percent). Averaging scores, especially averaging over time within the same standard, gives a distorted view of student achievement by allowing early attempts at learning to impact the final grade. It also communicates the message that high grades are contingent upon a fast start; a low or slow start will linger in perpetuity regardless of how much progress students make. This learner has obviously grown throughout the marking period, but delivering a final grade of C does not fully reflect that.

The same learner and his or her journey toward proficiency in a standards-based reporting system would look something like figure 10.2. Scoring assessments by standard and reporting in the same manner allow the teacher to communicate most recent evidence, as well as the student's learning journey.

Key for Academic Standards

4 = Mastery

3 = Proficiency

2 = Developing

1 = Novice

Standard	October 22	October 29	November 6	November 13
Use the four operations with whole numbers to solve problems.	2	2	3	4
Gain familiarity with factors and multiples.	2	3	4	4
Generate and analyze patterns.	1	2	2	3

Figure 10.2: Sample standards-based gradebook.

*Visit **go.SolutionTree.com/assessment** for a free reproducible version of this figure.*

By setting up the gradebook to look at the most recent evidence of the standards, teachers allow a more accurate picture of student achievement.

Reporting at the Classroom Level

Regardless of whether a standards-based reporting system is in place at the school level, teachers can take a standards-based approach to learning and reporting by rethinking the organization of their assessment evidence and report that progress in their online gradebooks to students and parents. They take a critical look at their grading practices, reorganize gradebooks to report by standards or strands (not tasks), and work toward greater accuracy.

If the goal is to communicate understanding of standards, teachers must redesign assessments to elicit evidence by standard to allow for more accurate reporting. While thinking about reporting, it is important to revisit the purpose of formative and summative assessment: respectively, to communicate to students where they are in relation to the academic standard and plan next instructional steps (formative) and to confirm the student's proficiency level at certain intervals or at the end of an instructional unit (summative). Since the purpose of summative assessment is verification, these ideally are the only grades in the gradebook. While this can be initially jarring and feel as though teachers are creating an even higher-stakes assessment environment, it is critical to remember that summative assessment is about use, not timing.

Dividing assessments by standard (see chapter 7, page 125) is a critical first step, but what teachers enter into the gradebook needs to align with that initial reorganization in order to more accurately communicate student achievement.

In a school where standards-based reporting is not the norm and interim grades are expected to be reported, teachers can enter formative progress by assigning that category zero weight. Figure 10.3 shows that approach. With this gradebook setup, teachers report progress toward proficiency without affecting the overall grade.

	Quarter 1	Quarter 2
Summative assessments	100%	100%
Formative assessments	0%	0%
Homework	0%	0%
Total	**100%**	**100%**

Figure 10.3: Formative assessments receiving zero weight.

With a setup similar to this one, parents can see the progress toward proficiency of the standards without early attempts at learning distorting the overall grade. As teachers collect new evidence for ongoing standards, they can use the same process by converting old summative scores to formative, thus not allowing them to affect the overall score for the standard. This is not ideal; however, we need to honor the readiness of parents and the school community, which means this interim step may be necessary to ease the transition to standards-based reporting. That said, the final grade must be based on summative evidence.

Beyond the weights, revising the way teachers enter scores into the gradebook can vastly change the way parents and students see and interpret academic scores. Many gradebooks allow teachers to attach standards to an assessment title. If the gradebook does not have this capability, simply changing the assessment's name to the assessed standard allows teachers to easily communicate that skill. Figure 10.4 shows an example of an online gradebook for different assessment scores a teacher has collected for three fourth-grade English language arts standards.

Standard	W.4.3—Write narratives to develop real or imagined experiences or events using effective technique, descriptive details, and clear event sequences.			W.4.3.a—Orient the reader by establishing a situation and introducing a narrator and/or characters; organize an event sequence that unfolds naturally.			W.4.3.b—Use dialogue and description to develop experiences and events or show the responses of characters to situations.		
Date	October 22	November 15	December 2	October 22	November 15	December 2	October 22	November 15	December 2
Student: Horatio	2	2	3	2	3	3	1	2	2

Source for standard: NGA & CCSSO, 2010a.

Figure 10.4: Online gradebook showing assessment scores for three fourth-grade ELA standards.

*Visit **go.SolutionTree.com/assessment** for a free reproducible version of this figure.*

Entering scores by standard instead of task means someone receiving these online scores can comprehend the learner's current understanding of the standards, as well as see overall growth. Having a standards-based classroom in a school that still uses traditional letter grades can be challenging, but teachers can manage it with thoughtful workarounds.

Converting to Letter Grades

Converting standards-based grades on a four-level scale to an overall letter grade can often prove difficult. When scores are separated by standard and progress is reported that way, accuracy and communication increase. Converting this meaningful communication into a singular grade might seem like a step backward (and in some ways it is). However, standards-based reporting is a newer concept for some schools, and the transition to a letter grade both for parents and future institutions may still be necessary. This is especially true at the high school level, where transcripts and other external communications are more common. Virtually all high schools require the reporting of a GPA for postsecondary institutions, and some scholarships require letter grades. Therefore, the conversion from standard scores to letter grades must be explored.

This section offers different methods for converting to letter grades and identifies their advantages and limitations. Each scale in the examples considers the final summative score for all the standards in a given marking period and their overall average.

The method in figure 10.5 offers the benefit of easy computation.

Average Summative Scores of Standards or Strands	Letter Grade Conversion
3.0–4.0	A
2.5–2.99	B
2.0–2.49	C
1.5–1.99	D
1.49 and below	F

Figure 10.5: Method 1 converting to letter grades.

*Visit **go.SolutionTree.com/assessment** for a free reproducible version of this figure.*

The benefit of the conversion shown in figure 10.5 is that it is mathematically easy to compute. However, with this system a student could have a deficit with a certain standard and it may not affect the overall score for the class. For example, the student could have received a 4 in four standards and a 1 in another standard; the average score would be 3.4, which equates to an A. Because of this, the student might not feel any need to continue learning with the skill that needs strengthening.

A modification of this scale appears in figure 10.6 (page 196). While this conversion scale might increase the reporting accuracy by not allowing students to have a low score for a standard, the grades become more complex to mathematically compute. This scale places a larger focus on reaching proficiency on *each* standard and communicates the message that doing so is important.

Average Scores of Standards	Letter Grade Conversion
3.0–4.0 (with no scores of 2 or below)	A
2.5–2.99 (with no scores of 1 or below)	B
2.0–2.49 (with no scores of 1 or below)	C
1.5–1.99	D
1.49 and below	F

Figure 10.6: Method 2 converting to letter grades.

*Visit **go.SolutionTree.com/assessment** for a free reproducible version of this figure.*

Yet another conversion method correlates a score on a four-level scale directly to a percentage score, as is illustrated in figure 10.7. This can be advantageous when implementing standards-based reporting in a school that still uses percentages. Although percentages are familiar, they bring with them the difficulties of a 101-level (0–100) grading system.

Standards Score	Percentage Score
4.0	100
3.0	90
2.0	75
1.0	60
Lack of evidence	50

Figure 10.7: Method 3 converting to letter grades.

*Visit **go.SolutionTree.com/assessment** for a free reproducible version of this figure.*

Many schools have tried to make the conversion using a scale like the one in figure 10.8, ranging from levels of A+ to F. However, because the intent is to move to a grading system with fewer performance categories—and each level with an accurate descriptor—to yield more reliable grades, reverting to a system with more levels (thirteen in this case) is counterproductive and inaccurate. Teachers should only use conversions such as those in figure 10.8 to determine final overall grades (should a school desire plus-minus distinctions) and they should avoid them when assessing individual assessments.

A+	3.75–4.0	A	3.5–3.74	A-	3.25–3.49
B+	3.0–3.24	B	2.75–2.99	B-	2.5–2.74
C+	2.25–2.49	C	2.0–2.24	C-	1.75–1.99
D+	1.5–1.74	D	1.25–1.49	D-	1.0–1.24
F	0–0.99				

Figure 10.8: Method 4 converting to letter grades.

The decisions about final grade determination are contextually driven by what each school or district decides is its purpose for reporting. Ensure that the purpose (and subsequent practices and processes) does not violate sound assessment principles, which ensure validity and reliable reporting.

Creating Grading Purpose Statements

When standards-based reporting is implemented at the school or district level, it is important that the appropriate amount of time has been invested in changing the mindsets of teachers, students, parents, and stakeholders first. Once the standards-based mindset is established, then doors to standards-based reporting at the school or district level can swing wide open.

Creating a shared purpose statement is an early implementation step at the school or district level. Just as teachers provide clear targets for students through standards, it is also important for the teachers themselves to have clear targets. Reform starts with productive conversations that help shape standards-based reporting systems, make sure that grades have meaning, and help all educators stay focused on a shared goal. To accomplish this, schools must first decide on the change's purpose and what the end result will look like.

To successfully reform outdated grading practices, a critical first step means having productive conversations about the meaning of grades and who those grades are for. These discussions work toward answering the following questions as a staff.

- What is the purpose of our grading and report cards?
- Who is the intended audience of our grading and report cards?
- What do we want to communicate through our reporting?
- How should the recipients use the reported information?

Generating a tangible purpose statement that all educators agree on will create a communication piece that teachers can share with students and parents. This purpose statement should represent a shared mindset among educators; they should communicate it to parents, students, and other stakeholders early and often. Schools should also clearly display it on websites, communications that students take home, and eventually report cards to ensure transparency. Some examples of grading purpose statements follow:

> The purpose of this report card is to describe to parents and guardians the progress their child has made and their most recent understanding of the current grade-level learning standards. This document should inform parents and guardians about successes and areas where their children need more guidance and instruction to improve.

From Deerfield Public School District 109 (2012):

> The purpose of this report card is to clearly communicate to parents and students about the most recent achievement of specific learning standards, as well as student work habits. It identifies proficiency levels against those standards, areas of strength, and areas where additional support and time is needed.

While the purpose may vary, the report card most often serves as the primary communication tool between school and home. As such, those who receive this document must understand its purpose and how they should use the information. A purpose statement gives parents clarity.

Creating a Standards-Based Report Card

Once the school decides on the report card's purpose, changes the language of learning, and helps stakeholders understand the purpose of standards-based reporting, only then is it time to start exploring a new report card. No matter what purpose the school decides on, quality standards-based report cards have a few commonalities. The most effective grading systems and report cards:

- Have a clear purpose statement
- Report process, progress, and product separately (Guskey & Bailey, 2010)
- Accurately communicate strengths and areas needing more attention
- Are detailed but digestible

The process of moving from reforming grading to implementing a standards-based report card can take a few years. During this journey, it is important to remember that the report card is only a piece of paper that reports proficiency at a chosen point in time. What truly matters is what happens in between those marking periods and how educators communicate with parents and learners.

Deciding What to Report

The end user—primarily parents—must be able to easily consume the information in standards-based report cards. Parents often have limited amounts of time to review their children's report cards, which means report cards should not overwhelm readers with too much information; the information conveyed should be powerful and meaningful. Because of this, many schools choose to report on strands or domains instead of standards. *Strands* and *domains* are groupings that encapsulate many standards. Teachers more commonly use these for reporting at the middle and high school levels because of the larger quantity of standards at those levels. Reporting on individual standards is more common at the elementary level. Figure 10.9 shows the difference between a mathematics domain and its standards within the CCSS.

Mathematics Domain: Operations and Algebraic Thinking
Standards Within Domain
Write and interpret numerical expressions.   • Use parentheses, brackets, or braces in numerical expressions, and evaluate expressions with these symbols. (5.OA.A.1)   • Write simple expressions that record calculations with numbers, and interpret numerical expressions without evaluating them. For example, express the calculation "add 8 and 7, then multiply by 2" as 2 × (8 + 7). Recognize that 3 × (18932 + 921) is three times as large as 18932 + 921, without having to calculate the indicated sum or product. (5.OA.A.2)
Analyze patterns and relationships.   • Generate two numerical patterns using two given rules. Identify apparent relationships between corresponding terms. Form ordered pairs consisting of corresponding terms from the two patterns, and graph the ordered pairs on a coordinate plane. For example, given the rule "Add 3" and the starting number 0, and given the rule "Add 6" and the starting number 0, generate terms in the resulting sequences, and observe that the terms in one sequence are twice the corresponding terms in the other sequence. Explain informally why this is so. (5.OA.B.3)

Source for standard: NGA & CCSSO, 2010b.

Figure 10.9: Difference in Common Core mathematics domain and its standards.

This makes the list of standards to report shorter and easier for the reader to consume. However, other schools feel that only reporting on domains or strands can be vague and choose to report on all standards. Still other schools choose to report only *priority standards* that they deem the most critical to report. When deciding on a reporting format, Ainsworth (2004) offers the following criteria for selecting reporting standards:

- **Endurance** (lasting beyond one grade or course; concepts and skills needed in life). Will proficiency of this standard provide students with the knowledge and skills that will be of value beyond the present? For example, proficiency in reading informational texts and being able to write effectively for a variety of purposes will endure throughout a student's academic career and work life.

- **Leverage** (crossover application *within* the content area and to other content areas, i.e., interdisciplinary connections). For example, proficiency in creating and interpreting graphs, diagrams, and charts and then being able to make accurate inferences from them will help students in math, science, social studies, language arts, and other areas. The ability to write an analytical summary or a persuasive essay will similarly help students in any academic discipline.

- **Readiness for the next level of learning** (prerequisite concepts and skills students need to enter a new grade level or course of study). Will proficiency of this standard provide students with the essential knowledge and skills that are necessary for future success? . . .

- **External Exams** (standardized tests, college entrance exams, and occupational competency exams). (pp. 25–27)

The following examples offer a glimpse into potential reporting formats. While these examples only show certain subjects, the report card in its entirety does report on all academic areas. Figure 10.10 is a report card from an elementary school that successfully implemented standards-based reporting.

The purpose of this progress report is to clearly communicate with parents and students about the achievement of specific learning standards and student work habits. It identifies students' levels of progress with regard to those standards, areas of strength, and areas where additional time and effort are needed.

Student name: _____   Student ID: _____

Teacher name: _____   Academic year: _____

School: _____

Academic Key			
Excelling With Standards: 4			
Meeting Standards: 3			
Working Toward Standards: 2			
Not Meeting Standards: 1			
Not Assessed at This Time: NA			
Reading			
Foundational Skills	Trimester 1	Trimester 2	Trimester 3
Applies phonics and word analysis when decoding words			
Reads with sufficient fluency to support comprehension			
Recognizes and reads sight words			
Literature	Trimester 1	Trimester 2	Trimester 3
Retells stories to include key details from text			
Compares and contrasts elements in stories			
Informational Text	Trimester 1	Trimester 2	Trimester 3
Identifies the main topic and key details of a text			
Compares and contrasts elements between two texts			
Uses text features to locate information in text			
Writing			
	Trimester 1	Trimester 2	Trimester 3
Writes to communicate ideas and information effectively			
Focuses on topic and adds details to strengthen writing			

Figure 10.10: Sample standards-based reporting report card for elementary school.

continued ➡

Language			
	Trimester 1	Trimester 2	Trimester 3
Demonstrates a command of capitalization			
Demonstrates a command of punctuation			
Spells grade-appropriate words			
Prints uppercase and lowercase words			
Speaking and Listening			
	Trimester 1	Trimester 2	Trimester 3
Participates in discussions with a group			
Asks and answers questions to clarify something that is not understood			
Habits of Success			

Habits of Success Key		Trimester 1	Trimester 2	Trimester 3
Consistently Demonstrates: 4	Respects others' rights, feelings, and property			
Usually Demonstrates: 3	Follows directions			
Sometimes Demonstrates: 2	Uses time effectively			
Seldom Demonstrates: 1	Organizes self and materials			
	Completes assignments with quality and punctuality			
	Exhibits effort, commitment, and perseverance			

Teacher Comments
Trimester 1:
Trimester 2:
Trimester 3:

Source: Adapted from Deerfield Public School District 109, 2012.

Figure 10.11 is a middle school example. Since it comes from the same district as the report card in figure 10.10, notice similarities in the proficiency scales and habits of success levels. One of the major differences is that the elementary school reports by *standard* (rewritten in student-friendly language) while the middle school reports by *strand*. Both have a common place for teacher comments, which often serve as one of the most powerful aspects of a standards-based report card. In this space, teachers can report growth or other information necessary to provide a better picture of the whole learner.

The purpose of this progress report is to clearly communicate with parents and students about the achievement of specific learning standards and student work habits. It identifies students' levels of progress with regard to those standards, areas of strength, and areas where additional time and effort are needed.

Student name: _____   Academic year: _____

Student ID: _____

Homeroom teacher name: _____

School: _____

Academic Key	**Habits of Success Key**
Excelling With Standards: 4	Consistently Demonstrates: 4
Meeting Standards: 3	Usually Demonstrates: 3
Working Toward Standards: 2	Sometimes Demonstrates: 2
Not Meeting Standards: 1	Seldom Demonstrates: 1
Not Assessed at This Time: NA	

English Language Arts	Quarter 1	Quarter 2	Quarter 3	Quarter 4	Habits of Success	Quarter 1	Quarter 2	Quarter 3	Quarter 4
Reading					Exhibits effort, commitment, and perseverance				
Writing					Follows directions				
Language					Respects others' rights, feelings, and property				
Speaking and Listening					Completes assignments with attention to quality and timeliness				

Figure 10.11: Sample standards-based reporting report card for middle school.
continued →

Teacher Comments									
Quarter 1:									
Quarter 2:									
Quarter 3:									
Quarter 4:									
Mathematics	Quarter 1	Quarter 2	Quarter 3	Quarter 4	Habits of Success	Quarter 1	Quarter 2	Quarter 3	Quarter 4
Ratios and Proportional Relationships					Exhibits effort, commitment, and perseverance				
The Number System					Follows directions				
Expressions and Equations					Respects others' rights, feelings, and property				
Geometry					Completes assignments with attention to quality and timeliness				
Statistics and Probability									
Teacher Comments									
Quarter 1:									
Quarter 2:									
Quarter 3:									
Quarter 4:									

Source: Adapted from Deerfield Public School District 109, 2016.

The major difference present in figure 10.12 is that this school reports on the standards in their entirety. While this is potentially challenging to comprehend, it does maintain the integrity of the standard and communicates the whole. Again, each school or district decides where to draw the line between thoroughness and verbosity.

Student name: _____ School year: _____
The purpose of this report card is to describe to parents and guardians the progress their child has made and their most recent understanding of the current grade-level learning standards. This document should inform parents and guardians about successes and areas where more guidance and instruction is needed to improve.

Proficiency Scale	**Learner-Quality Scale**
4: Mastery	C: Consistently demonstrates
3: Proficiency	S: Sometimes demonstrates
2: Emergent understanding	R: Rarely demonstrates
1: Significant gaps	

Learner Qualities	**Quarter 1**
Exhibits independence, takes initiative, and accepts responsibility for own behavior.	
Completes assignments with attention to quality and timeliness, and seeks assistance when necessary.	
Participates in and contributes to class and group activities.	
Shows respect for others' rights, feelings, and belongings; seeks positive solutions to conflicts.	

Standard	**Quarter 1**
Mathematics	
Interpret a multiplication equation as a comparison, e.g., interpret $35 = 5 \times 7$ as a statement that 35 is 5 times as many as 7 and 7 times as many as 5. Represent verbal statements of multiplicative comparisons as multiplication equations. (4.OA.A.1)	
Multiply or divide to solve word problems involving multiplicative comparison, e.g., by using drawings and equations with a symbol for the unknown number to represent the problem, distinguishing multiplicative comparison from additive comparison. (4.OA.A.2)	
Solve multistep word problems posed with whole numbers and having whole-number answers using the four operations, including problems in which remainders must be interpreted. Represent these problems using equations with a letter standing for the unknown quantity. Assess the reasonableness of answers using mental computation and estimation strategies including rounding. (4.OA.A.3)	

Figure 10.12: Example of entire-standard elementary standards-based reporting report card.

continued →

Find all factor pairs for a whole number in the range 1–100. Recognize that a whole number is a multiple of each of its factors. Determine whether a given whole number in the range 1–100 is a multiple of a given one-digit number. Determine whether a given whole number in the range 1–100 is prime or composite. (4.OA.B.4)	
Generate a number or shape pattern that follows a given rule. Identify apparent features of the pattern that were not explicit in the rule itself. (4.OA.C.5)	
Teacher comments:	

Source for standard: NGA & CCSSO, 2010b.

Figure 10.13 offers a high school report card. The major difference between this example and the others we present in this chapter is the presence of an overall grade. The myth of not being able to have standards-based report cards at the high school level is just that—*a myth*. Notice that the overall letter grade is present for grade point average, college admissions, and scholarships—but there is more. Even with allowing for teacher comments, this report card also offers another view at growth by communicating starting and ending scores with progress achievement.

The purpose of this progress update is to communicate with parents and students about the achievement of specific learning goals, classroom behaviors, and student growth. It identifies students' levels of progress with regard to those goals and behaviors indicating areas of strength, and areas where additional time and effort are needed.

Achievement Grades		Standard Marks		Process	
A	4.00–3.33	4	Distinguished	E	Excellent
B	3.32–2.67	3	Proficient	S	Satisfactory
C	2.66–1.67	2	Basic	N	Needs improvement
D	1.66–1.00	1	Needs improvement		
LoE[b]	Below 1.00	LoE[c]	Lack of evidence		

Student: Jane Smith   Subject: Chemistry

Reporting period: First semester

Teacher name and email address: George Lake glake@emailaddress.edu

Academic Achievement	Letter Grade: B
Asking questions and defining problems[a]	3
Developing and using models[a]	2
Planning and carrying out investigations[a]	3
Analyzing and interpreting data[a]	2
Obtaining, evaluating, and communicating information[a]	3
Constructing explanations and designing solutions[a]	3

Process Achievement	
Self-awareness	S
Responsibility	E
Participation	S
Problem solving	N

Chemistry description and comments:

Progress Achievement	Start	End
Asking questions and defining problems	2	3
Developing and using models	2	2
Planning and carrying out investigations	2	3
Analyzing and interpreting data	3	2
Obtaining, evaluating, and communicating information	1	3
Constructing explanations and designing solutions	2	3

a: Based on modified standard or standards.

b: Lack of evidence—At the end of the grading period all LoE will be changed into Fs.

c: Lack of evidence—At the end of the grading period all LoE will be changed into Os.

Figure 10.13: Example of standards-based reporting report card for high school.

Although report cards do count as a form of communication, teachers should talk to learners about their purpose and how to use that information before they receive them.

Talking to Learners

It is imperative that teachers involve learners in conversations surrounding reporting and help them understand its purpose. They must understand why teachers assign grades, what goes into reporting, and what A– or level 4 work looks like. Failing to accurately communicate the purpose and be transparent in grading and reporting methods leaves students trying to figure out the game of school.

It is vital that students understand that the academic scores that teachers report exclusively represent their most recent and consistent understanding of the academic standards. These academic grades are neither punishments nor compensation. Explain that if a student would like to see his or her grade improve, he or she needs to show greater proficiency. More learning is the only pathway to a higher grade.

Talking with learners about standards-based reporting follows the more important conversation about standards-based learning. Standards will provide clarity about what educators teach and assess in the classroom. Beyond that clarity, learners need to know that their teachers honor the natural process of learning, so they also (ideally) report information about both their behaviors and growth, but separately.

Beyond that, learners must understand that the report card itself is just a snapshot that reports achievement and progress at a point in time. Teachers will report proficiency of the academic standards in the gradebook and on the report card, but it is more important that learners understand that every moment in a standards-based classroom represents a new opportunity for learning.

Figure 10.14 offers questions students might ask when it comes to standards-based reporting, as well as possible teacher responses.

Student Question	Teacher Response
Why did the report card have to change?	Previously, I wasn't giving enough information. That one letter grade didn't tell how you were growing or about your class behaviors. It also didn't show what you needed to work on. The new report card will help with that.
How do I use the online gradebook?	Make sure that your focus is not on the overall grade, but on your proficiency with each standard.

Figure 10.14: Student questions and teacher responses about standards-based reporting.

Talking to Parents

Making the change to standards-based reporting, although a meaningful one, is a big change for parents as well. The traditional 101-level grading and reporting system is what parents know, and it is the school's responsibility to educate them about the value of a standards-based reporting system and how to use it. Explaining how grades have lost meaning over time will help them see clearly part of the reason for standards-based reporting.

Next, parents need to understand how grading and reporting will change, including formative versus summative assessment, honoring the natural process of learning, understanding the new grading scale, and how to look at progress by standard in the online gradebook. Finally, parents should learn what will look different, especially on the report card. The *why* and *how* are so much more important than the *what*, and that is where teachers and administrators invest a majority of time.

For additional communication in the beginning of the school year, schools might send home two sample reports, one traditional and one standards based, and ask parents which provides the most meaningful information and communicates the more accurate picture of the whole child. This allows parents to see the change without the additional stress of understanding how their children are achieving.

Communication is plentiful and ongoing, and it remembers that the student voice is powerful. Use class websites, newsletters, and any other communication platforms to share research, articles, and other pertinent information.

Getting Started With Standards-Based Reporting

Implementing standards-based reporting looks different in the classroom than it does at the school or district level. To honor that difference, implementation steps have been separated accordingly.

Implementing in the classroom:

- Work with your gradebook. How can you use it to effectively communicate achievement of the standards?

- Decide how you will communicate ongoing learning of students in the formative paradigm with learners and parents.

Implementing at the school or district level:

- Create your purpose statement for grading.

- Construct a common proficiency scale.

- Ensure that you have removed all behaviors from academic reporting.

- Determine expected behavioral characteristics and how you will communicate growth.

- Develop a long-term plan. You must change the mindset and grading practices of educators before changing the reporting.

- Form a committee of teachers and parents to start planning what the report card will look like.

Questions for Learning Teams

Pose these questions during teacher team meetings, planning meetings, or book study.

- What quote or passage encapsulates your biggest takeaway from this chapter? What immediate action (large or small) will you take as a result of this takeaway? Explain both to your team.

- What is your grading purpose statement? Does your report card structure align with its stated purpose? Is there anything you could do to enhance this alignment? Explain.

- To what degree have you removed all behavioral aspects from your summative grades? Can you identify any direct or indirect ways in which student behavior may still influence (in a small or large way) the final grades students earn?

- To what degree do the summative grades represent your learners' most recent understanding of the standards? Is there anything you can identify that could increase the accuracy of what you ultimately report about student achievement?

- How can you communicate academic achievement, classroom behaviors, and growth to students and parents more effectively?

Epilogue

Take the first step in faith. You don't have to see the whole staircase, just take the first step.

—Martin Luther King Jr.

It is both understandable and normal to feel overwhelmed at this point. The prospect of re-examining and revamping assessment and grading practices can be daunting, but it doesn't have to be that way. Remember that wherever you are in your own assessment journey is fine, as long as you commit to moving ahead. It's not the pace of change that matters; rather, it's the quality and sustainability of the change. Everyone is at a personal starting point, and certainly that influences how you read and react to what we've put forth here. In the end, it is our personalization of the standards-based learning journey that adds the necessary nuance and contextualization.

Putting standards-based learning into action is a process best executed in a series of short-term wins rather than a single major overhaul. Of course, having a long-term plan is desirable, but energy is best spent in immediacy. A simple way to start is by changing your language. Speak continuously in the language of *learning* as opposed to *tasks* and your students will do the same. Maintain a focus on the standards. With a laser-like focus on the destination, the journey becomes more manageable. All assessment roads lead to standards, so keep the standards in mind as you communicate with learners, identify the instructional goals, design activities, articulate effective feedback, verify that learning has occurred, and report to others about proficiency.

Know that the process can be messy. Expect and embrace missteps along the way and know they are simply opportunities to learn, reflect, and revise with greater strength. As the cliché goes, *experience comes from bad judgment*, and while we are not suggesting a cavalier approach to assessment, we want you to feel comfortable with an imperfect process. This journey has no perfect solution that works in every classroom for every teacher with every learner. Even with the best of intentions, missteps will happen. Finding a support system, whether it is within your school or outside, can be helpful. For example, many educators who are starting to put standards-based learning into action find support on Twitter (#atAssess and #sblchat) and other online forums that connect people from literally around the world. Many other educators are going through the same journey as you; they also need support. Share ideas, discuss strategies and resources, and grow together as educators.

Most important, know you are doing the right work! Keep consuming the research and practical implementation strategies so you can feel increasingly competent and confident responding to questions from students, parents, and colleagues. Some of this could be a (necessary) shock to the system, so the greater your depth and breadth of understanding, the more clarity you can provide. Be ready to educate and support others as you work through this change together. Making the change to standards-based learning has the power to increase student hope, efficacy, and achievement. This long and sometimes tough journey is meaningful, necessary work that is well worth it. Good luck!

References and Resources

Ainsworth, L. (2004). *Power standards: Identifying the standards that matter the most.* Englewood, CO: Lead + Learn Press.

Ainsworth, L. (2013). *Prioritizing the Common Core: Identifying specific standards to emphasize the most.* Englewood, CO: Lead + Learn Press.

American Institute of Certified Public Accountants. (2011). *CPA horizons 2025 report.* Accessed at www.aicpa.org/Research/CPAHorizons2025/DownloadableDocuments/cpa-horizons-report-web.pdf on July 29, 2017.

Andrade, H. L. (2010). Students as the definitive source of formative assessment: Academic self-assessment and the self-regulation of learning. In H. L. Andrade & G. J. Cizek (Eds.), *Handbook of formative assessment* (pp. 90–105). New York: Routledge.

Andrade, H. L. (2013). Classroom assessment in the context of learning. In J. H. McMillan (Ed.), *SAGE handbook of research on classroom assessment* (pp. 17–34). Thousand Oaks, CA: SAGE.

Balch, D., Blanck, R., & Balch, D. H. (2016). Rubrics—Sharing the rules of the game. *Journal of Instructional Research, 5*(1), 19–49.

Barnes, M. (2015). *Assessment 3.0: Throw out your grade book and inspire learning.* Thousand Oaks, CA: Corwin Press.

Black, P. (2013). Formative and summative aspects of assessment: Theoretical and research foundations in the context of pedagogy. In J. H. McMillan (Ed.), *SAGE handbook of research on classroom assessment* (pp. 167–178). Thousand Oaks, CA: SAGE.

Black, P., & Wiliam, D. (1998). Inside the black box: Raising standards through classroom assessment. *Phi Delta Kappan, 92*(1), 81–90.

Black, P., & Wiliam, D. (2005). Changing teaching through formative assessment: Research and practice. In *Formative assessment: Improving learning in secondary classrooms* (pp. 223–240). Paris: Organisation for Economic Co-operation and Development.

Bloom, B. S. (Ed.). (1956). *Taxonomy of educational objectives: The classification of educational goals.* London: Longmans.

Bloom, B. S., Engelhart, M., Furst, E., Hill, W., & Krathwohl, D. (1956). *Taxonomy of educational objectives: Handbook 1—Cognitive domain*. London: Longmans.

Boekaerts, M. (2006). Self-regulation and effort investment. In K. A. Renninger & I. E. Sigel (Eds.), *Handbook of child psychology, volume 4; Child psychology in practice* (6th ed., pp. 345–377). New York: Wiley.

Bonner, S. M. (2013). Validity in classroom assessment: Purposes, properties, and principles. In J. H. McMillan (Ed.), *SAGE handbook of research on classroom assessment* (pp. 87–106). Thousand Oaks, CA: SAGE.

Brookhart, S. M. (2003). Developing measurement theory for classroom assessment purposes and uses. *Educational Measurement: Issues and Practice, 22*(4), 5–12.

Brookhart, S. M. (2007). Expanding views about formative classroom assessment: A review of the literature. In J. H. McMillan (Ed.), *Formative classroom assessment: Theory into practice* (pp. 43–62). New York: Teachers College Press.

Brookhart, S. M. (2013a). Classroom assessment in the context of motivation theory and research. In J. H. McMillan (Ed.), *SAGE handbook of research on classroom assessment* (pp. 35–54). Thousand Oaks, CA: SAGE.

Brookhart, S. M. (2013b). Grading. In J. H. McMillan (Ed.), *SAGE handbook of research on classroom assessment* (pp. 257–271). Thousand Oaks, CA: SAGE.

Brookhart, S. M. (2013c). *How to create and use rubrics for formative assessment and grading*. Alexandria, VA: Association for Supervision and Curriculum Development.

Brookhart, S. M. (2017). *How to give effective feedback to your students* (2nd ed.). Alexandria, VA: Association for Supervision and Curriculum Development.

Brooks, V. (2002). *Assessment in secondary schools: The new teacher's guide to monitoring, assessment, recording, reporting and accountability*. Buckingham, United Kingdom: Open University Press.

Brown, B. (2009). *Standards-based education reform in the United States since "A Nation at Risk."* Honolulu: University of Hawaii College of Education.

Brown, G. T. L., & Harris, L. R. (2013). Student self-assessment. In J. H. McMillan (Ed.), *SAGE handbook of research on classroom assessment* (pp. 367–393). Thousand Oaks, CA: SAGE.

Butler, D. L., & Winne, P. H. (1995). Feedback and self-regulated learning: A theoretical synthesis. *Review of Educational Research, 65*(3), 245–281.

Chappuis, J. (2009). *Seven strategies of assessment for learning*. Boston: Allyn & Bacon.

Chappuis, J. (2015). *Seven strategies of assessment for learning* (2nd ed.). Portland, OR: Pearson Assessment Training Institute.

Chappuis, J., Stiggins, R., Chappuis, S., & Arter, J. (2012). *Classroom assessment for student learning: Doing it right—Using it well* (2nd ed.). Boston: Pearson.

Clark, I. (2012). Formative assessment: Assessment is for self-regulated learning. *Educational Psychology Review, 24*(2), 205–249.

Cook, J., & Jeng, K. (2009). *Child food insecurity: The economic impact on our nation.* Accessed at www.nokidhungry.org/sites/default/files/child-economy-study.pdf on June 5, 2017.

Cooper, H. (1989). Synthesis of research on homework. *Educational Leadership, 47*(3), 85–91.

Cooper, H., Robinson, J. C., & Patall, E. A. (2006). Does homework improve academic achievement? A synthesis of research, 1987–2003. *Review of Educational Research, 76*(1), 1–62.

Covey, S. R. (2004). *The Seven habits of highly effective people: Powerful lessons in personal change.* Glencoe, IL: Free Press.

Cross, L. H., & Frary, R. B. (1999). Hodgepodge grading: Endorsed by students and teachers alike. *Applied Measurement in Education, 12*(1), 53–72.

Deerfield Public School District 109. (2012). *Standards-based grading.* Accessed at http://dps109.org/standards-based-grading on November 3, 2017.

DeNavas-Walt, C., & Proctor, B. D. (2015, September). *Income and poverty in the United States: 2014.* Washington, DC: U.S. Government Printing Office. Accessed at www.census.gov/content/dam/Census/library/publications/2015/demo/p60-252.pdf on June 5, 2017.

Depka, E. (2015). *Bringing homework into focus: Tools and tips to enhance practices, design, and feedback.* Bloomington, IN: Solution Tree Press.

Depka, E. (2016). *Raising the rigor: Effective questioning strategies and techniques for the classroom.* Bloomington, IN: Solution Tree Press.

Dobbs, D. (2011). Beautiful brains. *National Geographic, 220*(4), 36–59.

Dueck, M. (2014). *Grading smarter, not harder: Assessment strategies that motivate kids and help them learn.* Alexandria, VA: Association for Supervision and Curriculum Development.

Dunning, D., Heath, C., & Suls, J. (2004). Flawed self-assessment: Implications for health, education, and the workplace. *Psychological Science in the Public Interest, 5*(3), 69–106.

Durlak, J. A., Weissberg, R. P., Dymnicki, A. B., Taylor, R. D., & Schellinger, K. (2011). *The impact of enhancing students' social and emotional learning: A meta-analysis of school-based universal interventions.* Accessed at www.casel.org/wp-content/uploads/2016/08/PDF-3-Durlak-Weissberg-Dymnicki-Taylor-_-Schellinger-2011-Meta-analysis.pdf on July 24, 2017.

Dweck, C. S. (2006). *Mindset: The new psychology of success.* New York: Random House.

Echevarria, J., Short, D., & Powers, K. (2010). School reform and standards-based education: A model for English-language learners. *Journal of Educational Research, 99*(4), 195–211.

Epstein, J. L., & Van Voorhis, F. L. (2001). More than minutes: Teachers' roles in designing homework. *Educational Psychologist, 36*(3), 181–193.

Erkens, C. (2016). *Collaborative common assessments: Teamwork. Instruction. Results.* Bloomington, IN: Solution Tree Press.

Erkens, C., Schimmer, T., & Vagle, N. D. (2018). *Instructional agility: Responding to assessment with real-time decisions.* Bloomington, IN: Solution Tree Press.

Feeding America. (2017, September). *Poverty and hunger fact sheet.* Accessed at www .feedingamerica.org/assets/pdfs/fact-sheets/poverty-and-hunger-fact-sheet.pdf on October 25, 2017.

Fink, L. D. (2003). *Creating significant learning experiences: An integrated approach to designing college courses.* San Francisco: Jossey-Bass.

Fullan, M. (2011). *Change leader: Learning to do what matters most.* San Francisco: Jossey-Bass.

Gill, B. P., & Schlossman, S. L. (2004). Villain or savior?: The American discourse on homework, 1850–2003. *Theory Into Practice, 43*(3), 174–181.

Griffin, P. (2007). The comfort of competence and the uncertainty of assessment. *Studies in Educational Evaluation, 33*(1), 87–99.

Guskey, T. R. (2015). *On your mark: Challenging the conventions of grading and reporting.* Bloomington, IN: Solution Tree Press.

Guskey, T. R., & Bailey, J. M. (2010). *Developing standards-based report cards.* Thousand Oaks, CA: Corwin Press.

Guskey, T. R., & Jung, L. A. (2016). Grading: Why you should trust your judgment. *Educational Leadership, 73*(7), 50–54.

Guskey, T. R., Swan, G. M., & Jung, L. A. (2010, May). *Developing a statewide, standards-based student report card: A review of the Kentucky initiative.* Paper presented at the annual meeting of the American Educational Research Association, Denver.

Hamilton, L. (2003). Chapter 2: Assessment as a policy tool. *Review of Research in Education, 27*(1), 25–68.

Hattie, J. A. C. (2009). *Visible learning: A synthesis of over 800 meta-analyses relating to achievement.* New York: Routledge.

Hattie, J. A. C. (2012). *Visible learning for teachers: Maximizing impact on learning.* New York: Routledge.

Hattie, J. A. C., & Timperley, H. (2007). The power of feedback. *Review of Educational Research, 77*(1), 81–112.

Heidemann, A. (2016, March 7). *How many times can you take the bar exam?* [Blog post]. Accessed at www.excellenceinlawschool.com/how-many-times-can-you-take-the-bar -exam on May 31, 2017.

Heritage, M. (2008). *Learning progressions: Supporting instruction and formative assessment.* Washington, DC: Council of Chief State School Officers.

Heritage, M. (2010). *Formative assessment: Making it happen in the classroom.* Thousand Oaks, CA: Corwin Press.

Heritage, M. (2013). Gathering evidence of student understanding. In J. H. McMillan (Ed.), *SAGE handbook of research on classroom assessment* (pp. 179–195). Thousand Oaks, CA: SAGE.

Hill, D., & Nave, J. (2012). *Power of ICU: The end of student apathy . . . reviving engagement and responsibility.* Lebanon, TN: JJ&ZAK.

Holme, J., Richards, M., Jimerson, J., & Cohen, R. (2010). Assessing the effects of high school exit examinations. *Review of Educational Research, 80*(4), 476–526.

Huitt, W. (1996). Measurement and evaluation: Criterion- versus norm-referenced testing. *Educational Psychology Interactive.* Valdosta, GA: Valdosta State University. Accessed at www.edpsycinteractive.org/topics/measeval/crnmref.html on May 31, 2017.

Illinois State Board of Education. (2010, June 24). *Illinois learning standards.* Accessed at www.isbe.net/Pages/Learning-Standards.aspx on November 3, 2017.

International Society for Technology in Education. (2016). *ISTE national educational technology standards.* Eugene, OR: Author.

Jones, D. (2007). Speaking, listening, planning and assessing: The teacher's role in developing metacognitive awareness. *Early Child Development and Care, 177*(6–7), 569–579.

Jung, L. A. & Guskey, T. R. (2012). *Grading exceptional and struggling learners.* Thousand Oaks, CA: Corwin Press.

Kalish, N., & Bennett, S. (2007). *The case against homework: How homework is hurting our children and what we can do about it.* New York: Crown.

King, M. L., Jr. (1999). In M. Marable & L. Mullings (Eds.), *Let nobody turn us around: Voices of resistance, reform, and renewal—An African American anthology.* Lanham, MD: Rowman & Littlefield.

Kluger, A. N., & DeNisi, A. (1996). *The effects of feedback interventions on performance: A historical review, a meta-analysis, and a preliminary feedback intervention theory.* Accessed at http://citeseerx.ist.psu.edu/viewdoc/download?doi=10.1.1.461.6812 &rep=rep1&type=pdf on August 29, 2017.

Kohn, A. (2006). *The homework myth: Why our kids get too much of a bad thing.* Cambridge, MA: Da Capo Life Long.

Kralovec, E., & Buell, J. (2000). *The end of homework: How homework disrupts families, overburdens children, and limits learning.* Boston: Beacon Press.

Lane, S. (2013). Performance assessment. In J. H. McMillan (Ed.), *SAGE handbook of research on classroom assessment* (pp. 313–329). Thousand Oaks, CA: SAGE.

Leko, M. M., Brownell, M. T., Sindelar, P. T., & Kiely, M. T. (2015). Envisioning the future of special education personnel preparation in a standards-based era. *Exceptional Children, 82*(1), 25–43.

Louisiana Department of Education. (n.d.). *Academic standards.* Accessed at www .louisianabelieves.com/resources/library/academic-standards on November 27, 2017.

Martínez, J. F., & Mastergeorge, A. (2002, April). *Rating performance assessments of students with disabilities: A generalizability study of teacher bias.* Paper presented at the annual meeting of the American Educational Research Association, New Orleans, LA.

Marzano, R. J. (2010). *Formative assessment and standards-based grading.* Bloomington, IN: Marzano Resources.

Marzano, R. J. (2017). *Making classroom assessments reliable and valid.* Bloomington, IN: Solution Tree Press.

Marzano, R. J., & Pickering, D. J. (2007). The case for and against homework. *Educational Leadership, 64*(6), 74–79.

McMillan, J. H. (2001). Secondary teachers' classroom assessment and grading practices. *Educational Measurement: Issues and Practice, 20*(1), 20–32.

McMunn, N., Schenck, P., & McColskey, W. (2003). *Standards-based assessment, grading, and reporting in classrooms: Can district training and support change teacher practice?* Paper presented at the annual meeting of the American Educational Research Association, Chicago.

McTighe, J., & Wiggins, G. (2013). *Essential questions: Opening doors to student understanding.* Alexandria, VA: Association for Supervision and Curriculum Development.

Meisels, S. J., Bickel, D. D., Nicholson, J., Xue, Y., & Atkins-Burnett, S. (2001). Trusting teachers' judgments: A validity study of a curriculum-embedded performance assessment in kindergarten–grade 3. *American Educational Research Journal, 38*(1), 73–95.

Messick, S. (1989). Validity. In R. L. Linn (Ed.), *Educational measurement* (3rd ed., pp. 13–103). New York: American Council on Education.

Minnesota Department of Education. (2007). *Minnesota academic standards: Mathematics K–12—2007 version.* Accessed at http://education.state.mn.us/MDE/dse/stds/Math on May 31, 2017.

Moss, C. M. (2013). Research on classroom summative assessment. In J. H. McMillan (Ed.), *SAGE handbook of research on classroom assessment* (pp. 235–255). Thousand Oaks, CA: SAGE.

National Commission on Excellence in Education. (1983). *A nation at risk: The imperative for educational reform* (Report to the Nation and the Secretary of Education, United States Department of Education). Washington, DC: Author.

National Council for the Social Studies. (2013). *The College, Career, and Civic Life (C3) framework for social studies state standards: Guidance for enhancing the rigor of K–12 civics, economics, geography, and history.* Silver Spring, MD: Author. Accessed at www.socialstudies.org/sites/default/files/c3/C3-Framework-for-Social-Studies.pdf on August 24, 2017.

National Governors Association Center for Best Practices & Council of Chief State School Officers. (2010a). *Common Core State Standards for English language arts and literacy in history/social studies, science, and technical subjects*. Washington, DC: Authors. Accessed at www.corestandards.org/assets/CCSSI_ELA%20Standards.pdf on May 31, 2017.

National Governors Association Center for Best Practices & Council of Chief State School Officers. (2010b). *Common Core State Standards for mathematics*. Washington, DC: Authors. Accessed at www.corestandards.org/assets/CCSSI_Math%20Standards.pdf on May 31, 2017.

Next Generation Science Standards Lead States. (2013). *Next Generation Science Standards: For states, by states*. Washington, DC: National Academies Press.

O'Connor, K. (2011). *A repair kit for grading: Fifteen fixes for broken grades with DVD* (2nd ed.). Portland, OR: Pearson Assessment Training Institute.

Parkes, J. (2013). Reliability in classroom assessment. In J. H. McMillan (Ed.), *SAGE handbook of research on classroom assessment* (pp. 107–123). Thousand Oaks, CA: SAGE.

Partnership for 21st Century Learning. (n.d.) *Framework for 21st century learning*. Accessed at www.p21.org/about-us/p21-framework on July 24, 2017.

Pascale, R., Sternin, J., & Sternin, M. (2010). *The power of positive deviance: How unlikely innovators solve the world's toughest problems*. Boston: Harvard Business Review Press.

Patall, E. A., Cooper, H., & Robinson, J. C. (2008). Parent involvement in homework: A research synthesis. *Review of Educational Research, 78*(4), 1039–1101.

Pfeffer, J., & Sutton, R. I. (1999). *The knowing-doing gap: How smart companies turn knowledge into action*. Boston: Harvard Business School Press.

Pintrich, P. R. (2002). The role of metacognitive knowledge in learning, teaching, and assessing. *Theory Into Practice, 41*(4), 219–225.

Ploegh, K., Tillema, H. H., & Segers, M. S. R. (2009). In search of quality criteria in peer assessment practices. *Studies in Educational Evaluation, 35*(2–3), 102–109.

Popham, W. J. (2008). *Transformative assessment*. Alexandria, VA: Association for Supervision and Curriculum Development.

Practice. (2017). In *Merriam-Webster's online dictionary*. Accessed at www.merriam -webster.com/dictionary/practice on January 28, 2017.

Ramdass, D., & Zimmerman, B. J. (2008). Effects of self-correction strategy training on middle school students' self-efficacy, self-evaluation, and mathematics division learning. *Journal of Advanced Academics, 20*(1), 18–41.

Randall, J., & Engelhard, G. (2010). Examining the grading practices of teachers. *Teaching and Teacher Education, 26*(7), 1372–1380.

Ratcliffe, C. (2015). *Child poverty and adult success*. Accessed at www.urban.org/sites /default/files/publication/65766/2000369-Child-Poverty-and-Adult-Success.pdf on October 25, 2017.

Reeves, D. (2015). *Elements of grading: A guide to effective practice* (2nd ed.). Bloomington, IN: Solution Tree Press.

Ruiz-Primo, M. A., & Li, M. (2013). Examining formative feedback in the classroom context: New research perspectives. In J. H. McMillan (Ed.), *SAGE handbook of research on classroom assessment* (pp. 215–232). Thousand Oaks, CA: SAGE.

Sadler, D. R. (1989). Formative assessment and the design of instructional systems. *Instructional Science, 18*(2), 119–144.

Schimmer, T. (2016). *Grading from the inside out: Bringing accuracy to student assessment through a standards-based mindset.* Bloomington, IN: Solution Tree Press.

Schunk, D. H. (2003). Self-efficacy for reading and writing: Influence of modeling, goal setting, and self-evaluation. *Reading and Writing Quarterly: Overcoming Learning Difficulties, 19*(2), 159–172.

Shavelson, R. J., Young, D. B., Ayala, C. C., Brandon, P. R., Furtak, E. M., Ruiz-Primo, M. A., et al. (2008). On the impact of curriculum-embedded formative assessment on learning: A collaboration between curriculum and assessment developers. *Applied Measurement in Education, 21*(4), 295–314.

Shepard, L. A. (2000). The role of assessment in a learning culture. *Educational Researcher, 29*(7), 4–14.

Shute, V. J. (2007). *Focus on formative feedback* (Research report RR-07–11). Princeton, NJ: Educational Testing Service. Accessed at www.ets.org/Media/Research/pdf/RR-07-11.pdf on June 1, 2017.

Slavin, R. E., Hurley, E. A., & Chamberlain, A. M. (2003). Cooperative learning and achievement: Theory and research. In W. M. Reynolds & G. E. Miller (Eds.), *Handbook of psychology, volume 7: Educational psychology* (pp. 177–198). Hoboken, NJ: Wiley.

Smith, C., Wiser, M., Anderson, C., & Krajcik, J. (2006). Implications of research on children's learning for standards and assessment: A proposed learning progression for matter and atomic-molecular theory. *Measurement: Interdisciplinary Research and Perspectives, 4*(1–2), 1–98.

Tiedemann, J. (2002). Teachers' gender stereotypes as determinants of teacher perceptions in elementary school mathematics. *Educational Studies in Mathematics, 50*(1), 49–62.

Tomlinson, C. A., & Moon, T. R. (2013). Differentiation and classroom assessment. In J. H. McMillan (Ed.), *SAGE handbook of research on classroom assessment* (pp. 415–430). Thousand Oaks, CA: SAGE.

Tomlinson, C. A., & Strickland, C. A. (2005). *Differentiation in practice: A resource guide for differentiating curriculum, grades 9–12.* Alexandria, VA: Association for Supervision and Curriculum Development.

Topping, K. J. (2013). Peers as a source of formative and summative assessment. In J. H. McMillan (Ed.), *SAGE handbook of research on classroom assessment* (pp. 395–412). Thousand Oaks, CA: SAGE.

Trautwein, U., Koller, O., Schmitz, B., & Baumert, J. (2002). Do homework assignments enhance achievement? A multilevel analysis in 7th-grade mathematics. *Contemporary Educational Psychology, 27*(1), 26–50.

Tsivitanidou, O. E., Zacharia, Z. C., & Hovardas, T. (2011). Investigating secondary school students' unmediated peer assessment skills. *Learning and Instruction, 21*(4), 506–519.

Vagle, N. D. (2013). *Balanced assessment: A conversation on meaningful assessment use* [PowerPoint presentation]. Accessed at http://michiganassessmentconsortium.org /sites/default/files/resources/Balanced_Assessment_Vagle_2013.pdf on June 5, 2017.

Vagle, N. D. (2014). *Design in five: Essential phases to create engaging assessment practice.* Bloomington, IN: Solution Tree Press.

van Gennip, N. A. E., Segers, M. S. R., & Tillema, H. H. (2009). Peer assessment for learning from a social perspective: The influence of interpersonal variables and structural features. *Educational Research Review, 4*(1), 41–54.

Van Zundert, M., Sluijsmans, D., & van Merriënboer, J. (2010). Effective peer assessment processes: Research findings and future directions. *Learning and Instruction, 20*(4), 270–279.

Vatterott, C. (2009). *Rethinking homework: Best practices that support diverse needs.* Alexandria, VA: Association for Supervision and Curriculum Development.

Vatterott, C. (2015). *Rethinking grading: Meaningful assessment for standards-based learning.* Alexandria, VA: Association for Supervision and Curriculum Development.

Walker, J. M., Hoover-Dempsey, K. V., Whetsel, D. R., & Green, C. L. (2004). *Parental involvement in homework: A review of current research and its implications for teachers, after school program staff, and parent leaders.* Cambridge, MA: Harvard Family Research Project.

Waltman, K. K., & Frisbie, D. A. (1994). Parents' understanding of their children's report card grades. *Applied Measurement in Education, 7*(3), 223–240.

Webb, N. L. (1997). *Criteria for alignment of expectations and assessments in mathematics and science education* (Research monograph no. 6). Washington, DC: Author.

Webb, N. L., Alt, M., Ely, R., & Vesperman, B. (2005). *Web alignment tool (WAT) training manual.* Madison: Wisconsin Center for Educational Research.

Welch, C. (2006). Item and prompt development in performance testing. In S. M. Downing & T. M. Haladyna (Eds.), *Handbook of test development* (pp. 303–328). Mahwah, NJ: Erlbaum.

Wiggins, G. (2012). Seven keys to effective feedback. *Educational Leadership, 70*(1), 10–16. Accessed at www.ascd.org/publications/educational-leadership/sept12/vol70 /num01/Seven-Keys-to-Effective-Feedback.aspx on June 5, 2017.

Wiliam, D. (2013). Feedback and instructional correctives. In J. H. McMillan (Ed.), *SAGE handbook of research on classroom assessment* (pp. 197–214). Thousand Oaks, CA: SAGE.

Wiliam, D. (2017). *Embedded formative assessment* (2nd ed.). Bloomington, IN: Solution Tree Press.

Williams, A-M. C. (2015). *Soft skills perceived by students and employers as relevant employability skills* (Unpublished doctoral dissertation). Walden University, Minneapolis, Minnesota.

Wormeli, R. (2006). *Fair isn't always equal: Assessing and grading in the differentiated classroom*. Portland, ME: Stenhouse.

Zimmerman, B. J. (2011). Motivational sources and outcomes of self-regulated learning and performance. In B. J. Zimmerman & D. H. Schunk (Eds.), *Handbook of self-regulation of learning and performance* (pp. 49–64). New York: Routledge.

Index

Essential Assessment
Cassandra Erkens, Tom Schimmer, and Nicole Dimich Vagle
Discover how to use the power of assessment to instill hope, efficacy, and achievement in your students. Explore six essential tenets of assessment that will help deepen your understanding of assessment to not only meet standards but also enhance students' academic success.
BKF752

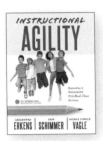

Instructional Agility
This highly practical resource empowers readers to become instructionally agile—moving seamlessly among instruction, formative assessment, and feedback—to enhance student engagement, proficiency, and ownership of learning. Each chapter concludes with reflection questions that assist readers in determining next steps.
BKF764

Softening the Edges: Assessment Practices That Honor K–12 Teachers and Learners
Katie White
Discover the difference between *soft edges* and *hard edges* regarding alignment between students' and teachers' needs and the assessment practices meant to meet them. Assessment must smoothly guide students through their learning, engaging them so their confidence grows.
BKF781

Beyond the Grade
Robert Lynn Canady, Carol E. Canady, and Anne Meek
To help all students succeed, vast changes in grading policies and scheduling are needed. In this research-based resource, the authors examine why current practices are ineffective and share how switching to a standards-based grading system can transform teaching and learning.
BKF726

a division of
Solution Tree | Press
Solution Tree

Visit SolutionTree.com or call 800.733.6786 to order.